The Question of Being in Husserl's *Logical Investigations*

PHAENOMENOLOGICA

COLLECTION FONDÉE PAR H.L. VAN BREDA ET PUBLIÉE
SOUS LE PATRONAGE DES CENTRES D'ARCHIVES-HUSSERL

81

JAMES R. MENSCH

The Question of Being in Husserl's *Logical Investigations*

Comité de rédaction de la collection:
Président: S. IJsseling (Leuven);
Membres: M. Farber (Buffalo), E. Fink† (Freiburg i. Br.),
L. Landgrebe (Köln), W. Marx (Freiburg i. Br.),
J.N. Mohanty (New York), P. Ricoeur (Paris), E. Ströker (Köln),
J. Taminiaux (Louvain), K.H. Volkmann-Schluck (Köln);
Secrétaire: J. Taminiaux.

JAMES R. MENSCH

The Question of Being in Husserl's *Logical Investigations*

1981

MARTINUS NIJHOFF PUBLISHERS
THE HAGUE/BOSTON/LONDON

Distributors

for the United States and Canada
Kluwer Boston, Inc.
190 Old Derby Street
Hingham, MA 02043
USA

for all other countries
Kluwer Academic Publishers Group
Distribution Center
P.O. Box 322
3300 AH Dordrecht
The Netherlands

B
3279
.H94
M46

This volume is listed in the Library of Congress Cataloging in Publication Data

ISBN 90-247-2413-9 (this volume)
ISBN 90-247-2339-6 (series)

Copyright © 1981 by Martinus Nijhoff Publishers bv, The Hague.

All rights reserved. No part of this publication may be reproduced, stored in a retrieval system, or transmitted in any form or by any means, mechanical, photocopying, recording, or otherwise, without the prior written permission of the publisher, Martinus Nijhoff Publishers bv, P.O. Box 566, 2501 CN The Hague, The Netherlands.

PRINTED IN THE NETHERLANDS

This book is dedicated to the memory of Jacob Klein
"Denn der Geist allein ist unsterblich"

ACKNOWLEDGEMENTS

I wish to acknowledge my gratitude to Professor James Morrison of the University of Toronto for his encouragement and aid in the preparation of this work. His generosity is an example of the genuine philosophic spirit. I should also like to thank Ernie and Frauke Hankamer as well as Hugo and Ruth Jakusch whose kindness sustained us in Munich and Dießen. Finally, mention must be made of the Canada Council without whose financial aid this book would not have been possible.

TABLE OF CONTENTS

INTRODUCTION   1

I. THE REFUTATION OF PSYCHOLOGISM   9
    Remark   24

II. ESTABLISHING THE GUIDING MOTIVATION: THE REFUTATION OF SCEPTICISM AND RELATIVISM   27

III. THE CATEGORY OF THE IDEAL   35
    1. The Category in the Context of *Ideen I*   35
    2. The Category in its own Context   42

IV. THE BEING OF THE IDEAL   53

V. SUBJECTIVE ACCOMPLISHMENT: INTENTIONALITY AS ONTOLOGICAL TRANSCENDENCE   73

VI. THE SUBJECT–OBJECT CORRELATION   95

VII. CATEGORIAL REPRESENTATION   133

VIII. ONTOLOGICAL DIFFICULTIES AND MOTIVATING CONNECTIONS   149

NOTES   193

BIBLIOGRAPHY   207

NAME INDEX   209

SUBJECT INDEX   210

INTRODUCTION

This study proposes a double thesis. The first concerns the *Logische Untersuchungen* itself. We will attempt to show that its statements about the nature of being are inconsistent and that this inconsistency is responsible for the failure of this work. The second concerns the *Logische Untersuchungen*'s relation to the *Ideen*. The latter, we propose, is a response to the failure of the *Logische Untersuchungen*'s ontology. It can thus be understood in terms of a shift in the ontology of the *Logische Untersuchungen*, a shift motivated by the attempt to overcome the contradictory assertions of the *Logische Untersuchungen*. In this sense our thesis is that, in the technical meaning that Husserl gives the term, the *Logische Untersuchungen* and the *Ideen* can be linked via a "motivated path."

We can, by way of an introduction, clarify our theses by regarding three elements. The first is the relation of epistemology to ontology. The second is the notion of motivation as Husserl conceives the term. The third is the fundamental distinctions that are to be explained via the notion of motivation.

1. We should begin by remarking that the goal of the *Logische Untersuchungen* is explicitly epistemological; it is that of answering "the cardinal question of epistemology, the question concerning the objectivity of knowledge" (*LU*, Tüb. ed., I, 8; F., p. 56).[1] For Husserl, his other questions — i.e., that of the theoretical bases of logic and that of the relation of logic to psychology — "essentially coincide" with this "cardinal question" (*Ibid.*). An important point here is that as Husserl conceives this question it has a certain regressive character. The inquiry is not just whether such knowledge can exist, but how it can. The inquiry is thus formulated in terms of the "conditions of the possibility of science in general" and "knowledge in general" — both being understood in the strong, objective sense of the terms (*LU*, "Prolegomena," §65, §66).

The relation of epistemology to ontology is set by Husserl's repeated assertion that metaphysics — a science of being *qua* being — is posterior to epistemology and in some sense can be thought of as growing out of the latter.[2] Given this formulation and given the *Logische Untersuchungen*'s explicit goal of securing the objectivity of knowledge, it is obvious that the ontology Husserl puts forward must be shaped by this goal. The relation, however, is more intimate than this suggests. It is such that Husserl's ontology and epistemology must be considered a related, organic whole. If we follow Husserl when he divides the conditions for knowledge into subjective and objective conditions, we find that they are ultimately ontological conditions. The question faced by Husserl is, what must the being of both subjects and objects be if objective knowledge is to be at all possible? The conditions for the possibility of objective knowledge are, as we shall see, ultimately understood as ontological conditions. In this regressive procedure in which we proceed from the assumption of objective knowledge to its essential ontological conditions, the intimacy of the relation is hereby expressed. In our view, it is such that ontological conditions so laid down serve as a consistency test for the *Logische Untersuchungen*'s conception of what it means to know.

Granting this, we can clarify our first thesis which sees the failure of the *Logische Untersuchungen* as a failure of its ontology. If the ontological conditions for knowledge are contradictory, then, according to the above, the whole project of the *Logische Untersuchungen*, its fundamental motivation of providing an answer to the problem of the objectivity of knowledge, is not satisfied.

2. The relationship of the *Logische Untersuchungen* and the *Ideen* has been subject to a number of interpretations without any clear consensus of opinion.[3] In Husserl's view, the works are different. There is a conceptual shift that takes place in the original interpretation of the *Logische Untersuchungen*. After the *Logische Untersuchungen* was written, "... there occurred not just additions but transvaluations (*nicht bloß Ergänzungen, sondern Umwertungen*) in the original sphere of research" (*LU*, Tüb. ed., I, viii–ix; F., p. 44). The reference of these remarks is the *Ideen*'s doctrine of transcendental idealism. The move to this latter position, according to Husserl, is to be understood in terms of a "motivated

path" that begins with the problem of the objectivity of knowledge ("Nachwort," *Ideen III*; ed. W. Biemel, Husserliana V, The Hague, 1971, p. 150).

To grasp Husserl's conception of this move, it is first necessary to understand the way in which he uses the terms "motivation" and "motivated path." In his developed phenomenology, the terms bear a certain technical sense. In constitutive phenomenology, for example, he speaks of the motivations that allow us to posit entities on the basis of evidence (See *Ideen I*, §52; ed. W. Biemel, Husserliana III, The Hague, 1950, p. 124). The source of the evidence is the interconnections of our perceptual experience. To make sense of our experience, to view it as the experience of relatively stable objects is, on the one hand, to be sensitive to the motivations arising from experience. On the other hand, it is to engage in what Husserl calls the thesis of rationality; the thesis is that the world is rational, that it presents itself as a collection of relatively stable objects which are there to be experienced, objects allowing of certain definite predicates. At its basis, the thesis is that our perceptual experience allows of inference, that we can infer objects, predicates and relations from it and thus come up with a world about which we can reason or infer (See *Ibid.*, §§136-37, §139, §142; Biemel ed., pp. 335-36, 341, 348-39).

More importantly for our own theme, the notion of motivation also plays a role in the explanation of the genesis of intellectual constructions: theories, sciences, ideologies, and so forth. It is in the context of this notion that Husserl's rather celebrated remark must be understood:

> The reigning dogma of a separation in principle between epistemological explanation and historical, even humanistic–psychological explanation, between epistemological and genetic origin is basically mistaken – at least insofar as we do not in the usual way inadmissibly limit the notions of "history," "historical explanation," and "genesis" ("Beilage III," *Krisis*; ed. W. Biemel, 2nd ed., Husserliana VI, The Hague, 1962, p. 379).

The inadmissible limitation referred to is the leaving out of account the notion of teleology. Thus, Husserl distinguishes his own account of philosophy from "that of a historical explanation in the usual sense" by asserting, "Our aim is to make comprehensible the teleology in the historical becoming of philosophy . . ." (*Krisis*, §15; Biemel ed., p. 71). In this context, Husserl speaks of the "primal establishment of the goals," goals which specify what philosophy as a task is, which live on in "sedimented forms" that can be "reawakened again and again" and which, by virtue of this, make philosophy an identifiable historical activity. Constantly revitalized, these goals give philosophers, active within their Western tradition, their ultimate or persistent motivation (*Ibid.*, pp. 72-73).

If we ask what sort of activity this is, we come to two further specifications of motivation, both of them negative. The notion of motivation does not involve causality; neither does it involve logical necessity. Its phenomenological notion for Husserl is "a generalization of that concept of motivation according to which we can say, e.g., that the willing of the end motivates the willing of the means." In the "pure phenomenological sphere," the concept exists "as a contrast to the concept of causality which is situated in the sphere of transcendent reality" (*Ideen I*, §47; Biemel ed., p. 112, fn. 1). Without getting into theoretical subtleties, we can explain this by saying that the not-yet, as opposed to what has already been, is the determinative factor in the motivation of a goal. We here equate the not-yet with the goal which has yet to be realized and casual determination with determination of the present by the past.

That motivation does not involve logical necessity may be put by noting that means for achieving an end are not necessarily determined by logical necessity. Such would be the case only if all choices except one were to be accounted illogical, i.e., logically impossible to conceive or execute. In distinction to this, in a motivated path, choices are open every step of the way. Genuine decisions are part and parcel of the becoming of the path.

The above is sufficient to indicate Husserl's criteria for a genetic of historical explanation. If we are to apply these criteria to his own work, several things are required. (1) We must see a certain continuous development in the work. Later books must not simply be restatements of earlier ones. (2) We must recognize a unique teleology in the work. This means the recognizable presence of a goal which defines a task, the accomplishment of the task specifying a unique and persistent motivation. (3) Finally, we must see all problems that arise in the work and all transformations that occur in response to these problems *as fundamentally related to the guiding motivation.*

This last criterion can be explained by saying that if an initial solution which Husserl puts forward satisfies the guiding motivation, then as a *motivated path* his work should stop. If it continues, it should only be because the solutions provided raise, when worked out, new problems with respect to the original motivation. We can speak here of the original motivation as determining the problems that arise in the given solutions, but not as determining the exact choice of response to these problems. This follows because a motivated path is neither causally nor logically determined — i.e., determined with the strict necessity of a syllogistic consequence. This leads to a further point of explanation. As words like "genesis" and "genetic" indicate, we must avoid a certain either-or standpoint with respect to stages in Husserl's development. In a genetic explanation earlier stages, when placed against later, are not rejected *tout court*. The adult is not a genetic rejection of the child, nor is the bloom such a rejection of the bud. Acknowledgement and acceptance of one stage here does not imply rejection of another. We can express this by saying that the notion of genetic development is distinct from the corresponding notion in the mathematical sphere of either-or decisions. Otherness does not mean a rejection of previous positions.

An example will make this notion clearer. The explicit goal of the *Logische Untersuchungen* is the securing of the possibility of objective knowledge. According to the "Nachwort" in the passage referred to, it is the same problem which leads Husserl ultimately to the doctrine of transcendental idealism. The solution to the problem of objective knowledge is thus the guiding motivation linking the two works. Now to secure the objectivity of knowledge, Husserl begins by separating logic and mathematics from psychology. The separation is expressed by a distinction between the real being of the subject and the ideal being of both the logical laws and the meaning contents these laws inform. The split in being becomes Husserl's answer to what being must be if objective knowledge is to be possible. What is important is the recognition that the failure of this ontology does not mean a return to a previous position — e.g., the position of the *Philosophy of Arithmetic*. If the arguments of the *Logische Untersuchungen* are correct, then the refusal to separate logic from psychology leads to psychological relativism — a position which forecloses the possibility of objective knowledge. This means that if the motivated path animated by this possibility is to continue, a certain "conceptual shift" in the interpretation of the original argumentation must occur. The arguments are no longer seen as sufficient conditions for achieving their goal. This does not mean, however, that they lose, *on the level on which they are presented,* their necessity and validity.

3. This conceptual shift is best expressed by the quotation about the motivated path. Defending his adoption of idealism, Husserl describes his work as follows:

> . . . it simply concerns a motivated path which, starting from the problem of the possibility of objective knowledge, wins the necessary insight that the very sense of this problem leads back to the pure ego existing in and for itself, the insight that this ego, as a presupposition for knowledge of the world, cannot be and cannot remain presupposed as a worldly being, the insight therefore that this ego must, through the phenomenological reduction and the epoché with respect to the being-for-me of the world, be brought to transcendental purity ("Nachwort"; Biemel ed., p. 150).

Implicit in this passage is the essential distinction between the *Logische Untersuchungen* and the *Ideen* — the distinction which must be bridged by our notion of motivation. It concerns the notion of the ego or subject. In the *Logische Untersuchungen,* the ego is declared to be an element in real being; in the *Ideen* it is taken out of this category. As Husserl writes, ". . . psychological subjectivity loses just that which gives it its actuality as something real in the world, the latter naively considered as something already there for experience; it loses its sense of being as a soul in an existing body within a pregiven spatial-temporal nature" ("Nachwort"; Biemel ed., p. 145).

The elements which give us this shift in the interpretation of the ego are the epoché and the phenomenological reduction. If we add a third element, that of the eidetic reduction, we have the essential schema for discussing the change of standpoint from the *Logische Untersuchungen* to the *Ideen.* A merely *preliminary* definition of these elements can be given as follows:

The *eidetic reduction* is the reduction of everything contingent in the object. The purpose of this is to see the species of which the object is an instance. Insofar as the species is considered part of *ideal being,* the result of the eidetic reduction may be classified simply as *das Ideal.* Here, we may note that in its complete context the eidetic reduction involves a thesis about the nature of being. The thesis involves the contingency and, thus, the reality of the instance we begin with and the non-contingency or ideality of the species that is uncovered by this reduction. The thesis is that what we may call worldly being exists on two levels, the contingent and the non-contingent, i.e., the real and the ideal. In this it is distinguished from the epoché.

The *epoché* is truly presuppositionless. It involves no thesis at all about the nature of being. It is simply the activity of withholding judgement on all forms of being in order to look at the evidence whereupon we form those judgements. There is here a certain kinship with Descartes' method of doubt, although as practiced by Husserl the method is primarily reflective. In it, we suspend objective considerations in order to reflect upon the subjective modes of consciousness in which objects manifest themselves. Now, although the epoché does not involve a thesis about the nature of being, it does lead us to another reduction that does.

The *phenomenological reduction* is the reduction of the conditioned to their conditions. The former are understood as the correlates of consciousness; they may be classified as worldy being, including both its ideal and real forms. The latter are understood as the experiences of consciousness, the modes of consciousness in which these correlates establish their givenness. Its thesis about the nature of being may be put in terms of what Husserl calls the "noematic X." This X, as representing an actual entity, is understood as more than simply the sum of its predicates. It is their underlying subject. As Husserl says, the predicates "are its predicates inconceivable without it, yet distinguishable from it" (*Ideen I*, §131; Biemel ed., p. 320). The thesis is that this X, which, as existent, is distinguished from its predicates, is nothing more than the "point of unification" of these predicates. It is that which we posit out of the unifiability of certain series of perceptually arrived at predications. It is thus no more than a title for certain rational connections of conscious experiences — i.e., those which allow us to infer that there is an object there about which we can make predictions (See *Ideen I*, §145; Biemel ed., p. 356).

As Celms says, the phenomenological reduction is a "leading back of objective being to the being of phenomenologically pure experiences" (*Der phänomenologische Idealismus Husserls*, Riga, 1928, p. 309). More properly, it is a leading back to the interconnections of these experiences. Objective being is related to these interconnections as conditioned to its explanatory conditions. The former is said to be dependent, the latter, "absolute" (*Ideen I*, §76; Biemel ed., p. 174). Insofar as the pure experiences of consciousness revealed by this reduction are placed in the ontological category of the irreal, the result of this reduction may be entitled *das Irreal*. The irreal exists in contrast to both real and ideal being (See *Ibid.*, "Einleitung"; p. 7).

Only the eidetic reduction occurs in the first edition of the *Logische Untersuchungen*. The epoché and phenomenological reduction are the products of Husserl's later theorizing. This points to the shift to be explained by our notion of motivation. It is a shift *from* the ego conceived as a part of worldly being, the ego as *suffering both real and ideal determination*. It is a shift *to* the ego conceived as irreal, as non-wordly. This latter conception views the ego as *determinative, in the sense of an explanatory condition*, of both forms of worldly being.

The elements that form the second conception are in the *Ideen* matters to be demonstrated in their own right. We close by remarking that we will not consider these demonstrations. Our task encompasses only observing the motivating connections that link the first conception to the second. For us, it will be sufficient to view them as motivated responses to the failure of the ontology of the *Logische Untersuchungen*.

CHAPTER I

THE REFUTATION OF PSYCHOLOGISM

One must establish that a thing is possible before one can begin the inquiry into the conditions of its possibility. One may, of course, assume the existence of the thing as a fact; but in an area where there is disagreement, there is at least a preliminary task that must be faced: that of answering the opposing arguments. Husserl meets these necessities in the "Prolegomena" to the *Logische Untersuchungen*. In a rather curious method of procedure, he argues that objective knowledge is possible because the denial of objective knowledge is *not possible*. More concretely, he may be regarded as arguing that any theory which denies the possibility of objectively valid knowledge slips into relativism. Relativism itself, however, collapses into scepticism – a position which undermines the possible validity of the original theory.

An important element in this methodology is the notion of metabasis. The question raised in this context is that of "$\mu\epsilon\tau\acute{\alpha}\beta\alpha\sigma\iota\sigma$ $\epsilon\grave{\iota}\varsigma$ $\ddot{\alpha}\lambda\lambda o$ $\gamma\acute{\epsilon}\nu o\varsigma$" (*LU*, Tüb. ed., I, 145; F., p. 161). Have we in an account so *transformed the genus* of the objects under study that we can no longer be regarded as talking about them at all? If this is the case, then we may be regarded as comitting the fallacy of substituting the explanation for the explained. The question is extended to the notion of explanation itself. A theoretical explanation which ends in a sceptical thesis about explanation *per se* may be regarded as transforming the very notion of explanation. By virtue of the transformation, its own claim to explain may be called into question.

We may begin with a preliminary definition of objectively valid knowledge. It is knowledge which agrees in its content with the object or, rather, entity in itself. At least in his initial statements, Husserl describes this last as a being which has its own categories independent of and prior to the categories which a contingently judging subject might impose on it (See *LU*, Tüb. ed., I, 15; F., p. 62; *Ibid.*, I, 228; F., pp. 225-26; *Ibid.*, II/1, 94-95; F., p. 325). The former categories stand as independent or *objective criteria* for the validity of the latter. Within this schema, we can say that a content of judgement which does agree with the object is objectively true. We can also say that insofar as it expresses the content of what is in itself — i.e., the *Sein-an-sich* — it expresses what is *true in itself.*

There are two further notions of objective being involved in this definition. They are that such being is not ambiguous and that, as a consequence, it permits of definite description.[1] If we combine these two with the first conception, we get the Husserlian assertion: "Nothing can be without being thus and thus determined, and that it is thus determined is the truth in itself which forms the necessary correlate of being in itself" (*LU*, Tüb. ed. I, 228; F., pp. 225-26).

The reason that being is declared to be unambiguous is easily put. Without it there could be no unique correspondence between truth and being. If being were not definitely describable then a number of descriptions could fit the same state of affairs. This would hold even if we broke the same state of affairs down to its most elementary spatial-temporal relations. A number of descriptions, given the basic ambiguity of being, would fit each relation. The consequence of this would be the inapplicability of the basic laws of logic — the laws of non-contradiction and excluded middle — to objective being. The laws demand that there be one truth, one determinate description that corresponds to an elementary state of affairs.

That the laws in question are essential to the notion of objective validity may be shown by borrowing a position from Kant. It is that the *objective validity* of a judgement and the *necessary universality of its content* in valid judgements are mutually equivalent terms. The first implies the second, "for when a judgement agrees with an object, all judgements concerning the same object must agree with each other." The second implies the first, for otherwise "there would be no reason why other judgements would necessarily have to agree with mine, if it were not the unity of the object to which they all refer and with which they all agree, and for that reason must agree amongst themselves" ("Prolegomena,"

§18, *Kants gesammelte Schriften*, 23 vols., Berlin, 1910-55, IV, 298).

Now, if we accept this equivalence of universal and objective validity, it is clear that if the first rests on the law of non-contradiction, so must the second. That the first does is obvious since universal validity as a conception rests on the assumption that the same content of judgement in appropriately well defined circumstances cannot be considered both true and false — i.e., valid and invalid. Granting this, we can say that objective validity — defined as equivalent to universal validity — rests on this law, and this last presupposes the definite nature of being. Otherwise put: only if being were definite and thus definitely describable would it allow all observers of the same relationship to come up with the same universal content of judgement.

This formal equivalence of universal and objective validity is what lies behind Husserl's statement: "Truth and being are both 'categories' in the same sense and obviously correlative. One cannot relativize truth and hold on to the objectivity of being" (*LU*, Tüb. ed., I, 131-32; F., p. 151). This follows since, if we remain within the equivalence, we define objective being as that which universally valid judgements refer to and agree with. It is the being which is there in its content for everyone to judge. We thus oppose it to what is private and subjective. This means that if we relativize truth, if we shrink our concept of universal validity to validity or truth-for-me, we necessarily relativize our conception of being. Being in itself becomes reduced to being-for-me.

With this, a first description of relativism can be formulated. It is, on the one hand, a denial of the conception of objective being. On the other hand, through its denial of universal validity, it is a denial of the fundamental laws of logic — those of non-contradiction and excluded middle. Now, Husserl's own definition of relativism can be reached by the following chain of reasoning. We begin by asking what is implied in this denial of logic. The answer that first comes to view is that we implicitly place logic outside of any framework in which it could serve as an objective criterion for competing truth claims. In Husserl's understanding, this means giving it only a contingent or hypothetical necessity. We conceive of it as a *fact* rather than as a *form of facts*. It is something which, even if it holds in a particular case, could be otherwise if certain contingent circumstances which ground it change. The conception thus involves the notion of logic as something contingent by virtue of being grounded on what is itself contingent — i.e., a fact. With this, we have Husserl's definition of "relativism in the widest sense of the word as a doctrine which somehow derives the pure principles of logic from facts" (*LU*, Tüb. ed., I, 122; F., p. 144).[2]

The foregoing remarks give us a framework to situate Husserl's attack on psychologism. Psychologism in the most general sense of the term may be defined as the attempt to explain the necessity of knowledge, not via an appeal to the object, but rather through an appeal to the psychological connections by which we grasp the object. Since logic makes up at least a formal part of this necessity, we have an attempt to clarify it psychologically by an appeal to just such connections.[3] Now, neither an epistemological examination of these necessary connections nor psychology itself as a special empirical science is attacked by Husserl. With respect to the latter, we can say there is a certain attempt to comprehend it such that it can ground and (in a different sense) be grounded by an objective epistemology, this being a theory of knowing that does not give up the presupposition of objective knowledge. What does call forth critical comments are certain elements embedded in the interpretation attached to this science. The elements are rejected when they lead to relativism and thus to a denial of objective knowledge.

This brings us to the point that the attack on psychologism is more general than it appears. Other forms of interpretation of knowledge fall under its censure. Thus, to mention only a few, a linguistic, an historical, a cultural interpretation of knowing is later considered by Husserl as refuted, at least insofar as it shares certain essential elements in common with the discredited brand of psychologism. All theories which lead to relativism, we should add, are considered as refuted by the general refutation of relativism put forward.

Relativism has been defined as a doctrine that attempts to derive logic from facts. Thus, the elements to be criticized are those which lead to this position. More specifically, they are those which lead to the following double thesis about knowledge and logic: The psychological conditions explanatory of our knowledge are considered to be facts. Logic, as expressing the formal conditions of our knowledge, is considered to express the factual nature of our presentation, thinking and judgement. Given the definition of facts as contingent, logic itself becomes contingent. The necessity of its laws is merely *hypothetical,* presupposing as it does the obtaining of circumstances which may alter (See *LU*, Tüb. ed., I, 146–47; F., p. 162). In its most crude form the position states that ". . . even logic alters with the development of the brain" (*Ibid.*, I, 147, fn. 1; F., p. 162).

According to its proponents, to reach this last position we must make logic a part of psychology, psychology being defined as an empirical science which investigates causal relations between individual facts. *The elements of interpretation* necessary for this inclusion are essentially three: *First*, we must identify *a content* of judgement with the *act* of judgement in which it is maintained. The content of judgement may be roughly defined as the content of meaning that logic considers in its examination of propositions. The act of judgement is understood as an individual fact. The necessity for this identification may be stated as follows. We must place the *logical relation* of contents of judgement on a level with the *psychological relation* of mental occurrences if we are to interpret the former in terms of the latter. This allows us our *second* identification. We identify the logical with the empirical law. The necessity of this is readily apparent. Psychology, as an empirical study of mental occurrences, formulates empirical laws of their relations. If logical laws are to be understood as psychological, they themselves must be empirical. This means that they must be considered to be laws based on the observed facts of mental processes and inductively drawn from the same. The *third* identification springs from the attempt of psychology to integrate itself with the other natural sciences. This leads it to speak of the psychological determination of mental events as the determination of real, spatial-temporal particulars. As Husserl observes, "The dependence will and can only be understood as causal" (*LU*, Tüb. ed., I, 120; F., p. 142).

If we include logic within psychology and make the analogy between psychology and a science like physics, we get the basis for Lipps's statement: "Logic is a physics of thinking or it is nothing at all" (*LU*, Tüb. ed., I, 55; F., p. 93). The underlying identification here is between the logical, psychological and causal law.[4]

Husserl's examination of these elements involves two points; the first is the metabasis that each identification implies. The second is the relativism that is the result of each metabasis. The ultimate metabasis, we should note in advance, is that of psychology in its claims to be a science. The metabasis involves the relativization of these claims.

These points are most obvious in the second identification. We, thus, begin with it first. If the logical and empirical laws are to be equated, then, as is readily apparent, there is a transformation of logic from an exact discipline into one whose laws can only be stated with a certain empirical indefiniteness. This occurs if we take the assertions of the psychologists Mill and Lipps and interpret them as saying that logic owes the whole of its theoretical content to psychology as *presently* established (See *LU*, Tüb. ed., I, 51; F., pp. 90-91). It also holds if we assume that psychology can one day reach the state of exact sciences like physics and chemistry. In its present state, Husserl observes, ". . . psychology lacks genuine and, hence, exact laws; the propositions that it honors with the name of laws are valuable if only vague generalizations from experience; they are statements about approximate regularities of coexistence and succession which make no claim to determine what must exist together or follow in exactly described relationships" (*LU*, Tüb. ed., I, 61; F., p. 98). Thus, admitting that "only vague rules can be established on vague theoretical principles," we have the transformation of logical rules from exact to inexact statements.

A similar transformation occurs even if we do allow psychology to reach the exactness of physics or chemistry. An exact law as above described is, in the empirical sciences, based on a certain "idealizing fiction." The fiction is that there is no such thing as observational error. In reality there is always a certain "zone of inexactness" in the empirical or observational sciences. This is a zone within the irreducible limits of observational error. By virtue of this zone, no truly unique law can be said to fit the observed data. Thus a number of laws, Husserl states, could do the same work as Newton's law of universal gravitation. The law recommends itself by virtue of its simplicity, but this does not make it *empirically* justified as a truly unique law. It is rather an approximation that fits the approximate state of the data (See *LU,* Tüb. ed., I, 63; F., p. 100). The consequences of conceiving a physical law as an approximation are, we should note, different from those of conceiving a logical law as such. Logical laws function exclusively as rules of inference. In chains of inference, the error of approximation should thus be multiplied. Thus, for example, if we view the laws of equational inference as approximations involving observational error, we should always, to reduce such error, choose the shorter rather than the longer inferential chain.

This leads us to our second metabasis: the logical law, whose content does not express the notion of probability, would be transformed into a statement of probability. This follows simply by giving the law an empirical basis. The principle, here, is that what is inductively established by experience can be overthrown by experience. The proof and the refutation, in other words, are to be regarded as on exactly the same level. Because of this, induction *per se* establishes not the holding of a law but the probability of the law. Each successive bit of evidence makes the holding of the law more probable; but within this probability, the possibility is contained that further evidence could overthrow the law. Thus, if logical laws are equated with empirical laws, they become statements of probability in the sense that their validity is to be regarded as *only probable.*

The consequences of this for science as mediately or inferentially arrived at knowledge can be indicated by noting the following. We have implicitly collapsed here the distinction between a rule of testing and that which is tested by a rule. Normally, we would say that contradictory empirical propositions cannot both be correct and that we must return again to the evidence on which they are based. The fact that they are contradictory in some sense serves as a *test* which throws their putative validity into question. If the rule of contradiction is itself only a probability which must be empirically grounded, then either this distinction does not hold or the law of contradiction, as an empirical proposition, must itself be tested by some other rule. This, if declared to be empirical, would demand a third rule and so forth. The result would be an infinite regress of probabilities. Viewed from one side, the series of them would be seen to descend to zero probability.[5]

The result would throw the whole of mediate knowledge, science included, into grave doubt.

The final metabasis that the second identification leads us to is that of a supposedly "pure" logical law into a law for matters of fact. This follows from the definition of an empirical law. As inductively derived from individual facts, it is a *generalization of the relations obtaining amongst these facts.* By virtue, then, of its origin, the empirical law should properly imply in its content the existence of such facts. The metabasis here implied by equating a logical and empirical law is stated by Husserl as follows:

> If psychologism were on the right track, one should in the doctrine of the syllogism expect only rules of the following type: It is an empirically established fact that under circumstances X, conclusions with the form C, provided with the character of apodictically necessary consequence, are connected with premises of the form P. Therefore, to syllogize correctly — i.e., to achieve judgements of this distinctive character through syllogizing — one must proceed according to the above and concern oneself with the realization of the necessary circumstances and the related premises (*LU*, Tüb. ed., I, 70; F., p. 105).

The difficulty with this metabasis is that it is difficult to see how logical or mathematical laws, as normally formulated in the usual symbolic fashion, imply individual facts in their content. As Husserl points out, what a proposition implies in its content should be deducible by syllogistic inference. "But," as he asks the proponents of this theory, "where are the forms of syllogism that allow the deduction of a fact from a pure law?" (*LU*, Tüb. ed., I, 71; F., p. 105.)

The relativism that grows out of these three metabases may be generally defined as the relativism of individual experience. It is the relativism of my set of empirical examples versus yours. In such a situation, we cannot be sure of sharing meanings or propositional senses in common. We may assume that our individual experiences roughly coincide; but this remains an assumption since experiences cannot, in an immediate sense, be shared and since the concepts we use to converse with each other are always based on our own contingent set of examples — i.e., the experiences which *we* have happened to have had.

With this, we may pass on to a discussion of the metabasis that occurs when we identify a content of judgement with the real act in which it is affirmed. The metabasis may be introduced by recalling the necessity for this identification. It is that of placing the *logical relation* of propositional contents on the same explanatory level as the *real relation* of corresponding acts of propositional affirmation. If the two relations are really the same, then there is no distinction between *real subjective capacity*, permitting the real relation, and *logical compatibility*, permitting the logical relation. The metabasis that occurs by virtue of this is, then, the transformation of a logical law into a law of subjective capacity. A law governing the logical compatibility of contents of judgement becomes, in other words, a law governing the real capability of a subject to affirm these contents in individual acts of propositional judgement. Because of this, we may begin with a statement like that of Lipps for a premise: "Logic is a psychological discipline just as surely as knowing only occurs in the mind and as thinking which terminates in knowing is a mental occurrence" (*LU*, Tüb. ed., I. 52, fn. 2; F., p. 91). But then our conclusion will be like the statements of Erdman and Mill where the logical law is reformulated in terms of possibility or impossibility of such real mental occurrences.

The implication of this is that real subjective and logical (or "objective") capacity are the same. As Husserl points out, there are a number of difficulties with this position. A number of important distinctions become undermined. To begin with, we would have no way of distinguishing the *objective* insolubility of a mathematical problem from its real insolubility by, e.g., a child or a layman. The latter's incapacity to provide a solution is a contingent incapacity. Objective insolubility, however, refers to the content of what is to be known. Thus, to take an example, it may be, as Husserl observes, that "the generalized solution of the n-body problem transcends all human capacity." But this does not in itself mean that the content of the problem fails to specify a solution (*LU*, Tüb. ed., I, 185; F., p. 191). The case is otherwise when we wish to reach a conclusion whose content is *not specified* by certain given premises. The conception, there, if it has any validity at all, is that it is objectively or logically impossible to syllogistically deduce the conclusion from the given premises — this independently of the capacity of the syllogizer.

A further distinction that is called into question is one between the contingent peculiarities of our scientific methods and the generality of their logical bases. To take a simple example, we prefer the Arabic to the Greek number system for reasons of subjective capacity. It is mentally easier to calculate in the former than the latter. This difference in subjective capacity, however, does not mean a difference in the objective relations specified by the concepts of addition, subtraction, etc. Only if we confused a sign with a thing signified would a change of signs by itself imply a change in our concepts of those relations. If we equate sign and signified, then translation into other systems of signs becomes impossible. If we do not make this equation, then it follows that it is in terms of the *concept of the thing signified* that various methods of symbolic procedure must have their bases. This allows us to distinguish between various special methods of science based on the peculiarities of our subjective capacity and their validating bases which show a common ground (See *LU*, Tüb. ed., I, 24; F., p. 69).

A final distinction should be mentioned here. It is that between the validity and the applicability of a law. For the law of contradiction to be applicable to our mental processes, we must be *subjectively capable* of maintaining constancy amongst our concepts. This condition for the applicability of the law is not the same as its validity. The latter depends only on certain relations obtaining once meanings are, in fact, held identical. It concerns the objective relations of the contents in question. Now, if we fail to distinguish between validity and applicability, then as Husserl says, we would have to call the law of contradiction *invalid* whenever we did not fulfill the condition of using expressions with the same meaning (*LU*, Tüb. ed., I, 99-100; F., p. 127). Under such assumption, the law of contradiction — regarded in one way — would itself be in violation of its own law.

This brings us to several general remarks whose purpose is to throw the results of this metabasis in a more comprehensive light. According to Husserl, the attempt to explain logic by an appeal to the theory of evolution only works by presupposing — not demonstrating — the metabasis in question. If we do not equate real subjective possibility with logical possibility, then the only thing evolution, as a biological notion, explains is the development of the conditions of the *applicability* of logic to our mental life — i.e., the development of the psychological ability to hold concepts stable. The same presupposition is at work when we assume that logic tells us something about the real relations of our mental states. If we do not assume that logic is such a "physics" of thought, then the following distinction must be drawn: On one side of the distinction, we have the *logical* incompatibility that concerns two contents — e.g., the content of some judgement we make and the content of the propositional assertion of some assumed law governing our mental life. On the other side, we have the *real* incompatibility of an act of judgement with its law-bound conditions. This second is the incompatibility of *a fact with certain factual conditions.* Given this distinction, a certain situation can arise. In Husserl's words:

> It appears quite possible that, precisely by virtue of the laws to which a creature's (e.g., a man's) entire thinking is subject, individual judgements may appear which deny the validity of those laws. The denial of those laws *contracts their assertion.* But the denial as a real act can be quite compatible with the objective validity of those laws, i.e., with the real operation of the conditions on which the laws make a general assertion (*LU*, Tüb. ed., I, 138; F., p. 156).

Husserl's point, here, is quite simple. It is that the above possibility arises once we do not equate "the ideal relation between contents of judgement" and "the real relation between the act of judgement and its law-bound conditions" (*Ibid.*). When we do not make this equation, then the ". . . ideal impossibility of a negative proposition does not clash with the real possibility of a negative act of judgement." In other words, we are free to say, ". . . the proposition is absurd, but the act of judgement is not causally ruled out" (*LU*, Tüb. ed., I, 141; F., p. 158).

That this possibility is, in fact, inherent in the situation under discussion is the point of an example Husserl brings forward. He invites us to consider the example of a calculator (See *LU*, Tüb. ed., I, 67–68; F., p. 103). If we are to speak here of laws, then it is obvious that certain mechanical laws must be called in to explain the machine's performance. *The same mechanical laws* — e.g., the laws of circuitry — are sufficient to explain machines which, from another point of view, give *correct or incorrect answers.* What this example points out is not just the *heterogeneity* of mechanical and arithmetic laws. It indicates the impossibility of doing a "physics" of thinking solely with regard to an empirical study of mental phenomena. In this attempt, we are in the same position as a man limited to an examination of the figures appearing on the face of the calculator. If he limits himself to empirical generalizations of what appears, it is obvious he cannot arrive at normative arithmetical laws which pronounce on the correctness or incorrectness of the machine's functioning. Neither, however, can he arrive at the mechanical laws which explain the machine's actual functioning.

To get these last laws, he must open the machine up. This implies, in terms of our analogy, that *psychology*, under the pressure of the attempt to relate logical laws to the real conditions of our minds, *collapses into physiology.* If we do not see these real conditions only as conditions for the applicability of the logical laws, but also see them as determining the validity of these laws, it also implies the disappearance of the objective, normative standards for the logical correctness of thought. The relativism this leads to can best be understood in the context of a third implication. It is that insofar as physiology is a study of material-causal relations, the understanding of logic enters this plane. The logical law becomes in some sense *identifiable with the causal law.*

The identification, of course, can only be partial. The logical law is not *per se* understood as a causal law, but rather as a *caused facticity.* In other words, continuing the identification between logical possibility and real subjective possibility of performing certain acts, we explain both in terms of material causality. The relations in question are between what immediately appears — i.e., psychological data supposedly conforming to the logical law — and certain physiological events of the brain that result in this appearance. The metabasis here is readily apparent, for the statement of the relations between physiological events or between physiological and psychological events — if the last relation *could* be formulated — need in no way resemble the statement of a logical law.[6]

The relativism inherent in this position may be expressed in terms of the concept of material causality. The law of such causality, as understood since Galileo's time, is that causal relations vary as the material makeup of the interacting bodies varies. A good example of this is the familiar Newtonian expression for gravitational force: The gravitational force existing between two bodies is directly proportional to the product of their masses and inversely proportional to the square of the distance between them. Keeping the distance constant, then, according as the mass of one or both of the bodies varies, so does the relation, i.e., the actual force existing between them. Causal facticities, in other words, are based upon the material (and spatial-temporal) makeup of nature. If we allow logic to be understood as such a caused facticity, it too varies with the material makeup of our nature. We thus come up with the statement quoted earlier, "logic alters with the structure of our brain."

The relativism implied by this, we may note, is, in a much more complete sense than previously expressed, a relativism of experience. The relativization of logic does not just imply that the forms of mediate knowledge − or explanatory validization − are relative. It implies, as a slight reflection shows, the relativization of the content and interconnection of direct experience. In other words, the whole empirical base for knowledge is implicitly relativized. To see this, it is only necessary to attempt to conceive of a being who was so constituted that he did not have to apply the law of non-contradiction to his statements of experience. The conception can be made easier by bringing out the full context of the possibility we are considering. It is that of considering the subject-object relation exclusively in terms of material causality. Here, we would have to say that the knowing or intentional relation that an existing subject has with an object depends upon the material makeup of the subject's perceptual and thinking organization, the material makeup of the object and the spatial-temporal relations existing between them. As any one of these varies, so will the caused fact, i.e., the perception and the knowing. Holding the object and the spatial-temporal relations stable, we can say that the perceiving and knowing of this object varies with the physical makeup of the subject.[7]

This sort of speculation has a definite point. It is to raise the question whether the appeal to physiology really puts us in any better position than we were before in our naive empirical attempt to do a "physics" of thinking. The question is one of the validity of an element in our analogy. Is our mind really like the example of a calculator so that we can, so to speak, "open it up"? The assumption that we can has been frequently made. Freud, for one, puts it in the following way. He writes, ". . . our mental apparatus . . . is itself a constituent part of the world which we set out to investigate, and it readily admits of such investigation." Granting this, it follows that ". . . the task of science is fully covered if we limit it to showing how the world must appear to us in consequence of the particular character of our organization" (*The Future of an Illusion*, trans. W.O. Scott, Garden City, 1964, pp. 91-92). The second statement follows from the first, we note, only if we assume an implicit identification. We must identify (1) the mental apparatus *that* "as a constituent part" of the world under investigation, *appears as a part* of this world with (2) the mental apparatus, as a "consequence" of whose "particular character," the world "must appear" as it does. The identification is between the *appearing* mental apparatus and the mental apparatus that is somehow *determinative of appearance*. Without this, we cannot base *on* appearance a study of that which is determinative *of* appearance. We can put this assumption in terms of causality. So expressed, it is that the mental physiology whose functioning we *observe* and *causally explain* is the same as the physiology by virtue of whose *causally determinative functioning* we make our observations and explanations. As is readily apparent, this assumption may be restated as the assertion that we are causally determined (by virtue of our apparatus) to get these *causal processes correctly*. Thus, we are also asserting that we can obtain the world as it is "in itself," i.e., get all its causal laws and processes as they actually function.

If this is the assumption in question, then it is clear that it is untenable. In the context we have set up, we have linked the subject and object via a causal relation. The world in this situation needs a physical percipient apparatus in order to appear; but according to the context, this means that its appearance must be relative to this percipient apparatus's physical makeup. Admitting that no physical apparatus could dispense with this relativity, we are at once forced to admit that the notion of a world as it is "in itself," as it is independently of the influence of a percipient mental apparatus, is an *empty* abstraction. The point also carries over to the laws which we ground on our observations of the world. To try to reason from these laws to what the world is "in itself," as it is in a *unique objective* sense, is to ignore what the context of causality tells us about these laws — namely, that they themselves, as empirically based, are relative to our specific perceptual apparatus.[8]

This relativism gets us into a certain circularity of explanation. Remaining within the context of causality, we can say that the circularity is vicious insofar as it involves the part-whole fallacy. The attempt to get at the determining structures of our mental apparatus assumes that *the real conditions of a part* of nature — the perceptual, mental apparatus — are *causally determinative* of the subject's vision and knowledge of the *whole* of nature; but the whole is assumed to include, as a particular determined *part* within its total nexus of real causality, *precisely the same real conditions of the thinking subject*. This means that the whole, as we know it in its natural laws, is explained by the determining conditions of a part of nature; and to explain just how the part in its real make-up determines this knowledge of the whole, we appeal to the whole as we know it — i.e., to its universal, natural causal laws. Thus the whole in its lawfulness is explained by a part which is itself explained by a whole which was to be explained.

It is obvious that, in terms of this circularity, the sciences are undermined. The result of this relativism is the metabasis of science itself. It is the metabasis from a notion of science *as an enterprise distinguished by its objective claim* to a notion of science *whose circularity of reasoning undercuts the basis of this claim*. We may at this point note that we can, without circularity, say that our knowledge of natural laws is determined by the laws of our thought. The circularity only arises when we interpret these latter laws as natural laws. It is then that we explain them in terms of that which they themselves were supposed to explain. The question is how else we are to conceive the laws of thought if they are not to be conceived of as natural, causal laws. Husserl's answers to this will become apparent in subsequent chapters.

REMARK

A final note may be added, though it goes far beyond the doctrine presented in the *Logische Untersuchungen*. Its actual reference is to certain remarks in *Ideen I*, §52. As Husserl there observes, to use causality *to explain appearances per se* is to make it a link between *appearance* and *what does not appear*. What does not appear must be the cause of appearance insofar as, in seeking a cause of the latter, we assume that it is not self-caused, i.e., that appearance *as such* must be explained by something else. Appearance in this position is understood as the concrete phenomenon of the appearing of the world to consciousness. What causes this phenomenon are certain causal processes of "physical being." This is the being which, on the one hand, is given the position of "an absolute reality." On the other hand, it is understood as "an unknown reality, which *itself*, in its own qualities, can never be apprehended" (Biemel ed., pp. 128-29). This position, according to Husserl, is simply the result of a *category mistake*. One has taken causality — which, as an empirical concept, has its basis in relations of dependency *amongst* appearance ("*Erscheinungs-abhängigkeitken*") — and one has attempted to use it as a relation *explanatory* of appearance *per se*.

The folly of this procedure can be seen by the fact that it is prevented from the start from achieving its intended result. Granted that causal relations are, at their basis, observed relations of dependency *amongst* appearances, they presuppose the fact of appearance — more particularly, the fact of the conscious *experience* of the world. This fact is thus involved in all talk of causality which has not lost its empirical basis. The consequences of this presupposition are twofold: (1) Causal relations, no matter how extended, cannot involve entities shut off from all possible experiences. (2) Causal relations as *presupposing experience* cannot explain experience *per se*. The nature of this presupposition may be seen by trying to derive it from causality alone. If we are limited to talk of space-filling physical processes causally determining other such processes, we never get to the fact of a conscious experience. On the conceptual level of such determination, it is as valid to say that the retina of the eye "sees" a color as to assert that the optic nerve, or certain cells in the brain, or certain molecules or atoms in these cells are perceivers of this color. Here, the rule that cause and effect must be similar in kind never allows us to talk of anything other than a space-filling process. The motion of perception applied to a chain of such processes sets up a whole series of "perceivers," one behind the other.

CHAPTER II

ESTABLISHING THE GUIDING MOTIVATION: THE REFUTATION OF SCEPTICISM AND RELATIVISM

All of Husserl's arguments thus far summarized have been confined to showing that the theory of psychologism leads to a certain relativism and scepticism. But if an opponent accepts this as a consequence of his theory, then Husserl's demonstrations do not *per se* constitute a refutation of psychologism. Only a refutation of scepticism and relativism would serve this purpose. Only then could Husserl consider his guiding motivation as established. We can put this more formally by saying that a denial of objective knowledge implies relativism, but only a proof that this consequence is false shows that the premise – the actual denial – cannot be valid. The same holds for the three identifications which went into the psychologistic denial of objective knowledge. Insofar as they involve this denial, they too will be proved invalid; but only insofar as the consequences of this denial – i.e., relativism and scepticism – are shown to be invalid. The ultimate result of the present argumentation is, then, to establish the motivation for actually searching for the conditions of objectively valid knowledge. As we shall see, the corollary of this result is the establishment of the priority of the epistemological standpoint.

The framework of Husserl's refutation of scepticism can best be introduced by bringing up a notion borrowed from Frederic Fitch. It is that of the "self-referential inconsistency" of scepticism.[1] As Fitch remarks, the sceptical view according to which "nothing is absolutely true" is actually a "theory about all theories." It, thus, casts doubt upon itself. Its theoretical thesis is that no proposition can be asserted as true for certain. Allowing for self-reference with respect to this assertion, it becomes inconsistent. On the one hand, it casts doubt on its own validity. On the other hand, if it is really valid, then it *wrongly* casts doubt on its own validity in casting doubt on the validity of *all* statements.

In Fitch's words, "... if it is valid, it is self-referentially inconsistent and hence not valid at all." We can also say that, as a *universal* statement, it is invalid since it must except itself from its own claims to universality.

This argument is basically the same as Husserl's. Sceptical theories are defined by him as those "whose theses either expressly state or analytically imply that the logical or noetic conditions for the possibility of any theory are false" (*LU*, Tüb., ed., I, 112; F., p. 136). If such theories are self-referring, then, in Husserl's words, they are "self-destroying." They have destroyed their own noetic and logical possibility. On the other hand, if they are not self-referring, they are meaningless. They have not the meaning given by the notions of noetical and logical possibility.

These notions, when referred to the conditions of a theory, concern both the subjective conditions for posing a theory and the objective ones for its actual validity. According to Husserl, the former are only "normative modifications" of the latter (*LU*, Tüb. ed., I, 239; F., pp. 233–34). Thus, as a piece of mediate knowledge, a theory presupposes, as an objective condition, the validity of the logical rules of inference by which mediate knowledge is obtained. It also presupposes the subject's ability to distinguish between a correct and incorrect inference. The same holds for appeals to experience. Experience must be recognized as having some objective validity and the subject must be able to recognize this — e.g., be able to prefer a direct experience of something to hearsay about the same thing.

Husserl's position can be put as follows. It is that a non-self-referring thesis about "the laws on which the rational possibility of any thesis and the proof of any thesis depend" is outside the horizon of sense constituted by these laws. As such, it has no meaning as defined by the latter. In a formal sense, this occurs because a non-self-referring thesis is a different *order* or *type* than that which it speaks about. If it were the same type, then some self-reference would implicitly occur.[2] In a more than formal sense, the force of Husserl's position can be understood by referring to certain remarks in *Ideen I*, §52. Their import is that the subjective and objective conditions for knowledge must be understood *as motivations for taking a stand* on a thesis. The laws that formalize such conditions are, in other words, laws which express the motivations for rationally taking a position on an assertion – i.e., for rationally assigning it a truth value. In this sense, to abstract from these laws is to *deprive oneself of any epistemological motivation.*

Such motivations are simple and may be detailed as follows. With respect to direct perception, we have the motive of trusting our own experience rather than that of hearsay. More specifically, the trustworthy witness is preferred over the untrustworthy, and our own direct experience has generally a greater motivating power than the reported experience of the first. With respect to what has not yet been perceived by us, we have experientially based motivations. Within the flow of experience, certain anticipations can grow up. They relate to possible experiences and objects of experience. They also relate to the general form of experience. The statement of such anticipations is a statement of what we *expect* to experience on the *motivating basis* of past experiences. Thus we expect that recurrent phenomena will continue to recur; we expect that the world will continue to look tomorrow much the same as it did today. The anticipation also grows up that experience *per se* will continue to exhibit the same general structure. A series of perspective views, we assume, will still be continuous. Objects will not disappear if we turn them around. On the basis of such anticipations, we can make general inductive statements about the general structure of possible objects of experience.

Since what is inductively established by experience can be overthrown by it, the motivated statements in this sphere are only statements of probable validity. What we have are empirical motivations which give assertions a greater or lesser probability. This is sufficient for the main point. It is that, abstracting from such motivations, all such probabilities are placed on the same level. One empirical thesis is as probable as the next, and since the number of such possible theses may be potentially infinite, the probability of each becomes zero. Thus, a thesis whose assertion is beyond any *identity of type with what we actually experience* is experientially motivationless. It is also, we can say, beyond the horizon of experiential sense. If the thesis is still within the horizon of logic, if it is not formally inconsistent, then it is still what Husserl calls an experientially "empty logical possibility."

If, however, it is also asserted to have no identity of type with logic, the thesis may be regarded as completely motivationless and empty. All commentary, all sense that experience and logic could lend to it are rejected. This means that a *non*-self-referential thesis about experience and logic is in the position of rejecting all immediate and mediate evidence — all argument and proof— which could be brought forward to make it intelligible. At this point we can say that the thesis is both infallible and empty. It is infallible because nothing can be brought forward to oppose it, empty because it is equally insupportable.

It is important to realize that the above argument concerns theses about experience and logic as non-self-referential, not as sceptical *per se*. What it does indicate is that when an epistemologically sceptical thesis about experience and logic is not to be considered as meaningless, it must be considered to be self-referential. It is at this point that, as involving appeals to experience and logical arguments, it becomes inconsistent with itself.

An interesting notion, here, is that this inconsistency places the thesis in the *category of logical contradictions.* A typical example of such paradoxes is the Epimenides: "Epimenides the Cretan said that all Cretans were liars." We can, as is obvious, apply the same characterization to this statement as was applied to the sceptical thesis. The *denial of the validity* of the statements made by Cretans is (self-referentially) inconsistent with the *validity of this denial.* The denial itself constitutes an *exception* to the denial and, thus, destroys its own claims to universality. As the characterization indicates, logical contradictions are inconsistent precisely to the point that they implicitly assume the validity of what they explicitly deny. In other words, they are inconsistent because they *presuppose in their own case* the opposite of their explicit theses.

The conception allows us to bring out the underlying movement of Husserl's arguments against scepticism and relativism. He is arguing that scepticism and relativism are self-referentially inconsistent because their assertions involve a denial of presuppositions which their own assertions implicitly assume. Thus, just as Epimenides' statement, if really valid, presupposes the negative of his assertion — i.e., *not* all Cretans are liars — so, here, the argument is that scepticism and relativism work only by presupposing in their own cases the negative of their theses. If correct, the conclusion present in this may be thus stated: it is that the theses of scepticism and relativism are not really statements but rather logical paradoxes. To use a Wittgensteinian phrase, the "language game" of such theories is that of the logical contradictions.

The previous arguments may be considered sufficient to cover the case of scepticism. If not meaningless, the epistemologically sceptical theory may be considered to be inconsistent with itself. Its own truth claim implicitly violates the claim of its denial. As for relativism, we may, following our previous discussion, classify its denial as ultimately one of a conception of being-in-itself. The denial follows upon the relativistic reduction of the conception of universal validity or truth for everybody. A corresponding reduction of the conception of the object of this truth must, as we said, take place.

The scope of the reduction in the validity of an assertion allows us, according to Husserl, to distinguish individual from specific relativism. The individual relativist asserts, "For each man, that is true which appears to him to be true; one thing to one man, the opposite to another if that is how he sees it." Specific relativism, when it takes the form of anthropologism, asserts: "Every judgement rooted in what is specific to man, in the constitutive laws of mankind, is a true judgement for human beings" (*LU*, Tüb. ed., I, 114-15; F., p. 138). Now, these statements of limitations placed on the validity of a judgement are understood by Husserl as theses asserting limitations on the corresponding concepts of the objects of these judgements. His remarks on these theses can be correctly interpreted as showing how they presuppose their opposites. The dominant argument is that the denial of objective being only works by presupposing it.

To begin with the first thesis, it is clear that to remain within the limits of his thesis, the individual relativist must treat the fact of his making his assertion as true for himself and not as true in itself. Moreover, as Husserl remarks, "Even the fact of his subjective thinking, he will treat as merely true for himself and not as true in itself" (*LU*, Tüb. ed., I, 115-16; F., p. 139). This implies that all his judgements — even the most immediate perceptual judgements concerning his own contents of consciousness — must be denied objective value. Thus, his thesis recommends itself to those who believe that the "being-for-me of a conscious content could not as such also be a being-in-itself," that "subjectivity in a psychological sense could conflict with objectivity in a logical sense" (*Ibid.*, I, 116, fn. 1; F., p. 139).

This argument is left by Husserl in an unfinished state. Its conclusion can be drawn out by observing that the self in such a doctrine can only be the above mentioned conscious contents. Anything else — e.g., a physical body — would imply an objective status. This implies, however, that if conscious contents are relative to the self, they are relative to themselves. But to be relative to one's self — and not to another — is a definition of objective being, of being in itself. The thesis, then, if it is to have an intelligible sense within its own limits, must violate these limits. It has, as a presupposition, a notion of the objective being of the point to which it declares things relative. The individual relativist must, in other words, *except his own being* from the universality of his category of being-for-me.

The same sort of argument, though in a much more explicit manner, is given for the case of specific relativism. The original assertion that truth for a species is relative to the specific constitution of the species implies that there is actually such a thing as this specific constitution. It also implies that such a constitution has, objectively speaking, definite properties determining the species' grasp of the truth. These last assertions, which are objective, refer to the constitution of the species as something objective. Insofar as they are consequences of the original statement, it too must presuppose their notions. Thus, once again, the denial of objective being must except the point to which it declares things to be relative. As Husserl says, "The relativism of truth presupposes once again an objective being as a point of relation — the contradiction of relativism lies in this" (*LU*, Tüb. ed., I, 132; F., p. 151). Since the contradiction is with its own thesis, the thesis is *inconsistent with itself*.

The same inconsistency follows even if we attempt to avoid the above objections. In such an attempt, we would have to say that the objective being of a specific constitution is not presupposed in making the thesis. As Husserl observes, the implication would then be that the objective being of the constitution in question would depend on the species being determined to hold it as an objective truth that it had such a constitution. Since, however, the constitution itself is held by the thesis to be the determining factor, the constitution must be understood as a *"causa sui"* (*LU*, Tüb. ed., I, 120–21; F., p. 143). Once again, the inconsistency with the original denial is apparent. The notion of a self-caused cause is a notion of something absolute and objective — not dependent and relative. A constitution relative to itself in this way is, by definition, objective.

The conclusion of these arguments — which have been rather drastically summarized — may be stated in its final form. The conclusion is based on a notion of objective being, defined such that its denial leads directly to relativism. Insofar as relativism must presuppose this notion to state its own thesis, its statement may be called self-referentially inconsistent and, hence, invalid. The notion of being at issue is that which is correlated to objectively valid knowledge. Thus, by such argumentation, Husserl may be understood as establishing the motivation for the search after the conditions of the possibility of this knowledge. In a certain sense, we can say that a "space" has been opened for this type of inquiry.

Somewhat more precisely, the situation may be described in terms of the epistemological standpoint. This is the standpoint that begins with the knowing relationship. To generalize from Husserl's arguments on psychologism, we can say that scepticism is engendered whenever some other relation is declared to be prior to the knowing relationship. In the particular case of psychologism, it is the relation of causality. But the arguments against it can be generalized to include the relationships of history, language, culture, etc. All we have to do is to see these relationships as *outside* the knowing relationship and as somehow *prior* in the sense of determining its content. The Husserlian position on such theories should be clear from the above. If they attempt to avoid the sceptical consequences which undermine their own claims, they must justify themselves as items of knowledge. At this point, however, they become inconsistent with themselves, for they presuppose the independence and priority of the knowing relationship with respect to their own justification.

The question, here, is how to understand the priority of the standpoint of this relationship. In other words, what are the conditions of its possibility?

CHAPTER III

THE CATEGORY OF THE IDEAL

1. THE CATEGORY IN THE CONTEXT OF *IDEEN I*

The last chapter ended with establishment of the guiding motivation, but did not state how it was to be satisfied. Here, as always, the factor of freedom must be recognized in following a motivated path. The stages which make up its journey are, within certain limits, determined by open choices.

One of these choices may be delineated as follows. If we reflect on the asserted priority of the epistemological standpoint, then this priority seems to necessitate a reinterpretation of what consciousness is. The priority assumes that the knowing relationship is prior to all other forms of relationship includes the causal. A first understanding of this indicates that consciousness in its relation to the world cannot be interpreted causally. The same conclusion arises from Husserl's criticism of the identification of the logical with the causal law. The identification, as we said, leads to a certain circularity of interpretation. The circularity can be avoided only if we assume that the laws of thought are *not the same* as natural causal laws (See above, p. 23). We can then say that the knowledge of the natural laws is structured by the laws of our thought. But we do not interpret these laws solely as natural laws and, thus, commit the fallacy of explaining them in terms of what they were supposed to explain. A further motivating connection for this conclusion can be drawn from our Remark to Chapter I. The import of this Remark is that it is a category mistake to take causality, when understood as an empirically based concept of relations of dependency amongst appearances, and use it to explain appearance *per se.* Such relations presuppose the fact of consciousness as providing the realm in which they may appear. The category mistake is an attempting to use them to explain this presupposition. As the Remark concluded, if we do attempt this, then we will never return to the presupposition — i.e., to the fact of consciousness.

The implication of these reflections can be seen to indirectly lead to certain positions of *Ideen I*. Over and beyond the epoché — conceived as a suspension of judgements concerning existence — there is in *Ideen I* a realization. The realization is not itself a restraint from these judgements. It is rather a return to the process of judgement after it has been purified of certain presuppositions belonging to what Husserl calls the "natural attitude." These presuppositions rest on the assumption that the world of "nature," as investigated by the scientific or natural attitude, embraces the whole of being. Now, the realization is that consciousness is ontologically distinct from this world. More precisely stated, what one is supposed to realize is that there are *two* spheres of being, one absolute, the other dependent (see *Ideen I*, §49–§50). The former is "pure transcendental consciousness"; the latter is worldly being, which is "transcendent" to consciousness. It goes without saying that the phenomenological reduction, as defined in our Introduction, is not possible without this realization. Thus, Husserl, after completing his description of the two spheres of being, writes that what is essential is "the not so easily obtainable evidence that the phenomenological reduction is possible as a shutting off of the natural attitude and its general theses . . ." (*Ideen I*, §55; Biemel ed., p. 136). This shutting off depends upon the fact of the two spheres of being which *are there to be realized*. Otherwise, a turn from transcendent to immanent or conscious being would not get us out of the natural scientific interpretation given to this being. It is only when transcendental consciousness shows itself as a different realm of being, that Husserl can say that "the phenomenological reduction does not mean a mere limitation of judgement to a connected part of the totality of real being" (*Ideen I*, §51; Biemel ed., p. 120). Now the first evidence that the reduction to consciousness is not a move to a part of real being is found in the arguments given above that consciousness cannot be explained causally.

Having said this, we should also observe that the reduction, as grounded in the above realization, is not the same as the eidetic reduction. Husserl is quite clear on this point. He writes, "Since the reader already knows that the dominating interest of these meditations is a new eidetic, he might at first expect that the world as fact falls to the reduction, but not indeed the world as

THE CATEGORY OF THE IDEAL 37

eidos nor any other sphere of essence." He contradicts this surmise with the words, "We, however, do not take this path nor does our goal lie in this direction . . ." (*Ideen I*, §33; Biemel ed., p. 70). The direction taken is the examination of "pure experience, pure consciousness" with its "pure correlates of consciousness"; that is, one fixes one's glance on the "sphere of consciousness" and studies what is "immanent" in it (*Ibid.*; p. 71).

Why is the study of what is immanent in consciousness opposed in this way to the eidetic? Husserl adds several remarks which give us a clue to the direction of his thought. Taking consciousness as the field of its experiences, he notes:

> Entrenched as we are in the natural standpoint . . ., we, like the psychologist, take all that we find here as real world events, as the experiences of animal beings. It is so natural for us to see them only as such that, acquainted as we are with the possibility of a change in standpoint and searching after a new region of objects, we do not realize that these spheres of experience are themselves that out of which, through the new standpoint, the new region springs; that is, we do not realize that with the absolute method of the epoché, psychological experience, which psychology itself gives us, changes into a new type of experience. Connected with this lack of realization is the fact that, instead of keeping our glance on this natural psychological sphere, we turn away from it and seek new objects in the ontological realms of arithmetic, geometry and the like, whereby, in fact, nothing new can be won (*Ideen I*, §33; Biemel ed., p. 71).

This passage can be read as containing a number of assertions. The first is that when we take conscious experiences as "real world events," we are motivated to seek "a change in standpoint." The standpoint would be one where the psychological relativism implied by this view of experience would no longer obtain. The result is a turning to the ideal realm of "arithmetic, geometry and the like," a turning which, in fact, involves the eidetic reduction. When we read the passage in this way, its final words can be taken as making a crucial distinction between the eidetic and phenomenological reductions. They, then, contain the thought that until we overcome the naturalization of consciousness — i.e., overcome through the phenomenological reduction the belief that experiences are "real world events," this turning does not reveal a realm where something "new can be won."

The reason why this passage is so interesting is that, thus understood, it can be seen as describing the path of thought in the *Logische Untersuchungen*. This is a path we shall presently study in detail. Before we do, it might be well first to pause for a moment and speculate on why the *Logische Untersuchungen* does not embrace the *Ideen*'s solution of the non-worldly reality of consciousness. The reason that can be given may be entitled "the abyss of the self-determination of consciousness."[1] An entry into this abyss is made by the recognition of the special status of consciousness; it is a status which is given once we admit that the fact of consciousness cannot be derived from any series of physical processes, no matter how extended. The radical interpretation of this is that consciousness is *not* a physical reality and, therefore, does not stand under material-causal determination. The abyss first appears when we ask what determines consciousness in its attempt to get objectively valid knowledge of the world. If we assume that the world is physical in its reality, while consciousness is not, then a notion of determination which would span such totally different regions of being seems to be excluded.

Direct solutions to this problem must naturally involve bridging the assumed difference in the regions of being. Now, the solution of the volumes of the *Ideen* is to overcome the difference in favor of consciousness: the spatial-temporal world is not really other than consciousness — at least, if we mean by otherness, that it forms a region of being whose principle is other than that of consciousness. Consciousness, rather, becomes "the primary category of being in general"; it is "the original region in which all other regions of being have their roots, the region to which they are essentially related and on which, hence, they are all essentially dependent" (*Ideen I*, §76; Biemel ed., p. 174). As for the region of spatial-temporal reality, "It is a being that consciousness posits in its experience . . . beyond this, it is nothing at all, more precisely, for this being the notion of a beyond is a contradictory one" (*Ideen I*, §49; Biemel ed., p. 117).

The abyss, implicitly present, becomes apparent when we reflect on these remarks. If consciousness is the region of being on which all others are dependent, then it cannot be dependent on any one of them. This means that in its relations to them, it must become *totally self-determinative*. The given actual world becomes at this point only "a special case of many possible worlds." These worlds exist "only as correlates of essentially possible transformations of the idea of 'experiencing consciousness' with its more or less ordered interconnections of experience" (*Ideen I*, §47; Biemel ed., p. 111). As for the forms which we may, through the eidetic reduction, abstract from a given world, they too, as a specific region of being, become dependent on the forms and interconnections of the experiences of consciousness (See *Ideen III*, §13-14, *Formal and Transcendental Logic*, §61, §84).

The above remarks are sufficient to indicate that this solution is not directly derivable from the *Logische Untersuchungen*'s criticisms of the naturalism of psychologism.[2] The motivations for this radical position are, as we shall show, not fully intelligible without a careful study of the positions of the *Logische Untersuchungen*. It is only then that we can judge why Husserl feels compelled to face this abyss.

The earlier work, in fact, takes the alternate path for bridging the gap between consciousness and the world. As the remarks we quoted above indicate, the resolution is in favor of the world. Thus, the *Logische Untersuchungen* takes mental experiences as "real world events." It also attempts to get out of the relativism this implies by seeking a new standpoint "in the ontological realms of arithmetic, geometry and the like." The fundamental distinction in this solution is not between immanent and transcendent being, between "being as consciousness and being as 'manifesting' itself within consciousness" (*Ideen I*, §76; Biemel ed., p. 174). It is rather a distinction between the real and the ideal being of the world. In this, consciousness with all its experiences is assumed to be part of *Realität*. We have, then, the assertion, repeated again and again, that "mental being is also real being" (*LU*, Tüb. ed., II/1, 133; F., p. 359).[3] We also have, however, the assertion that over and above the real, there is the realm of ideal being. This is the realm where the contingency of the real does not exist. The duality of the situation can be expressed as a hope. It is that, if we can somehow find a standpoint in the ontological realms of "arithmetic, geometry and the like," we can avoid the contingency of the real in the positing of knowledge. As is obvious, the assumption of this standpoint is the assumption of the possibility of the eidetic reduction. If such a reduction can be assumed, without also assuming the special status of consciousness, then the abyss mentioned above can be avoided.

Now, although Husserl asserts in the *Ideen* that "nothing new can be won" from turning to the ontological realms of arithmetic, geometry and the like, each of these, regarded in the *Logische Untersuchungen*, does have an advantage which recommends itself to him. The logical laws fit into this collection of realms, and Husserl has argued that an *empirical interpretation* of all such laws is an intolerable metabasis. The conclusion of these arguments shows the *advantage* of these realms. It is that, as *non*-empirical, they are absolutely silent on the real — including the real psychological circumstances of our judgements concerning them. The laws which we draw from them, in other words, show us by their content that they are not empirically derived, inductive generalizations of the singular facts of experience. As such, they do not in their content concern individual facts or make existential assertions about them (e.g., the assertion that a fact of type A will be such as to spatially-temporally follow a fact of type B). From this Husserl concludes that their validity is independent of the fact world. This means, for example, that the fact that we do at times think illogically has in itself no bearing on the truth or falsity of logic. It means, more generally, that the *validity of these laws,* which in their content make absolutely no assertion about facts, is *absolutely independent of all facts* including, most importantly, the facts which constitute our contingent thinking organization as studied by the psychologist and the evolutionary biologist (See *LU*, Tüb. ed., I, 74; F. p. 107).

A radical conclusion is drawn from these assertions. It is that there are *two different types of laws,* and, corresponding to them, *two different types of sciences.* Sciences of the real set forth general, inductively derived laws relating to spheres of fact. The extension of their general concepts is one of individual, temporally determinate singulars. Sciences of the ideal — sciences of arithmetic, geometry, logic and so forth — on the other hand, set forth ideal general laws, grounded with intuitive certainty in general concepts. The extension of *their* general concepts is one of lowest specific differences (See *LU*, Tüb. ed., I, 178; F., p. 185).[4]

This distinction of the two sciences in terms of the *range of instances* falling under their concepts indicates Husserl's first reaction to his own arguments against psychologism. His initial procedure — which is continued in some sense throughout the *Logische Untersuchungen* — may be represented by two elements. In an attempt to get out of psychological relativism, he *assumes with psychology the reality (Realität) of the subject*. He then goes on to point out that the laws of logic, mathematics and so forth have *nothing to do with reality* conceived of as the domain of spatial-temporal singulars and, therefore, they are not laws for the psychologically real subject.[5] In fact, in terms of this first perspective, we must reach beyond the real subject if we are to get at the objects of these ideal laws.[6]

Two preliminary points may be mentioned about this method. The first is that the ideal is defined in terms of its *transcendence.* The ideal transcends the factual contingency of the real; the transcendence, in other words, is one of *Wesen* over *Tatsache*. Since the subject, interpreted in terms of psychological reality, remains in the realm of *Tatsache,* the *eidetic reduction* of the *Logische Untersuchungen*, the reduction that leaves as a "residuum" the world of essences, can be *understood as passing beyond this interpretation of the subject.* In other words, in the first instance (i.e., in the "Prolegomena"), one turns away from the real subject, as interpreted as a contingent product of biological development, and considers things that are true in themselves — true, that is, independent of and prior to all such factually existing subjectivity. The point, we note, simply follows from the division of the two types of sciences in terms of their concepts' range of applicability. If the range of those of ideal sciences does not extend to temporally determinate singulars, then we must say, for example, about the laws of arithmetic: "They are absolutely silent concerning what is real; they tell us nothing about either real things counted or real acts in which they are counted, i.e., acts in which such and such indirect number characteristics constitute themselves" (*LU*, Tüb. ed., I, 171; F., p. 180). The latter, insofar as they are factually real, must be abstracted from to get at the objectively valid arithmetical laws.

The second point is that such a procedure, while apparently avoiding psychological relativism, tells us absolutely nothing about its own grounds of possibility. Thus we are, on the one hand, told that we do have "intuitive certainty" with respect to the general concepts upon which the ideal laws are based; but, on the other hand, we are not told how this is possible for us as real psychological subjects. The eidetic reduction's possibility for us – as factually contingent subjects – is, in other words, left hanging. The difficulty here is that the possibility of the eidetic reduction, as mentioned above, is the possibility of entering the non-relativistic standpoint. One may also observe that the difficulty concerns the relation of the real and ideal in the epistemological context. Once one begins with the real in order to argue to the ideal (as Husserl does when he argues that the laws of the psychologically real subject are *not* the ideal laws of logic, mathematics, etc.), one is stuck with both the real and ideal and their conflicting, though apparently equally valid, claims on the knowing subject.[7] This ontological difficulty in the conditions for the possibility of knowing reaches its climax in Husserl's attempt to concretely describe the real subject's process of eidetic abstraction.

2. THE CATEGORY IN ITS OWN CONTEXT

This description and the doctrines it involves cannot be understood by us without a thorough study of the text of the *Logische Untersuchungen*. In this, we leave behind our preliminary comparison of the *Logische Untersuchungen* with the *Ideen I* and enter into the path of Husserl's self-understanding of his particular method. The first part in this understanding may be described as a general extension of his thesis. The original thesis is that the truths of logic, mathematics and so forth cannot be described as causal facticities. The thesis is extended by Husserl to include the case of the truths of perceptual knowledge. To put this first part in the proper context, we observe the following: Its proof of the independence of the truths of perceptual knowing is not *per se* a proof of the truths of the perceptual knowing which *we* carry out. As so often, Husserl splits the problem. He first demonstrates that the perceptual meaning can be conceived as ideal in relation to the perceivers and thus does not have the real being which would put it into causal relation with the perceivers. He then attempts to demonstrate the second part of this thesis, namely that we, as real subjects, can grasp this meaning and that this meaning is the meaning or sense of the object itself. To introduce a word of caution, it is to be observed that the two parts of this demonstration are not necessarily consistent with each other.

The first part can be regarded as beginning with giving the ideal the characterization of an idea or species. To possess such characteristics is to satisfy certain requirements with respect to universality and particularity.[8] We may take as an example the ideal (non-contingent) truth that $7 + 5 = 12$. If it is indeed true in itself that $7 + 5 = 12$, then every particular assertion that has this as its content is true. This single objective content, this self-same identical meaning, is thus present in all particular true assertions about the sum of $7 + 5$, its presence, indeed, being that which makes them true. Even if, however, no one were to make this sum correctly (e.g., supposing that factually no thinking being ever knows how to count beyond 10), this self-same identical meaning or content would remain true in itself. The content, then, can be present in the many without destroying its self-subsistent unity. Now, such a content, Husserl argues, can be considered not only as present in all correct judgements concerning this sum but also, by virtue of its self-subsistent unity, as *standing against* the many judgements about it. It is, in other words, the one thing which decides whether all the many factually possible judgements concerning this sum are true. Insofar as in its unity (in its singleness as an objective criterion) it does stand against the many, it can be considered as ob-jective (*gegen-ständlich*). The objectivity, here, is not that of a physical reality, but rather of a content manifesting itself as one in many.

We have just opposed the objectivity of a *content* to the objectivity of a *physical entity*; yet in another view, it is clear that the epistemological objectivity of the latter depends upon that of the former. The physical entity, to be grasped as objective (as there for everybody), must have a definite and definitely describable content. The content must be capable of the same one-in-many phenomenon. Implicit in this notion is, of course, the characterization of objective being which the refutation of scepticism and relativism indirectly establishes. To review its conclusions, the refutation of the opposite thesis leaves us with a necessary conception of the notion of objective being as one of being in itself. This means being as it is prior to and independent of all contingent interpretation of the real thinking organism. Thus, whatever a factually contingent subject may think, objective being, according to the argument, still maintains its objective relations. Corresponding to these relations of being considered in itself is truth in itself, objective truth. Thus, if the sun and the earth, for example, have a certain objective relation, the content which expresses this relation is true in itself, true, that is, independent of and prior to all factually possible statements about this relation. Once we accept these notions, the same argument follows about the content of a perceptual judgement as about the content of an essential judgement – e.g., the content of the judgement that $7 + 5 = 12$. Thus, the content, "the earth revolves around the sun," is present in all particular true judgements about this factual relation, its presence being that which makes them true. If, however, no particular judgement were, in point of fact, ever made with this as the content of its assertion, the content would still be true in itself. It would still be true that the earth revolved about the sun, assuming, of course, that their objective relations remained the same.

Even this last, the condition of the temporal *enduring* of the objective relationship, can be eliminated as a condition for the truth of our factual assertion. All we have to do is make our factual assertion complete by adding to our assertion of a spatial relationship the assertion of a time when. Given its original objective truth, the content continues to remain true forever. The mere passage of time does not affect the truth of the assertion about the obtaining of a relation at a particular time. With this modification, the truth of a content of a perceptual assertion manifests itself under the modality of the one and the many that characterizes an idea. Its presence in the many judgements does not undercut its own self-subsistence as an objective criterion.

Now, if we ask what is implicit in the notion of this modification, we have the Husserlian thesis that *truth overcomes its occasional character by including in its content the occasion of what it asserts*. In this, it is self-understood that when the assertion includes a reference to the speaker, the occasion of the *act of assertion* is also included. In other words, it is by virtue of such inclusions that the assertive statement escapes the fate of being occasionally true — i.e., having a truth value capable of being nullified by a change of time and place from the occasion of its original utterance.

Before we examine Husserl's defense of this thesis, we should mention the necessity in the given context for it. In his description of real being, Husserl asserts, "Temporality for us is a sufficient characteristic of reality" (*LU*, Tüb. ed., II/1, 123; F., 351). Granting this, truth must be considered to be a-temporal in order to be placed in the category of the a-temporal ideal. The same conclusion follows when we note that it is only as an *objective criterion* that truth functions as an idea with respect to its many temporally located assertions. If the time or circumstances of the assertions could invalidate its nature as a criterion, then the criterion would not be self-subsistent with respect to its instantiations — a second necessary characteristic for the conception of truth as an idea or species. What this means for Husserl is that he can assert:

> Each truth is an ideal unity with regard to an infinite and unbounded multiplicity of possible true statements having the same form and content (*LU*, Tüb. ed., I, 187; F., p. 192),

only after he has repeatedly asserted:

> Truth, however, is "eternal" or, better, it is an idea and as such beyond time. It makes no sense either to give it a position in time or a duration, even if it lasts through all time (*LU* Tüb. ed., I, 128; F., p. 148).

The Husserlian thesis, then, can be restated as follows: It is by virtue of the *inclusion of its occasion in its content*, that the truth value of a statement *escapes being temporally determined by its particular instantiations embodied in spoken or written assertions.*

The justification for this centers on a single point. It is that ". . . every subjective expression allows itself to be replaced by an objective expression . . .," the latter being one that can explicitly specify its own circumstances (*LU*, Tüb. ed., II/1, 90; F., p. 321). Husserl also states this in the following way: "The content, which in a specific case the subjective expression means in orienting its meaning to the occasion, is an ideal unitary meaning in exactly the same sense as a content of a fixed expression" (*Ibid.*). This statement may be regarded as equivalent to the first; for if the referent of a subjectively occasional expression is an ideal meaning unit and, thus, can be expressed by a fixed, objective expression, then the latter can replace the former.

To do this, of course, the objective expression must include in its content the elements whose *absence* makes the expression occasional. These are the references to the relevant circumstances in which the expression occurs. Now, in terms of the *content* of these circumstances, this expressibility remains what Husserl calls an *ideal or objective* possibility. This possibility remains, even though, for certain languages with certain limitations in the means of expression, it is not a *factual* possibility. The guarantee of the former, objective possibility is a notion of being established by the refutation of relativism. It is being as definite in content and thus as having, in terms of this content, the possibility of *definite description*. According to the refutation, this characteristic is inherent in the *necessary* notion of objective being. The notion is defined within the logical horizon constituted by the law of non-contradiction. As we said above, the horizon presupposes for its applicability a notion of being as determinate in its content (See p. 11).

According to Husserl, in the case of real being, its determinate nature includes its "specific . . . position in space and time" (*LU*, Tüb. ed., II/1, 90; F., p. 321). This means that when, in the manner of the refutation, we take truth to be the *objective sense of being,* then truth expresses the sense of real being only by including such spatial-temporal determinations. Only in such cases is it truth, in the sense of being a correlative category to this being. When it is not, it is occasional. This brings us to the point that most of our statements, *according to the meaning of our words,* are occasional. Although being *per se* is definitely describable, we do not for reasons of practicality definitely describe it.[9] Thus, in most cases, as Husserl says, it is necessary when hearing a statement "to orient its present actual meaning to the occasion, the speaker and the situation" (*LU*, Tüb. ed., II/1, 81; F., p. 315). Now, the fact that, by virtue of this orientation, we do understand the statement has for Husserl two important implications. The first is that such circumstances must implicitly enter the content of the *understood meaning*. The second is that the *words* that make a statement occasional must in some sense function as *indicators*, pointing to these circumstances and allowing them to become an implicit part of the statement's meaning.

The two implications may be brought out by considering Husserl's treatment of the occasional expression: "I wish you luck." The words *I* and *you*, function, according to Husserl, as "universally operative indicators" (*LU*, Tüb. ed., II/1, 82; F., p. 316). As such an indicator, the word *I* means only "your vis-à-vis intends himself." Like other occasional words – such as *here, now, today, yesterday*, etc. – *it points to a circumstance* in which it is used *without expressing the circumstance's particular content*. This means, according to Husserl, that every occasional expression implies a distinction between the "indicating (*anzeigende*) meaning" of a word and the "indicated (*angezeigte*) meaning" of the circumstance it points to (*LU*, Tüb. ed., II/1, 83; F., p. 316). A further conclusion is that, in understanding an occasional expression, we must pass from the former to the latter.[10]

The above analysis yields, for Husserl, the desired result. It is that, in an occasional expression, *meanings per se* do not alter. The indicating meanings, as simply pointers, remain the same. So do the indicated meanings of the various objects pointed to by the occasional expression. Thus, the fact that someone else uses the word *I* to refer to a different subject neither affects the inherent content of my own subject nor changes the content of the word *I* as a universal indicator. What changes in each case, as Husserl says, is "the act of meaning" – i.e., "the subjective act which gives the expression its (understood) meaning" (*LU*, Tüb. ed., II/1, 91; F., p. 322). The change, in other words, is in the movement from the indicating meaning to the various possible meanings, which as a pointer it can refer to. Granting this, Husserl's original assertion follows. The content meant or referred to by the occasional expression is not itself occasional. It is just as much ideal – i.e., capable of being held constant in a definite description – as the content of a fixed expression.

As Husserl makes clear, this argument follows only on the assumption of certain premises. Thus, we must assume that the things themselves have a definite meaning. This last must be regarded as a meaning that is in some sense independent of the particular usage of a particular language. In our specific context, this means that there must be such a thing as an *indicated* meaning to which we can move from the occasional expression. Since in most cases, it is the *intuitive presence of the indicated circumstances* that allows us to understand the occasional expression, a further premise may be put as follows: It is that of the *inherence of sense in intuitive presence.* This is what allows intuition to specify in the normal manner our understanding of the occasional expression (See *LU*, VI, §5). Summed up, the premises amount to the assertion that being has an inherent sense which shows itself in intuitive presence. In Husserl's view, the possibility of this assertion can be considered to be already established — at least insofar as its opposite thesis leads to relativism. The real strength of this argument is thus the strength of his refutation of relativism.[11]

The modification of making truth include its occasion has, as we said, one purpose: that of placing truth in the category of the ideal. The placing of truth in this category naturally affects our conception of verification — i.e., our conception of grasping a truth *as true*. If truth is ideal, it must be apprehended as such. It must be apprehended as something *one* in *many*. The consequence of this is drawn by Husserl when he writes, "We are conscious of truth as we are in general conscious of a species — e.g., redness" (*LU*, Tüb. ed., I, 128; F., p. 148).

The necessity for this remark can be drawn by returning to our original comments on the Kantian equation between objective validity and necessary universal validity (See above, pp. 10–11). If the claims for the one are equivalent to those of the other, then a certain line of reasoning can be seen to plausibly follow. We assert that the recognition of the objective validity of a content of judgement is *the same as* the recognition of its necessary universality. To recognize the latter is to see the content as the *one* content that can be present in all valid judgements about a well-defined relation. The recognition, in other words, involves the grasp of the content as one in many, i.e., as a species. Since the species is ideal and since necessary universality also implies objective validity, we get Husserl's statement: "The ideality of truth is what implies its objectivity" (*LU*, Tüb. ed., I, 191; F., p. 195). We also get Husserl's repeated assertions that truth can be grasped as true only by virtue of an act which can grasp it as a species, the act being that of ideation or, in our terms, eidetic reduction (See *LU*, Tüb. ed., I, 128-29; F., pp. 148-49; *Ibid.,* I, 229-30; F., pp. 226-27).

We can express the move that this act makes possible in terms of the Kantian notions of a judgement of perception and a judgement of experience. The first may be defined as a judgement which is valid insofar as it expresses a relation to our own subject. It expresses what is there for me at this moment. The judgement of experience, on the other hand, claims validity as expressing a relation to the object. Its claim is to be valid not just for me but for everyone else in the same way. Otherwise put: it asserts that there is something there which I am experiencing and which others could also experience. Now, the move from the first to the second can be described as an admission of the necessary *universality* of our judgement of perception's content (See "Prolegomena," §18, *Kants ges. Schr.*, IV, 298). Granting this essentially Kantian conclusion and granting also the Husserlian addition that one must in a specific act recognize this content to be universal, we have an important consequence which determines Husserl's later investigation of subjective accomplishment. It is that all states of affairs, all correlates of judgements asserting an objective relationship, must be grasped as having an ideal character. In other words, the act of ideation must be extended to play its part in the grounding of every objective assertion.

Although we are not in any sense ready to discuss the question of subjective accomplishment, we may for a moment pause and, in a deeper sense than hithertofore, consider the necessities for this position. They center on the issue of verification as simple reperformance. This last can be introduced by noting a certain Humean problematic. It begins with the assertion that what can be established by individual perceptual experiences can be overthrown by them. If this is the case, then such experiences can ground only probabilities and the question arises of how we can assure ourselves of the validity of any of our individual assertions. Within the view put forward by this problematic, the reperformance of a cognitive act cannot be seen as *per se* validating it. The reperformance, as simply *another look* at an object, can have its own validity called into question and thus demand a further reperformance. In other words, if reperformance *per se* assured validity, its own validity would be dependent on reperformance.[12]

The Husserlian reply to this difficulty may be put in terms of a separation of two questions. On the one hand, we have the question of the stability of nature as it persists through time. On the other, we have the question of the validity of an assertion. The two questions are not the same. Thus, reperformance, conceived simply as an attempt to repeat a cognitive act and get the object as apparently the same, can answer only the first question — i.e., whether nature remains apparently stable. As for the second question, reperformance is only helpful to a limited degree. According to Husserl, it is useful only if, in reproducing an initial experience, it leads us to focus on the *content* of this experience. In other words, its role is limited to producing a *number* of experiences with *one and the same* content. With respect to the second question, then, its useful role is that of an act *preparatory* to ideation.

The guiding insight, here, is that what we attempt to validate in the process of verification is not the *existence* of an individual experience which, as such, has temporally passed away. It is also not the stability of nature. On the contrary, according to Husserl:

> "Validity" or "objectivity" and their opposites do not pertain to an assertion as a temporal experience, but to the assertion *in specie*, the pure and identical assertion ... (*LU*, Tüb. ed., I, 191; F., p. 195).

This insight may be expressed in terms of our discussion of occasional and non-occasional expressions. The expression of the full assertion, as *non-occasional*, includes, as we said, the content of its occasion. This means that the content of a judgement about real being should include a reference to time and place. Since a judgement's claim for validity is limited to its proper content, the consequence is obvious: A non-occasional judgement of fact claims validity only for its own occasion. Its verification includes the claim for its occasion; but it does not — if it is a judgement of a contingent state of affairs existing at a moment — involve a claim beyond this occasion. This limitation, as we shall see, does not affect the notion of the objective validity — or validity for everyone — of the assertion. It does, however, point out that the question of such validity is other than the question of the stability of nature.

The discussions of this chapter are naturally limited by their abstraction from the question of subjective accomplishment. Within this limitation, we can bring them to a natural conclusion by mentioning what Husserl sees as serving as a subjective instance of truth *qua* species. This will allow us to bring up again the presuppositions for the arguments of his enterprise. Now, according to Husserl, this subjective instance is an individual consciousness of *original givenness*, this consciousness being that which forms the evident judgement (See *LU*, Tüb. ed., I, 190; F., p. 194). We accordingly ascend to a conception of a particular judgement as an instance of a particular *species* of truth when we recognize this conscious experience as one of many experiences of a similar type. In other words, we recognize it as only an example of a genuine grasp of the object. It is seen to be one of many possible conscious experiences, each of which could display the object with this specific content and display it with the evidence of original givenness.

The presuppositions for this description are (1) that being in itself has a definite sense which can be originally given; that (2) consciousness itself possesses a standard for recognizing this original givenness; and that (3) this standard is, in fact, one of perceptual presence. A further presupposition is, of course, that once we do have an example of original givenness "individualized in the experience of evident judgement," an act of ideational abstraction can take place which will allow us to see the instance as an instance (See *LU*, Tüb. ed., I, 229-30; F., pp. 226-27).

The first presupposition Husserl considers as established by his refutation of relativism. The last presupposition has been the subject of our immediate discussion. It is with the second and third that we concern ourselves now. Their basis is in the readily apparent assumption that the sense of the object which we derived from an act of cognition cannot be the same as the object's inherent sense *unless the object itself can be originally given.* "Originally given" has in this context two senses, the second, in fact, being a presupposition for the first. Husserl takes it to mean *given as it is in itself.* He also understands it to mean *given in a relation that is original in the sense of being sui generis* — i.e., a relation not essentially dependent upon some other relation. This last presupposition has been mentioned by us before. It is simply that of the primacy of the epistemological standpoint (See above, p. 33). Within the present context, it means that cognition itself must possess a standard for validating itself; for if we assert the opposite, then we are asserting that cognition cannot be cognitively validated — i.e., that its validity depends on some *other* relation. Since original givenness has been equated with the evidence that validates, this comes down to the assumption that cognition must in itself possess a standard for recognizing original giveness.

This standard within cognition for the original giveness of an entity is, according to Husserl, the entity's perceptual presence. The reason that he chooses this as a standard may be described as essentially Cartesian. Following Descartes, he recognizes degrees in the "clarity and distinctness" of our perceptions. These degrees give rise to the conception of an *inherent* standard. Within perception itself, in other words, the notion of a completely adequate perceptual presence arises as a goal for perceptual, cognitive experience. This is the presence that has the highest degree of richness of detail and also the highest degrees of vivacity and "reality" of the content portrayed (*LU*, Tüb. ed., II/2, 83-84; F., pp. 734-35). The notion of "reality" refers in this context to the features of the object that are not, as it were, read into this presence — be this through association, imagination or some other process. It refers to the features that are actually present in what Husserl calls the *pure* perceptual content. When such a standard is reached or approached, the "object itself" is given according to Husserl. It is given "as it is in itself."[13]

CHAPTER IV

THE BEING OF THE IDEAL

We have so far avoided any reference to the being of the ideal. But without a discussion of this point, the considerations of our last chapter lack a certain measure of intelligibility. We shall accordingly focus on two issues and then relate the results of our inquiry to our previous discussion. The issues before us are, first, Husserl's argument for positing the ideal as a distinct region of being and, second, his discussion of the nature of the ideal considered as it is in itself. A grounded discussion of these issues requires a necessary propaedeutic. A mention must be made of Husserl's doctrine of sense and reference. The doctrine is crucial for understanding the way in which the ideal can be considered to describe a region of being.

We begin with a definition of the relevant terms. By *sense* is meant the *inherent meaning* of an expression. *Reference* is understood as the expression's "characteristic of directing itself as a name to this or that objectivity" (*LU*, Tüb. ed., II/1, 149; F., p. 289). Husserl, it should be noted, does *not* follow Frege's terminology, according to which sense is *Sinn* and is so distinguished from reference as *Bedeutung* (See *Ibid.*, II/1, 52-53; F., p. 292).

The two principles of Husserl's doctrine can be stated at once. They are that *sense implies reference* and that *reference, as the above defined characteristic of an expression, does not imply the existence of the designated object.* The second follows naturally from the first. For not all expressions with an inherent sense can be correlated to an existent object. Thus the expression, "the present king of France," if taken to refer *through* its sense, cannot be understood such that its reference implies existence.

The understanding of this, of course, depends on the first of these principles. Its origin is (somewhat surprisingly) a definition Husserl borrows from Frege. Frege, to do justice to the fact that many different expressions can refer to one and the same object, distinguishes the sense of an expression from its objective reference by defining the sense as the "mode of presentation of that which is designated" ("On Sense and Reference," *Translations from the Philosophical Writings of Gottlob Frege*, eds. and trans. P. Geach and Max Black, Oxford, 1970, p. 57). Husserl uses this definition throughout his work. He writes, for example, "The presentations *equilateral triangle* and *equiangular triangle* differ in content, though both are directed, as can be made evident, to the same object. They present the same object but in 'differing modes' " (*LU*, Tüb. ed., II/1, 414; F., p. 588). This Fregean distinction between the mode of presentation and the object presented also receives what Husserl considers to be an equivalent formulation. He expresses it as distinction between "the object as (*sowie*) it is intended and the object, simply, which is intended" (*LU*, Tüb. ed., II/1, 400; F., p. 578).

These definitions are sufficient for Husserl to make his point. He argues that we cannot talk about a mode of presentation without mentioning the presented *per se*. Equivalently, we cannot talk about the sense of the object, the object *as* it is intended, without bringing in the object which is intended (See *LU*, Tüb. ed., II/1, 54; F., p. 293; also *LU*, I, §13). The converse also holds for Husserl. He considers it a matter of definition that in the sphere of signs that function by virtue of an inherent sense, reference to an object must involve sense. In this sphere, in other words, "Reference to an object is possible *a priori* only by being a definite mode of objective reference" (*LU*, Tüd. ed., II/1, 416; F., p. 589). This statement, we should observe, includes the case of proper names — e.g., *Socrates, the city of Athens,* etc. Husserl engages in an immense and complicated argumentation to show that these names can only refer by virtue of an inherent sense. His argument, in other words, is that "certain meanings correspond to these names, and *through these* we refer to objects" (*LU*, Tüb. ed., II/1, 140; F., p. 366, italics added).

We cannot, without deviating from our own purposes, provide the particulars of this argumentation. It will have to be sufficient to observe that it involves Husserl in a lengthy discussion of Mill's distinction of connotative and denotative names and an even more extended discussion of the relation between naming and positing

(See *LU*, I, §1-§16, §26-§28, V, §33-§36, §38, §40). Its essential point is that the name, as bearing an inherent sense, can refer without presupposing the existence of its referent. But the inherently *meaningless* sign, functioning simply as an indicator, *definitely* refers only in the presence of the appropriate circumstances which serve to activate it. In other words, to refer to a specific correlate, it must presuppose the existence of the referent towards which it only points in an indefinite manner. Since naming is not positing – i.e., since the named object need not be understood as existing at all – the distinction between the two is made on the level of sense. The name, in other words, must possess an inherent sense to definitely refer without presupposing existence.

The exact reasons for this will be given by us later when we discuss sense as sense. This last is considered to have an ideal character which expresses what Husserl calls a "pure possibility." Existing on the *level of the ideal*, it does not have *the required relation to the real* which would allow us to draw from it the implications of real "matters of fact" (See below, p. 65).

Before we pursue this line of inquiry, which concerns the ideal simply in its own nature, we should mention what seems to be the premise of Husserl's lengthy argumentation about the nature of a name. It is that being cannot be thought apart from sense, but the latter can be conceived in abstraction from the former. We can concretely express this by stating that in direct perception we grasp an object both as existing and as bearing a definite sense; but in a report of this perception, we transmit, not existence, but the sense of existence. The hearer of our report, in other words, can only ultimately confirm its validity with respect to the object by a perception of his own.

There is here, perhaps, only one essential point. It is that the confirmation occurs not by matching sense *conceived as one thing* with existence *conceived as abstracted from this*, but by grasping *both together*. The way in which we do grasp *both together* is by synthesizing our perceptions of the supposed referent. If the perceptions fit, or are "harmonious" with one another, we say that the object bears an *intelligible sense*. We also say that we are not experiencing a hallucination – as well we might if a series of perspectival views did not fit together. We say rather that we are experiencing the object as *something existent*.

The fact that these two theses are *in this case* essentially coincident has an important bearing on the notion of a name. Its implication is that to each actual object "there belongs a possible synthesis of perceptions, a possible individual meaning, a possible proper name" (*LU*, Tüb. ed., II/2, 31; F., p. 693). The name, Husserl argues, must embody the meaning which the synthesis of perceptions manifests. It cannot be attached to any single perception or imagination or pictorial illustration of the object. For, as Husserl observes, with respect to the name of a person:

> The same person makes his appearance in countless possible intuitions, and all these appearances have not just an intuitive but also a recognitive (*erkenntnismäßige*) unity. Each individual appearance from such an intuitive multiplicity can be used with the same right as a basis for the synonymous naming through the proper name. Whichever experience is given, the person using the name means one and the same person or thing. He means it not in the way of simply being intuitively oriented to it, as in the consideration of an individual object foreign to him. Rather he recognizes it as this definite person or thing. In naming, he recognizes Hans as Hans, Berlin as Berlin (*LU*, Tüb. ed., II/2, 30-31; F., p. 693).

The point stressed by Husserl in the context of this remark is that if we did not have the ability to recognize an object as itself, we could never use a name to refer to an object in a new orientation. This implies, however, that for a name *to refer in this normal way* it must bear within itself the characteristics of meaning. It must show itself as one thing applicable to many. The name, in other words, has to contain in itself the sense that unifies an indefinite range of possible perceptions – i.e., those which show themselves to be perceptions of one and the same object.[1]

As Husserl is careful to point out, the name embodies the thought of a unified range but does not presuppose the actual presence of its individual members. Because of this, we can namingly refer in the *absence* of the referent.[2] And in the case of the object that no longer exists – or, in fact, has never existed – we can use the name to set up the thought of a remembered or, alternately, an imaginary synthesis of possible perceptions. In such cases, as Husserl says, the name, with respect to instances of *actual* intuitive presence, has "no range" at all. "Its universality is an empty pretension" (*LU*, Tüb. ed., II/2, 30; F., p. 692). It still, however, intends one thing in many. It still sets up a possible recognition of a common content in a multitude of possible intuitions; but the intuitions which form the range of this content cannot be present. The putative recognition is only thought.

The ability of a name to do this is grounded by Husserl in his ontological description of sense *qua* sense – i.e., in his description of ideal being considered just as it is in itself. This will be discussed by us later. For the moment, we confine ourselves to pointing out that the above discussion gives, by definition, a referring power to a name independently of whether or not the designated object exists. The underlying reason for this is the coincidence, in the case of naming an actual object, of the theses of *Sinn* and *Sein*. When the thesis of sense is detached by way of a verbal report, it carries, implicitly with it, its intention to the other thesis. Whether or not this thesis can be justified depends, of course, on the presence of the actual intuitions which can be subsumed under its putative range. But as intending one thing in many, it still contains the thought of a possible existent which stands as the correlate of a synthesis of perceptions. This applies to all significant expressions. Thus, Husserl can say: "To use an expression significantly (*mit Sinn*) and to refer expressively to an object (to form a presentation of it) are one and the same." He can also immediately add to this: "This does not at all depend on whether the object exists or is fictitious or even impossible" (*LU*, Tüb. ed., II/1, 54; F., p. 293).

To draw an obvious conclusion from this last remark, what Husserl wants in his doctrine of sense and reference is to *separate* as well as relate the theses of sense and being. The separation occurs when we say that sense implies reference, but reference does not imply (in the sense of presuppose) the existence of the correlate to which we refer. The separation may be expressed in terms of the traditional distinction between essence and being. In this distinction, the question of the former refers to *what* a thing is – i.e., its inherent sense. The question of the latter refers to *whether* the thing is – i.e., its actual being. Now, if we assume that the question of *what* does not presuppose a yes or no answer to the question of *whether*, we have the distinction traditionally drawn between the two concepts.[3] The distinction may in *some* sense be considered as transferred to Husserl's doctrine. The reason for this is that sense and reference, when regarded in themselves, stand on one side of this metaphysical distinction. Regarded in themselves, they do not presuppose an answer to the question of actual existence. The consequence of this is that in the *Logische Untersuchungen a purely linguistic ontology is not possible*. Questions of essence and existence cannot be worked out on the level of sense and reference as characteristics of expressions because, as such, they are silent on the question whether something is. Husserl's point in this regard has already been indicated in the above discussion. It is that existence is not a function of meanings by which we refer. It is rather a function of the confirmation of meaning by intuitive presence. Such confirmation, in terms of real being, occurs when the putative range of intuitions unified by our meaningful expression are actually filled up by genuinely present examples. It is, in other words, the intuitive givenness of the object which makes us move beyond meaning into being. The implication of this, as our next chapter will show, is that a dialectic of *sense and presence* is ultimately regarded as much more important than that of sense and reference.

The conclusion, we should note, should have been expected. It follows from the refutation of relativism and the remarks that were made in the last chapter. The refutation leaves us with the doctrine that "truth and being are categories in the same sense and are clearly correlative" (*LU*, Tüb. ed., I, 131-32; F., p. 151). The last chapter put forward the Husserlian position that intuitive givenness was the instance of truth. If we combine these positions, then we come up with the double thesis that we can speak of being only in the context of truth and that this last implies the context of possible intuitive givenness. In terms of Husserl's technical phraseology, we are asserting that "being in the sense of truth" is "to be defined as the identity of the object at once meant and given in an adequation or (in conformity with the natural sense of the words) as the adequately perceivable thing as such . . ." (*LU*, Tüb. ed., II/2, 126; F., p. 768). Here, intuitive givenness becomes the sign of being.

This doctrine has been fashioned by Husserl with a definite purpose in mind. It allows him to grant ideality but *not being* to a certain class of meanings. This is the class of false or inconsistent meanings. Since logic deals with meanings only insofar as they manifest an ideal character — i.e., insofar as they are mutually comprehensible as identical contents by *many* — it is obvious that false or inconsistent propositional meanings must be given this character. Otherwise, logic could not deal with falsity or inconsistency. Thus Husserl writes, "Even in such cases, we distinguish from the fleeting experiences of affirmation and assertion their ideal contents, i.e., the meaning of the assertion as the unity in multiplicity" (*LU*, Tüb. ed., II/1, 44; F., p. 285). Now, to grant being to all such meanings does not just imply a certain overstocking of the ideal realm. It also implies that this realm or region of being is useless in interpreting the region of the real. In other words, if we take the ideal region of being as composed of *principles* of the region of the real, then these principles cannot be allowed to be indefinitely multiplied. An infinite number of principles for a given region makes the region unintelligible by a finite mind.

Because of this, Husserl writes:

> It is naturally not our intention to place the *being of the ideal* on the level with the *being-thought-of* of the fictitious or inconsistent. This last does not exist at all. In an authentic sense, nothing can be categorically predicated of it; and if we do speak of it as if it were existent, as if it had its own mode of being — i.e., that of being "merely intentional" — on closer consideration this shows itself as an improper way of speaking. There are, in fact, only certain lawfully valid connections between "objectless presentations," which by virtue of their analogy with truths bearing on objective presentations suggest this talk of merely presented objects which, in fact, do not exist (*LU*, Tüb. ed., II/1, 124; F., p. 352).[4]

Husserl's point here is readily intelligible in the light of our previous discussion. In the case of direct perception, the theses of being and of sense are coincident. This allows us to form an incorrect analogy according to which we can talk about the being corresponding to some given sense when, in fact, the being does not exist. In such a case, we only *think* the connections between presentations which, as harmonious, would allow us to posit the being. The same point carries over to positing objects of purely ideal concepts — e.g., the object referred to by the concept π.[5] The object as existent is distinguished from its concept by virtue of the possibility of its intuition. There are, as we shall see when we discuss eidetic intuition, certain features which must be present to make the coincident theses of the sense and being of the ideal. Again, by an incorrect analogy, they can be transferred to a case where such intuition is not possible. The fact is, however, that in such cases, we cannot genuinely talk about the being of an object. For, over and beyond a unitary reference to an object, being involves intuitive presence. In other words, the ideal's character as *meaning* — as capable of being understood by many — is not sufficient.

With this, we have laid the groundwork for Husserl's argument for positing the ideal as a form of being. The argument, as we should expect, is one of positing on the basis of truth. We must first grant that truth and being are correlative categories. Admitting this, we can speak of ideal being. In this context, as Husserl states, "A person who takes this talk at first simply as an indication for the validity (or supposed validity) of certain judgements and interprets this being as the correlate of the subjects of these judgements can find no objection" (*LU*, Halle ed., II, 101). In fact, as the second edition adds, the person is "evidently obliged to affix the title 'actually existent object' to the correlate of the judgement's validity, to that which it judges about" (*LU*, Tüb. ed., II/1, 101; F., p. 300). The argument here is extremely simple. It is that in addition to truths about real objects, ". . . we also grasp with insight certain categorical truths that are related to . . . ideal objects. If these truths are valid, then everything that their validity objectively presupposes must have being" (*LU*, Tüb. ed., II/1, 125; F., p. 352).

As is obvious, the above follows only by virtue of an analogy. We can assume that truth and being "are categories in the same sense and clearly correlative." We can also assume that the mention of being serves "at first simply as an indication of the validity (or supposed validity) of certain judgements." We can then interpret "this being as the correlate of the subjects of these judgements." This, however, is not sufficient to secure the argument for the ideal being of the species. We must also assume that there is a *common sense to the predicate "truth"* that allows us to call not only statements about matters of fact, but also statements about ideal relationships "truths." Only then will the correspondence between truth and being assure us that there is a common or *universal sense to the predicate "being"* such that we can say that real and ideal objects both "truly are."

The implications of making this analogy concern both truth and being. Since the context of truth involves intuitive givenness, there is here a demand that the ideal and the real have *certain essential features in common* with respect to the way they become intuitively present to consciousness. This sets up a task with respect to Husserl's description of the subjective accomplishment of ideation. This task (and the limitations it implies) is crucially important and will be considered by us in Chapter VII.

With respect to being, there is, of course, the implication of a universal sense of being corresponding to the universal sense of truth. *Husserl identifies the former with that of object.* According to Husserl, "the conceptual unity of what-is" is "the same" as that of "object in general." The "universal sense of being" is, thus, equated with that of "object in general" (*LU*, Tüb. ed., II/1, 125; F., p. 353).

An explanation of this identification can only be preliminary. It can, however, be begun by noting two elements in the Husserlian conception of object. The first is the conception of object as *Gegen-stand*, i.e., as that which *stands against* consciousness. This means, for Husserl, that being is objective insofar as, in standing against consciousness, its own actuality does not depend upon the actuality of our grasp of it.[6] It also means that the object in its own content stands against consciousness as an objective criterion of the validity of the way consciousness grasps it. The second element is the conception of object as something standing in relation to consciousness. Equally with the first, its context is that of truth. Here, however, the aspect emphasized is the fact that, as posited out of this context, the notion of object functions only in the sphere of knowledge. Being *qua* object, in other words, is understood as being *qua* object of knowledge and is used exclusively in this sense (See *LU*, Tüb. ed., I, 228-29; F., p. 226).

The intended result of these two elements is to describe being as an object and to mean by this that *being stands in relation to consciousness* precisely *through its character of standing against it.* This standing in relation *by virtue of* standing against is, for Husserl, what characterizes *epistemological presence,* as opposed to the mere *bodily presence* which things have to one another. Things are not "objective criteria" of the truth or falsity of their relations to each other. As such, the relation of "mere" things is not epistemological.

There are two implications of this doctrine which we shall mention but leave to our next chapter to discuss. The first is the elimination of the Kantian thing-in-itself, at least if we describe this as something standing outside of any possibility of the knowing relation of consciousness. The second is a certain dialectic of sense and presence by which the conflicting claims of standing against and standing in relation are sorted out.

This last concerns the topic of subjective accomplishment. For the present we will consider only the *formal* resolution of the characteristics given to the notion of being as object. The question is how can we say that the actuality of a being does not depend on the *actuality of our grasp* and yet say that being *qua* object is understood as object of knowledge. For Husserl, the resolution of the two is given in terms of a notion of *possibility.* The fundamental assertion is that being is objective because its own possibility includes the possibility of a *subjective grasp of it.* In other words, the possibility of a being is *the same* as the possibility of its being in relation to consciousness. This last, again, is itself *the same as* the possibility of its being an object for us.

To understand this resolution two things are necessary. We must gain an understanding of Husserl's doctrine that the ideal considered in its own being represents what he calls a "pure" or "mathematical" possibility. Equally, we must comprehend how this reflects back on the argument for positing on the basis of truth. The linking point here is that each truth, as a species, has its own ideal being.

Now, Husserl asserts with regard to the species that possibility (*Möglichkeit*) and essentiality (*Wesenhaftigkeit*) are the same (*LU,* Tüb. ed., I, 240; F., p. 234). He also equates the being (*Sein*) of universals (*Allgemeinheiten*) with the being of ideal possibilities (*LU,* Tüb. ed., I, 129; F., p. 149). A number of clarifications must be made to avoid any misunderstanding of this equation. Thus, we must not assume that ascribing possibility to a species is asserting that a species is *merely* possible in the sense that it itself may or may not be. On the contrary, to predicate possibility of a species is to predicate being, at least in the sense that a species' *ideal being* expresses possibility. What is possible in the sense of being *merely* possible "is the existence of objects falling under the relevant concepts" (*LU*, Tüb. ed., I, 240; F., p. 235). The possibility of a species refers, here, not to actual existence, but rather "to the possible being of empirical individuals falling under the universals" (*Ibid.*, I, 129; F., p. 149).

This leads to a second clarification. It is that the possibility of a species does *not* depend on the actuality of its instances. Because, in this sense, the species do not make a *claim* on the actuality of real existence, Husserl can write ". . . possibilities themselves are ideal objects. Possibilities can as little be found in the real world as numbers in general and triangles in general" (*LU*, Tüb. ed., II/1, 115; F., p. 345). The reason that they do not make this claim can be indicated by first observing that Husserl refers to mathematical definitions to illustrate the equivalence between the possibility and essentiality of a concept (See *LU*, Tüb. ed., I, 240; F., p. 235). This points to a crucial refinement in his notion of possibility. It is that he conceives of ideal (as opposed to empirical) possibility in mathematical terms. Thus Husserl, speaking of the ideal existence of the species, writes:

> This "it exists" ("*es gibt*") has here the same ideal sense as it has in mathematics. To bring it back to the possibility of the corresponding individuals is not to reduce it to something other, but merely to express it through an equivalent phrase. This is so, at least when possibility is understood as pure and, therefore, not as empirical possibility, and when it is understood as "real" in *this* sense (*LU*, Tüb. ed., II/2, 103; F., pp. 749-50).

The above remarks and the doctrine they imply can best be understood in terms of a position borrowed from Frege. It is that in mathematics, *definition specifies the range of a concept*; but such specification involves only the *possibility, not the actuality, of the objects of the range*. Frege can be understood as arguing this in the following way: He first observes that we define a concept by specifying what properties objects must have to fall under the concept. In doing this, we specify the objects only insofar as we specify an indefinite range of them. How far they are thus specified can be brought out by the fact that it is a mistake to assert, for example, that the concept *square* is itself square — i.e., has the properties of rectangularity *as a concept.* The conclusion, here, is that *properties of objects* specified by a concept are not themselves *properties of this concept.* Frege's particular point is that mathematical definition is not creative of mathematical objects. In fact, such definition does not involve the assertion, in a positing sense, of a single object that has the properties defined by the concept. The *concept that is asserted* does not have the properties, and the existence of the corresponding objects is *not asserted.* In Frege's words: "Whether such objects exist is not immediately known by means of their definitions . . . Neither has the concept defined got this property, nor is a definition a guarantee that the concept is realized" ("Preface," "Selections from the *Grundgesetze*, Vol. I," *Trans. from the Phil. Writings of G. Frege*, ed. cit., p. 145).[7]

From this, the notion of "pure" or "mathematical" possibility is easily derived. The distinction Frege makes between *properties* of objects and the marks of concepts which specify these properties extends for Frege to concepts whose range is one of individual real objects. The relation of concept to object is the same as in the case of strictly mathematical concepts. This means that their assertion as concepts does not involve claims for the real existence of their objects. Such objects are conceived only in terms of their possibility. This is why — in *some* sense, following Frege — Husserl says that "possibilities are ideal objects." It is also why he asserts that to point to the existence of possible instances falling under a species to explain this species' existence is not to explain this in terms of something else — i.e., a realm of real as opposed to ideal being. This follows because in defining concepts, we simply *state the conditions* of a range of possible objects falling under the concepts and make no presuppositions about the reality of such ranges.

The attractions for Husserl of this doctrine are numerous. They follow from its fundamental position that if we remain on the level of possibility conceived in this "mathematical" way, no presuppositions about individual real existents need be made. This has an obvious reference to the conception of a proper name as a species containing the idea of a unified range of perceptions of some object. If the pure thought of a name as a species implies only possibility in the above defined sense, then a name's power to refer does not imply existence. The thought of a name involves the formal possibility of the corresponding perceptions, but not their given actuality. A much more general advantage is the underpinning of the distinction between real and ideal sciences. The two, we may recall, are distinguished by their general concepts according as these are conceived as species or empirical generalizations. The empirical generalization, by virtue of its origin, presupposes the existence of its range of empirical instances. It is, in its own content, in some sense defined by its range. The species, however, if we define it in the above terms, *does not in itself contain the thought of the real existence of its range.* Like a mathematical definition, it defines its range of possible instances rather than being defined by it. With this, we have the basis for Husserl's later notion of the presuppositionlessness of *Wesenschau.*[8] A pure regard to species or essences — if, indeed, they are to be conceived as possibilities in the mathematical sense — involves absolutely no presuppositions with respect to real existence.

There are two further elements in Husserl's notion of possibility. Together, they complete the list of clarifications which we have been making. There is first the division of possibility into prior and posterior, in which the "ideal existence" of the species stands as the "original possibility" with respect to its instances (*LU*, Tüb. ed., II/2, 106-107; F., p. 752). There is, secondly, a corollary to this which states that the obtaining of a posterior possibility guarantees the obtaining of a prior possibility.

The insight which grounds the notion of the existence of a species as an "original" possibility may be simply put. It is the insight that the being or existence of a species represents the possibility of being-one-in-many. This means for Husserl that the species must itself *first be one* before it can be *one-in-many.* The upshot of this is the doctrine, "Unity as such grounds possibility" (*LU*, Tüb. ed., II/2, 109; F., p. 754). Unity, in other words, represents the original possibility of a species' being one in many.[9]

The insight, we should mention, has especial force in the case of complex species. What it states is that the component elements of such species must themselves be unifiable before they can have the possibility (as a unified, complex species) of *unifying* a range of instances.[10]

As is obvious, the notion of priority is inherent in this schema. To put this in the Fregean terms of concept and object, we can say that the concept *qua* species must be one in order to specify an unambiguous unitary range of objects. If the species is complex, then the unifiability of its contents expresses the *prior possibility* of their being objects whose properties are specified by the species' contents.

This whole conception finds a natural extension in Husserl's treatment of a *logic of content*. Investigations III and IV examine the unifiability of contents into complex wholes. The two fundamental notions in this logic are those of foundation and whole. Non-independent "moments" or contents of objects are called by Husserl "founded contents" (*fundierte Inhalte*). A content is founded or dependent on another if it needs the other in order to be. More precisely, as Husserl says, "A content of type A is founded in the content of type B, if A, by its essence (i.e., lawfully, on the basis of its specific character) cannot exist without B also existing" (*LU*, Tüb. ed., II/1, 275; F., p. 475). This determines the notion of a whole which, according to Husserl, is "a sum of contents covered by a unitary foundation without the help of any further contents" (*Ibid.*). An example of dependence would be the dependence of a content of *color* on that of *extension*. An example of a founded whole would be one made by the *loudness, pitch* and *duration* of a tone. The first and second of these contents — in the Husserlian sense of the term — mutually "found" one another. They are both dependent or are "founded" in the third content; but beyond this they have no further dependencies.

Inherent in this is, of course, the notion of certain minimal requirements for forming a whole. Thus, a moment of color and the three moments of tone cannot *by themselves* form a whole, for they lack a common ground of foundation. We must, in this case, add the moment of extension: a red tone is not a possible whole; but a red sounding extension is such. Another factor that prevents the formation of a whole is the placing of conflicting demands on a necessary ground. Thus, the non-independent moments of squareness and roundness both require a moment of extension; but since they place conflicting demands on this latter, a round square is not a possible whole.

The relation of this "synthetic" logic to the above discussion is immediately set once we realize that what is at issue is not just the relation of perceptual contents but rather the relationship of properties of objects. As Husserl says of its distinction between non-independent moments and a whole, "It transcends the sphere of contents of consciousness and becomes a highly important distinction in the area of *objects* as such" (*LU*, Tüb. ed., II/1, 225; F., 435).[11] The links here are the equation of object and being and the notion of perceptual presence as the sign of being. Perceptual senses cannot conflict if we are to posit being; and this means that the basic condition of the perceptual presence of an object is the unifiable, non-contradictory nature of the senses it bears. The same condition is transferred *mutatis mutandis* to the properties of objects as showing themselves in the senses of perceptual contents. The idea of a whole then becomes the idea of a possible object having the whole's contents as its properties. At this point the laws of content and whole become laws specifying the prior possibilities of objects.

The corollary to the notion of prior possibility follows almost as a matter of definition: If the posterior possibility demands the obtaining of a prior possibility, then the posterior cannot obtain without the prior also obtaining. As was said above, the obtaining of the posterior thus guarantees the obtaining of the prior possibility.

Husserl combines this corollary with the conception of the species expressing a pure or mathematical possibility in the following passage:

> There is certainly a good sense in speaking of the unifiability of contents whose factual union has always remained and always will remain excluded. But if two contents are united, their unity proves not only their own unifiability but also that of an ideal infinity of other cases, namely all pairs of contents that are like them in belonging to similar kinds (*LU*, Tüb. ed., II/2, 105; F., p. 751).

The conception of a species as a pure possibility does not include the conception of its factual instances. We can thus speak of the untion of the contents of the species without referring to these instances. On the other hand, the obtaining of a single instance proves, by virtue of the corollary, an ideal infinity of other possible cases. This infinity points to the complex species which permits, via its indefinite range, this infinite instantiation. As Husserl observes, it is this *species* which, as a prior possibility, is guaranteed by the obtaining of the posterior possibility — i.e., the single case of actual instantiation (See *Ibid.*).

Now, the interest for us of this doctrine is its application to the notion of positing on the basis of truth. Each individual truth, according to Husserl, is an ideal species — one that can be intuited through an act of ideation. The interpretation of species as representing pure or prior possibilities, gives us the following account of truth:

> Truth is thus also an idea. We experience it like every other idea in an act of ideation based on intuition (this is, here, naturally the act of insight), and we also gain the evidence of its identical unity over against a dispersed multiplicity of compared concrete instances (i.e., here, evident judgements). And just as the being or validity of universals, as in other cases, is *equivalent to ideal possibilities* — namely, in respect to the possible being of empirical instances which fall under these universals, so we see the same thing here. The assertions, "the truth is valid," and, "there are thinking creatures possible whose judgements comprehend the relevant contents of meaning," are equivalent.

The remarks that continue this passage show that the possibility of such thinking creatures is understood in the pure or mathematical sense:

> If there are no intelligent creatures, if the natural excludes them, if they are thus impossible in a *real* sense — or if there are no creatures capable of knowing certain classes of truths — then these ideal possibilities remain without fulfilling actuality. The apprehension, knowledge, bringing to consciousness of truth (or certain classes of truth) is nowhere

THE BEING OF THE IDEAL 69

ever realized. But such truth remains in itself what it is; it keeps its ideal being. It is not "somewhere in the void," but is a unity of validity in the timeless realm of the ideas (*LU*, Tüb. ed., I, 129-30; F., p. 149).

In terms of our above discussion, the meaning of this passage should be clear. The ideal being that is kept is the being of a pure possibility. This means that although the range of a truth *qua* species is composed of individual judgements that manifest its content, the assertion of the *validity of a truth* is not the same as the assertion of the *reality of its range*. The pure thought of the former, as grasped in an act of ideation, *is presuppositionless with respect to the real acts of judgement in which the truth is maintained*. Truth, in other words, in its character as a species, remains true whether or not anyone grasps it. This last simply follows from the refinement Husserl has made in the notion of a species. A species, in order to be such, must be able to be present in the many without destroying its own self-subsistent unity. The Husserlian refinement is that it is the thought of a species as a pure (or mathematical) possibility that grounds the description of the self-subsistence of this unity.

This has a natural application to the positing of being on the basis of truth. According to the argument of such positing, if we do have insight into certain truths, then everything presupposed by the validity of such truths must have being. The above requires us to translate this into a statement of possibility. Thus, the ideal validity of a truth is understood as the possibility of ourselves, as species of judging creatures, having insight into the truth. The positing of being on the basis of truth becomes, accordingly, the possibility of such positing. Further, since the context of truth is intuitive givenness or presence, the possibility of a grasp of the truth becomes the possibility of the presence to consciousness of the objects and relationships presupposed by the truth.

With this, of course, we arrive at the Husserlian resolution indicated above. As defined within the context of truth, the possibility of being is understood as the possibility of being in relation to consciousness, i.e., being an object for consciousness. Since possibility is understood in a "pure" sense, this means that if a truth is not grasped, if the objects and relations presupposed by the truth are not *actually* present to consciousness, nevertheless the possibility of their presence remains. The attempt here, as is obvious, is to use possibility to establish an objective sense of being *without violating the sense of its inherent relation to consciousness*. Since the possibility of presence remains even though a truth is not factually grasped, the sense of being *as this presence* is in some manner a sense independent of the actuality of its apprehension.

The whole of this discussion allows us to clarify certain points we made above about Husserl's notion of verification. The notion is based on the principle that the comprehension of a truth as a truth involves the grasp of it as a species. Now, since the species is a pure possibility, the grasp of truth as such must be interpreted in these terms. This necessitates a certain refinement or reinterpretation of the equation made between objective validity and necessary universal validity. We said above that to comprehend a content of judgement as objectively valid is, necessarily, to comprehend it as universally present in all judgements concerning the self-same relation. We can now say that to comprehend this content as a species of truth is to understand it as expressing the *pure possibility* of its presence in an indefinite range of these judgements.

This refinement both strengthens and limits the claim of objectively grasping the truth about some relation. If we express this claim in terms of a correspondence between our assertion and its object, then we do not *assert* the actuality of any correspondence other than our own. This follows since truth, in this regard, is grasped only as the *pure possibility* of such correspondence occurring. As expressing the thought of this pure possibility, the concept of a truth does not express the assertion of any actual correspondence other than the particular one on which it is based. This last, however — given the schema of posterior and prior possibilities — is sufficient to validate truth in the only way it can, *as a species,* be validated. As we quoted Husserl above, the single actual instance is sufficient to guarantee the possibility of an infinity of other instances similar in kind. It does not thereby guarantee the actuality of any other instance; though it does guarantee the species itself which is exactly equivalent to this possibility.

We may, in closing, observe one final point. It is that problems in the concept of verification arise when we equate universal validity with objective validity, but do not make the above refinement. In Husserl's view, it is the conception of the species as a pure possibility which distinguishes it from an empirical generalization. The latter needs a number of examples in order to be founded. Its probability increases with the empirical evidence for it. To conceive of universal validity in these terms is to conceive of it as establishable by numerous instances of reconfirmation. The confusion of this attempt to validate is, in the *Logische Untersuchungen*'s view, apparent. It is the confusion of the thought of a range of *actual* instances with the thought of a range of *possible* instances. Truth as a species involves the latter, not the former.

CHAPTER V

SUBJECTIVE ACCOMPLISHMENT: INTENTIONALITY AS ONTOLOGICAL TRANSCENDENCE

With the above, we have stated the preliminary ontological conditions for the view of consciousness as *Einsicht* or *Anschauung*. This is the conception of consciousness as possessing insight or intuition into objective being. As indicated in our first chapter, this conception requires an essential precondition. We must get the intentional relation — the relation of a subject directed to an object — out of real causality.

The problem is: how are we to do this? Husserl's answer, to be fully intelligible, requires that a mention be made of his concept of real causality — i.e., the causality characteristic of real being.[1] Temporality is viewed as a sufficient characteristic of this being; and this means for Husserl that causality is attached to this temporality. More precisely expressed: causality is viewed as temporal determination in which the conditions of the past determine those of the present. If we express these conditions as a series of variables, then these variables — when associated with a particular time point — are considered to be both determined and determinative (See *LU*, Halle ed., II., 249-50). The unity founded through such a series of determinations is a unity existing *through* time. It is a "thing-like" unity; and Husserl characterizes it by comparing it to the notion of unity brought forward in his logic of content. The latter concerns relations of dependencies between *coexistent* contents. The unity of a thing, however, is achieved by adding to these relations the relations of dependencies between *succeeding* contents (See *Ibid.*, II, 248, 250-51).

It is these relationships that make up *temporal or real existence* — at least if we consider such existence as that of *unities enduring through time*, no matter how short this time may be. The position, then, is that being, *insofar as it manifests a temporal character, manifests a causal unity*. In other words, by virtue of its temporality, it falls under causal relations. We achieve knowledge about these relationships "*a posteriori* by way of induction," but by virtue of the above schema we can say with Husserl, "such relations are possible *a priori*. They are evident as possibilities" (*LU*, Halle ed., II, 284). As our last chapter indicated, for Husserl, the evidence for a possibility is the evidence for an idea or species. It is achieved by insight into the essence of the entity under question.[2]

Insofar as the individual subject is essentially temporal, it is part of real being and falls under causality. Thus, Husserl applies to it the above specifications. There is, first, a unity belonging to "the phenomenological ego of the moment." This is the "unity of consciousness" which is determined by the specific dependencies of its contents — e.g., an experience of color requires an experience of extension. There is, further, the unity of the subject existing through time. Husserl describes this unity in the following terms:

> Just as the outer thing is not the momentary individual complex of characteristics, but rather constitutes itself as a unity persisting in change in first passing through a multitude of actual and possible changes, so the ego first constitutes itself as a subsisting object in the unity that spans all actual and possible changes of the complex of experiences. And this unity is no longer a phenomenological unity; it has its basis in causal lawfulness (*LU*, Halle ed., II, 332).

In other words, as subsisting through time, the ego falls under causality. As Husserl also puts this, the ego "counts for us as no more than a 'unity of consciousness,' as an actual 'bundle' of experiences, or even better as the continual thing-like unity, which constitutes itself in the experiences belonging to one 'ego' because this unity is demanded by both the specific and causal characteristics of these experiences" (*LU*, Halle ed., II, 356).

This sets the context of the problem Husserl faces in attempting to get the intentional relation out of causality. Granting that real relations, as involving thing — like unities, are causal relationships, the above states that these relations must involve the subject — at least, insofar as it is an enduring thing — like unity. The conclusion cannot be avoided by Husserl, for it is by virtue of his positioning of the subject as a temporal reality that has distinguished its laws — i.e., the laws of empirical psychology — from the ideal a-temporal laws of logic and mathematics. The difficulty, of course, is that to remain within this conception of the subject is to fall into relativism. One thinks the object not as it is in itself, but as one has been causally — i.e., contingently — determined to think it. The result is, then, the destruction of the "transcendence" or "reaching out" of thought, precisely the thing that is supposed to characterize the intentional relation.

The context imposes severe limitations on Husserl's options. He takes what seems to be the only way out. His solution has already been indicated by our discussion of the necessary ideality of meaning and truth, i.e., their capability of being one in many. Husserl lifts the intentional relation out of the causal nexus by *declaring its objective pole to be ideal.* In other words, over and above any "inherent actual" contents of consciousness, he posits the existence of an "ideal intentional content" (*LU*, Halle ed., II, 16).[3]

With this move, we get Husserl's early notion, so subject to confusion in its interpretation, of the *intentional object*. On the one hand, he declares that the intentional relationship is not a causal one — i.e., not one between two *Realitäten* (See *LU*, Tüb. ed., II/1, 391; F., p. 572). On the other hand, he asserts that the intentional object is the actual object — the actual object, for example, of a straightforward perception of this tree here in my garden (See *Ibid.*, II/1, 425; F., 595). These apparent contradictions can be resolved once one realizes — to take our example — that what one intends to see is precisely "this tree in the garden," that is, the perceptually embodied meaning by which the tree shows us *what it itself is*. The appearance of the tree, Husserl argues, is not "mere appearance" (as contrasted with reality), but rather the appearing of the tree through which the tree, by virtue of its very being as a spatial-temporal object, shows us what it itself is. Now, the tree shows us what it is by the *perceptually embodied* meaning, what Husserl also calls the *fulfilling* meaning. That perception embodies meaning is apparent for Husserl from the fact that we can, on the basis of perception, predicate certain characteristics of the appearing tree, report them to others and have our report confirmed by an independent observer. Perception could not be transformed into a report or a report confirmed by a perception unless there were an *identical content of meaning* present in them both (See *LU*, Tüb. ed., II/2, 95; F., pp. 743-45).

An inherent part of this doctrine is that meaning —whether perceptually embodied or present in a report — involves both *sense* and *reference*. It is because of this that we can have an intentional relation to a perceptually embodied meaning and say that this relation is also to an actually existent object. In terms of our example, we can say that the tree through its perceptually embodied meaning *refers to itself* as actually existent. An intentional relation to such a meaning is, by virtue of this self-reference, a relation to an actual object. The underlying point here is one that we mentioned above. It is that the objectivity of a physical object depends upon what we called the epistemological objectivity of its content. The former, to be grasped as objectively actual (as *there* for everybody) must have a content that is ideal in the sense of being one thing capable of being grasped by many. This ideality is not something that contradicts the object's existence as a real entity; it is rather that through which it must show itself as such. We can also put this in terms of the coincidence, in the case of perception, of the theses of the being of the object and the sense of the object. An intentional relationship to the object's sense is a relationship to what *per se* is ideal. By virtue of the coincidence of the theses, it is also a relationship to the being of the object which, in the case of the tree, is real. The tree manifests an intelligible sense, a coherent perceptual meaning. The harmonious fitting together of perceptions that allows this also allows the grasp of the object as something existent — as something there of which we are having perceptions. Insofar as the thesis of being is also a thesis of the presence of an intelligible, coherent sense, a relation to this sense is also a relation to being.

In a report, the theses of being and sense become separated. Yet as we pointed out, there is a reference in a report to the perceptions which would fill out the range indicated by the sense. The sense still remains that which unifies an indefinite range of possible perceptions. It is thought of as one thing manifesting itself in many possible perceptions. When the report is verified, the theses of being and sense are reunited. The perceptions are actually given; and, by virtue of their harmonious synthesis, the object appears as one thing in many perceptions — i.e., as the one thing of which we are having perceptions. The sense that it manifests in this appearance can be compared with that of the report. In both the report and the actual perceptual experience, the ability to be intended as one in many is, as Husserl says, the "ideal character" that makes the intentional object an object of thought or (in the case of perception) an object of knowledge (*LU*, Halle ed., II, 9).

Here, of course, we must observe that, as merely thought, in the sense of being significantly referred to, the object need not exist. There is simply the thought of a possible existent which stands as a correlate to an imagined synthesis of perceptions. If we call this the *intentional* object in the sense of an object *intended* or referred to by our thought, the notion of existence is not included in this concept. We have to say, "the intention, the *reference* to the object as bearing certain characteristics exists, but not the object" (*LU*, Tüb. ed., II/1, 425; F., p. 596). Even in this case, however, the intentional "object" equals the actual object in the purely analytical sense that the *intended* object of our reference is by definition the *actual* object of our reference, in the sense that we refer to no other (See *Ibid.*). As for the object intended or referred to by a coherent perceptual sense, the question of the identity between the intended and the actual object (the object as it is in its own nature) is a question of the adequacy of the given perception.

For Husserl, at this point, the question of whether the appearing tree is really the appearance of the tree in itself is answered by responding to what he considers the primary objection for identifying the two. This is that the subject-object relation is causal and thus contingent on certain material factors which enter into any physical account of causality. This, he has prepared for by the arguments related in the last two chapters. The account of the ideal, non-contingent nature of truth both demands and is supposed to demonstrate that the perceptual meaning can be considered as ideal in relation to perceivers. If meaning *qua* meaning is ideal, then the relationship involving it cannot be causal.

We see here the complex nature of the "intentional object," as identified with the unified, coherent perceptual meaning. On the one hand, it is the meaning, perceptually embodied, *of* this one thing — in our example, a real thing. On the other hand, as a meaning, its nature is ideal. It is one thing, yet available for many. We can talk in common, for example, about "this perceived tree." "This perceived tree," in other words, maintains its unity of meaning in all talk about it. It is, in fact, the one in the many, the intentional unity drawing together the statements about it. There is, in this context, a fundamental fact as Husserl puts it, "The fact, namely, that all thinking and knowing is directed to states of affairs whose unity relative to a multiplicity of actual or possible acts of thought is a 'unity in multiplicity' and is, therefore, of an ideal character" (*LU*, Halle ed., II, 9).

Several conclusions can be drawn from this. The first is that the transcendence or reaching out of consciousness is based on the characterization of sense or meaning as ideal. It is, in other words, based on an explanation of "how the same experience can have a content in a twofold sense, how next to its inherent actual content, there should and can dwell an ideal, intentional content" (*LU*, Halle ed., II, 16). This intentional content is *the content of the object that we intend to see*. As ideal — and Husserl stresses this again and again — it is no real (*real*) part of consciousness conceived as a physical reality (See, e.g., *LU*, Tüb. ed., I, 171, 175-76, II/1, 94-95; F., pp. 180, 183-84, 325). The transcendence of consciousness is thus *a reaching out beyond its reality to grasp an ideal content of meaning*. In other words, for Husserl in the *Logische Untersuchungen*, without the ideal, there is no *transcendence* by consciousness (as a natural reality) *of the real causal nexus*.

The above is, of course, only an ontological framework. To fill it out, we must ask how consciousness actually does this. How does it transcend its position as a physical reality among other physical realities? How does it achieve an *epistemological* as opposed to a *mere bodily relation* with the object? These are the questions of subjective accomplishment. Husserl's reply to them is an early form of his *Konstitutionstheorie*. The theory is presented in the first instance as an attack on the sense data theories of psychologism. According to such theories, at least as Husserl reports them, perception can be reduced to the influxes of the data of sensation, such "data" being taken as titles for real physical events, the real stimulations of consciousness by an external world. To counter this view, Husserl posits the *objectifying act* as essential to every perceptually oriented intentional experience. The function of this act is interpretive, it interprets the sensations that consciousness receives as sensations of some one thing – i.e., of an object which is there for consciousness. The doctrine here is that it is in "the animating interpretation of sensation that what we call the appearing of the object consists" (*LU*, Tüb. ed., II/1, 351; F., p. 539). Without going into the particulars of this theory, several points may be mentioned.

1. The theory may be regarded as an attempt to explain the circumstance that we do not *per se* "see" our sensations but rather objects of which we have sensations. Thus, we see, e.g., one and the same box however it may be turned. The perceived object remains the same, although the actually experienced contents shift with each turn of the box. In Husserl's words, "Very different contents are thus experienced, but in spite of this the same object is perceived. Thus, to give a general principle, the experienced content is not itself the perceived object" (*LU*, Tüb. ed., II/1, 382; F., p. 565).[4]

2. The distinction indicated above is actually threefold. For if we admit that the objectifying interpretation makes the difference between the actually experienced *sensations* and the *appearing of the object* through these sensations, then the act of interpretation can itself be neither of these. Husserl makes this point several times. In the "Appendix" to the First Edition, he writes:

> It is readily apparent that these interwoven sensations cannot themselves be considered as appearances, neither as appearances in the sense of acts nor as appearances in the sense of appearing objects. They are not the first because under the title *sensations*, we comprehend non-acts, which at most experience an objectifying interpretation by virtue of acts. They are not the second because to the phenomenal objectivity of sensations, acts themselves would have to belong. They would have to direct their intention to these sensations (*LU*, Halle ed., II, 707–708).

3. This last quotation brings us to a further point. It is that acts of interpretation are required to perceive even our own mental contents. As Husserl says:

> Outer perception is interpretation, thus the unity of the concept demands that inner perception be such. It belongs to perception that something appears within it, but *interpretation* makes up what we term appearance — be it correct or not, anticipatory or overdrawn. The *house* appears to me through no other way but that I interpret in a certain fashion actually experienced contents of sensation. I hear a *barrel organ* — the sensed tones I interpret as *barrel organ tones*. Even so, I perceive via interpretation what mentally appears in me, the *penetrating joy*, the *heartfelt sorrow*, etc. They are termed "appearances" or, better, appearing contents precisely for the reason that they are contents of perceptive interpretation (*LU*, Halle ed., II, 704-705).

4. What Husserl wishes to establish by this and similar passages is a distinction between the division of inner and outer perception, on the one hand, and the division of adequate and inadequate perception on the other. Both inner and outer perception can be adequate, and both can be inadequate. The doctrine that inner perception can be inadequate follows from the notion that perception *per se* is interpretation — on the most basic level, the interpretation that allows one to "attend to" or focus on a referent. Since interpretation can be correct or incorrect, so can the perception that is this interpretation. The deeper reason for this position (which is diametrically opposite to that of *Ideen I*) is to be found in the interpretation of the subject. The subject is asserted to be a part of real being. But to real being *per se* a definite type of perception is said to correspond (See *LU*, Tüb. ed., II/2, 145-46, 151; F., pp. 787, 791). The result, then, is that the subject itself, as a part of reality, must be perceived in the same fashion as any external reality.

5. A further point is that the theory is the forerunner of the noetic-hyletic distinction of *Ideen I*, §85. At its basis is the conception of the noeses, the "acts" of consciousness informing or shaping the contents of sensation which are with respect to such acts "hyletic" (from the Aristotelean term for matter). As is

obvious, the Aristotelean notion of form "informing" its matter is used here in an opposite sense from Aristotle's original intention. For Aristotle, consciousness (*nous*), as it exists in straightforward perception, was a "*tabula rasa*" with respect to its object. It did not inform its object but rather was informed by it; it became its object, taking on the object's form. In fact, Aristotle's "passive intellect," insofar as it did not have any form or structure, stood as "matter" with respect to the informing form of the object. For Husserl, on the contrary, it is consciousness that takes the active part. Its interpreting intentions inform the external matter of sensation.

6. The reason that Husserl reverses the Aristotelean position (a position which was designed to insure our grasp of objective being) is to be found in the theoretical necessities of his own position. The psychological relativism, against which he is arguing, equates the real act of judgement with the content of judgement. It also embraces, as a basis of this, a similar equation between the real act of perception and the perceptual content (the sense of the object that is grasped). Its position, concretely speaking, is that "presentation and what is presented are one and the same." Both are to be *reduced* to "the mere having of sensations" (*LU*, Tüb. ed., II/1, 507; F. p. 658). By virtue of this, it can equate the perceptual sense of the object, the sense which forms the basis of perceptual judgements, with certain real events – i.e., sensations – in a real, biophysically describable consciousness. The way is thus open for the physiological relativism discussed above. In Husserl's view, this reduction is actually "a refusal to take into account the phenomenological moment of interpretation . . ." (*Ibid*.). It is actually an ignoring of the perceptual act of interpretation and a direct equation between perceptual sense and the physical presence of sensations. This follows insofar as, admitting the existence of this act, one must, in Husserl's view, admit the distinctions drawn in points 2 and 3. Thus, it is the act of interpretation that results in the distinction between the data of perception and the appearing object. The act itself cannot be confused with either. Husserl's assumption of this interpretative, informing act is, then, itself intended to break up an equation that threatens our grasp of objective being.

Against the assumption of this equation, Husserl attempts to show that the presence of the sense of the object cannot be identified with the presence of real sensations. Now, he cannot dismiss *tout court* the arguments of the psychologists by denying the reality (*Realität*) of consciousness; for he has made this reality the basis of his argumentation that the ideal laws — e.g., the laws of logic — are not the laws that psychology derives from the real subject. From this, indeed, he achieves the double perspective that is characteristic of the *Logische Untersuchungen* — namely, the perspective of both the *reality* of the subject and the *ideality* of knowledge as the content of the known. Husserl, thus posits the existence of an objectifying interpretative act. The presence of the sense of the object is taken as pointing to the objectifying interpretation that consciousness places on its sensations. In other words, when we suppose ourselves, in the flux of differing contents of sensation, to be in contact with one and the same object, we are really presupposing a corresponding factor of interpretation. There must, Husserl argues, be a certain *identity of interpretation* that corresponds to the *grasp of identity*, i.e., to the grasp of the object that shows itself as the same when viewed from different sides (See *LU*, Tüb. ed., 382-83; F., p. 566). From this, Husserl draws the conclusion: "Interpretation never allows itself to be reduced to an influx of new sensations; it is a character of an act, a 'mode of consciousness,' a mode of 'mindedness.' Perception of the object in question is what we term the experience of sensations in this way of being conscious" (*LU*, Tüb. ed., II/1, 381-82; F., p. 565).

Since, in fact, what consciousness in its interpretative activity does to its sensations is "make sense" of them — i.e., place them in an interpretative framework of *identity of multiplicity* — the result is the presence of the perceptually embodied "fulfilling sense." Sense *qua* sense is ideal; and this means that it is the presence, or being-there, of the ideal that is the result of this activity. This is why Husserl immediately adds after the above quotation about interpretation, "The being-there (*Dasein*) of the sensory content is, thus, totally other than the being-there of the perceived object which is presented through the content but is not inherent within consciousness" (*LU*, Halle ed., II, 361).[5] This totally other presence is the presence of the object *according to its sense* and not according to the contents of sensation which are caused by it.

The point of this argumentation should be readily apparent. It is to assert that consciousness transcends the real influence of the real object on itself — i.e., the real presence of contents of sensation — by virtue of the interpretation it places on this real influence. We cannot predicate of the ideal what we predicate of the real. The latter has the characteristics involved with spatial-temporality; the former lacks these qualities. Thus, Husserl also can assert, ". . . what is predicated of the appearing is not also predicated of what appears in it" (*LU*, Tüb. ed., II/1, 350-51; F., p. 539). The appearing, understood as the presence of sensations, is a process subject to real psychological description. What appears, however, is not a "real part of my concrete seeing" (*LU*, Halle ed., II, 326). It is an "ideal intentional content" — i.e., the content of the object grasped as a sense.

The result of this is twofold. On the one hand, we have an ontological underpinning of the notion of intentionality, according to which we can say that the "truly immanent contents . . . of consciousness are not intentional." In other words, consciousness must transcend itself to reach the intentional object, i.e., "what is, in truth, not really immanent and mental" (*LU*, Tüb. ed., II/1, 373-74; F., p. 559). On the other hand, we have the assertions that the subject-object relation is not a "psychologically real one (*ein psychologisch-reales*)" and thus does not concern "a real process or real relation (*einen realen Vorgang oder ein reales sich Beziehen*)" (*LU*, Tüb. ed., II/1, 371-72; F., pp. 557-58). The connection of the two is obvious from the above. The position Husserl counters assumes the transcendence of the object as a spatial-temporal fact. Because this transcendence is merely a matter of spatial-temporality (i.e., the subject here, the object there, and all relations between them taking place in time), the relationship that bridges this transcendence is interpreted as causality. Husserl, then, in his struggle against the relativism of psychology, in his struggle to show that consciousness is capable of objectively valid *Einsicht* and *Anschauung*, feels compelled not only to demonstrate that the object is transcendent, but to define this transcendence in such a way that causality does not follow in its train. The result, then, is that a specifically epistemological transcendence is interpreted as one of the ideal over the real.[6]

7. To complete this discussion with a final point, we must bring a second notion of transcendence to the fore. Sense *qua* sense may transcend the real-causal nexus, but does it also transcend the interpretation of consciousness? In other words, can we describe it as both the *result* of the interpretative activity of consciousness and as an *objective criterion* for this activity? The question draws its obvious validity from the fact that Husserl is attempting to secure the possibility of objective knowledge. Inherent in the concept of this last is the possibility of the object's presence as an *objective criterion* for our knowledge.

To answer these questions, Husserl engages in a lengthy discussion of what we may call the dialectic of *intention and fulfillment*. Every intentional act, every act relating consciousness to an object, is based, Husserl says, on an objectifying act (See *LU*, Tüb. ed., II/1, 493-94; F., p. 648). More concretely, perception *per se*, as we quoted Husserl above, is interpretation and the point of interpretation is to make something objective. To intend an object in the pregnant sense of intending to see it is, thus, to engage in an objectifying act. It is, as we indicated, to try and inform one's data of sensation with a single objective sense. Now, Husserl argues that it is a fact of experience — e.g., in the cases of "mistaken identity" — that not every intention of consciousness is fulfilled. There is, in other words, a dialectic between intention and fulfillment. It is a dialectic which affirms that although every sense of the object is a sense intended by consciousness, consciousness in its intending the object cannot, in its act of interpretation, inform the object with every possible sense (See *LU*, Tüb. ed., II/2, 74; F., p. 727, *Ibid.*, II/2, 188; F., p. 821). Only those senses, then, which are fulfilled or embodied by the intuitive presence of the object pertain to it as such (See *Ibid.*, II/2, 93; F., pp. 741-42). This dialectic, as Husserl's extremely careful rhetoric makes apparent, is one of strict mutuality. Neither intention nor fulfillment is given the edge over the other. The most one can say is that consciousness' interpretive, intending sense informs the object's intuitive presence only to the point that the object's intuitive presence fulfills or embodies the interpretive, intending sense of consciousness. Since in actual perception, we do make the theses of *Sinn* and *Sein* together, the point of this dialectic is to guarantee that when the object is there with a definite sense, it stands as an objective criterion for our statements about it.

This final point leaves us with a question. We may ask how far this dialectic, with all its delicate balancing, can assure us that we do have objectively valid intuition. This cannot be answered by us at present. What we can say is that the Sixth Investigation may be regarded as considering this guarantee as insufficient. The guarantee works within the double perspective of the reality of the subject and the ideality of the content of knowledge. Since both the subject and object (as the basis of our perception) maintain their reality, what is to prevent the laws of reality, the laws of causality, from invading the sphere of ideality? To make this concrete, we need only note that, although it may be the case that interpretation can never be reduced to an influx of sensations, this in itself is not sufficient to distinguish the intentional relation from a real process or real relation.

The act of interpretation, as belonging to a consciousness whose unity "has its basis in causal lawfulness," may itself be considered to be causally determined. In other words, as long as it is seen to be a real act in a real, factually contingent consciousness, the effect of interpretation — the sense of the object — is seen to be equally contingent.

The effect of this, from the perspective of the Sixth Investigation, is not to overthrow the above conceptions, but only to show them in their preliminary character. We may put this more precisely by saying that it is one-sided to talk only about the presence of an "ideal intentional content." According to Husserl, we must mention "the further fact that a form of thought dwells within all thinking, a form which stands under ideal laws that circumscribe the objectivity or ideality of knowledge as such" (*LU*, Tüb. ed., II/1, 8; F., p. 254). The purpose of this form of thought with its accompanying ideal lawfulness is to limit the factual contingency of consciousness and, thereby, to limit *the contingency of the act and the effect of the act of interpretation*. Its full import is to provide a *structuring ontological ground* for the mutuality of intention and fulfillment.

Let us consider the second point first. We can introduce it by considering three ways of viewing the subject-object relation. They differentiate themselves according to where they place what we may call "the weight of being." There is first the natural attitude which is both an attitude characteristic of our every-day encounter with the world and characteristic as well of the natural scientist when he does not allow epistemological difficulties to interfere with his pursuits. Here the *weight of being* falls on the objective side of the subject-object relation. We may also say that the object is assumed to have *independent being,* while consciousness — as consciousness *of* the object — is assumed to have *dependent being.* As Aristotle, in one sense the father of the natural attitude, puts this, the mind formally be-comes what it knows. It can do this because it has no categories of its own. As passive to the object, it stands as a wax tablet and is informed by the form of the object much like wax by a seal. This attitude is shared by the modern scientist — at least insofar as he has faith in what he perceives and does not slip into relativism. He differs, however, from Aristotle in his weaving in of the subtleties of modern physics to explain the "informing" and ultimately, thereby, in substituting the mathematical formula for the form (See *Ideen I,* §85).

When the natural attitude is somehow disturbed, when faith in perception comes into question, we may achieve what can be interpreted as the Kantian attitude. With this, we split the weight of being evenly between the subjective and objective poles of the relation. *Both* have independent being; both have their own categories. Thus, neither can be said to become the other. As before, the subject is interpreted as "that which experiences." But experience *qua* experience is given definite informing forms — i.e., the twelve categories. The result of this may be seen in the notion of causality. If, in the natural attitude — which for Kant is represented by Newton — the question is posed, "Why do I see the object appearing in just the forms in which I see it?", the natural answer is "because the object *causes* me to see it is so." Kant undercuts this answer by making causality one of the forms of our experience, a *category* which *we* impose in the synthesis of our perceptions according to the form of time. For Kant, then, the answer to this question is that consciousness as such has its own categories and that these categories — involving time and space — are the forms which conscious experience must assume. As for the objects considered simply as things in themselves, their own categories (at least on the basis of experience) are unknowable. The notion of consciousness operative here can be directly (if somewhat crudely) put as follows: Consciousness, in its independence, is considered as *one thing* over and against the object which, in its own independent being, is considered *another*. The weight of being falls upon each equally but in such a way that each is *independent* of the other.

The result of this schemata is the famous thing-in-itself. The *Ding-an-sich* is, of course, not posited out of experience. *As unknowable*, it can, in fact, only be conceived as a term required by the Kantian interpretation of what it means to experience. Once one states that consciousness — taken as a title for individual subjectivity — imposes certain formal categories on its experience of objects, the question logically arises as to what these objects are in themselves. It is a question, so to speak, of the "remainder." Granted that experience, to be experience of objects, must have certain forms — on the most basic level, the forms of spatial-temporal synthesis — the question still remains, what is the object in itself apart from and prior to these forms which belong to the essence of the experiencing subject as such. The question is, what is the nature of the object apart from experience, i.e., the *Ding-an-sich*. On the *basis* of experience, the question is, of course, unanswerable.

With this, we get what, for Husserl, are both the advantages and disadvantages of the Kantian system. By making causality a category of the subject, he avoids the notion of the causal *determination* of knowledge and, thus, that of the causally determined *relativity* of the same. In this, Kant's argument is *not* if knowledge is subjective, then it is *a priori*. It is rather that by virtue of being *a priori*, it must be subjective. Thus, one could place the structuring logical and perceptual forms of knowledge within the subject and yet have the subject, along with these forms, change with time. We have then a changing "historical" subject. On the other hand, if we say that the purpose of "time, space and the categories . . . is to make experience possible" and mean by this that human experience is only possible within certain fixed *a priori* limits, we have a conception of knowledge that is both subjective and *a priori*. Here, the *contingency* of knowledge, when regarded *empirically* in terms of its objects, is overcome by these structuring, *a priori* forms of the subject.

This strength, however, is also the weakness of the position. For, according to its schema, the non-relativity of knowledge is bought at the price of an unknowable thing-in-itself. Otherwise put: The necessary *universality* of knowledge is guaranteed, but not its *objective validity* as Husserl defines the term. Thus the *object* or thing *in its own categories* is said to be unknowable. The forms of experiencing consciousness can be said to *cover up* rather than *reveal* these categories.

This conclusion raises a certain question about the nature of the *a priori* itself. In contact solely with the forms which make experience possible, we can raise the question whether these forms represent the only possible mode for knowing things, or whether they represent merely an *a priori* for specifically *human* subjectivity. It is in terms of the thought of the second that Husserl criticizes certain attempted *a priori* treatments of consciousness as forms of specific relativism (See *LU*, Tüb. ed., I, 123-24; F., p. 145). It is also in terms of this that he extends this criticism to the neo-Kantians and to Kant himself (See *Ibid.*, I, 93; F., p. 122).

The basis of this criticism can be seen in a passage of the *Prolegomenon,* a work which Husserl studied extensively before writing the *Logische Untersuchungen.* After having said that the sole purpose of the categories of the understanding is to make experience possible, and that, hence, to make a claim to understand something beyond our possible experience of it is itself an absurdity, Kant adds the following remark:

> But it would, on the other hand, be an even greater absurdity if we did not admit any things in themselves or wanted to pretend that our experience were the only possible experience of things and therefore that our intuition in space and time were the only possible intuition, our discursive understanding the archetype of every possible understanding and, consequently, wanted to have the principles of the possibility of experience known as the conditions of things themselves (*"Prolegomenon,"* §57, *Kants ges. Sch.*, IV, 350-51).

The absurdity, here, according to Kant would be the interpretation of transcendental (or immanent) principles as "transcendent" and thereby "the setting up of the limits of our reason as limits of the possibility of things themselves..." (*Ibid.*, p. 351).

Now, if we interpret the above as asserting that there are indeed other possible ways of experiencing and understanding things, that our own way is but one of many contingently possible ways, then we have the basis for Husserl's charge of specific relativism. Correct or incorrect, his basic accusation is that Kant "lacked the phenomenologically pure concept of the *a priori*" (*LU*, Tüb. ed., II/2, 203; F., p. 833). To gain an insight into this *a priori*, we have to make another transition. When we do, we will realize that the Husserlian view is precisely the final "absurdity" mentioned by Kant above.

The transition is a shift in the weight of being such that the Kantian *independence* of subject and object becomes a *mutual dependence*. In Husserl's understanding, mutual dependence means much more than the simple, almost analytically derivable truth that subject and object are relative terms, each demanding, by its meaning, the other. While it is true that subjectivity as consciousness *of* . . . demands, in order to be such, an object *of which* it is conscious; and while it is also true that an ob-ject as a *Gegen-stand* demands a subject against which it can stand (for objects are never ob-jects to other objects), this in itself does not go far enough. For while a *thing* may need a subject in order to be an *object*, without such a subject (or even the possibility thereof) it can still remain a *"thing-in-itself."* And the *Ding-an-sich* does not demand for the possibility of *its* being the possibility of a relation to a subject. To establish a mutual ontological dependence one must, then, eliminate the notion of the thing-in-itself, and this by radically transforming the outlook that raises the question of the "remainder."

The transformation occurs when we put the weight of being on the *subject-object relation per se*. We then say that the relation has *independent* reality, while individual subjects and objects have only a *dependent* reality. The laws which govern the relationship are, in other words, interpreted as definitive of the possibility of there being individual subjects and objects at all. The *Ding-an-sich* is thereby eliminated, for the new schema limits the possibilities of a thing's being to the possibilities of its entering into a subject-object relation. The possibility of an entity's being (or existing) *is* the possibility of its being known. This conclusion is the same as that presented in the last chapter

(See above, pp. 69-70). What we here present is only the underlying schema by which Husserl *attempts* to ground the metaphysics of possibility as it works within the conception of positing on the basis of truth.

According to this schema, the subject is the necessary condition for the possibility of the object and *vice versa*. *Essentially* regarded, they are dependent moments which "found" each other to form one independent whole. The results of this schema are threefold. We say first, the subject is *in essence* intentional — i.e., a consciousness of something. Second, we must say that the object is something that *can* be given (i.e., can be intuited or perceived). There is, thus, no thing in itself interpreted as *essentially* unknowable. The third thing we must say is that constitution, as presented in the *Logische Untersuchungen*, never equals creation. The subject to be such requires an object, and this means that constitution, in the sense of an objectivity presupposing the acts of subjectivity, is never understood to mean that the object is created or brought forth by the subject.[7]

These conclusions have a natural reference to the dialectic of intention and fulfillment. The mutuality of the two is structured by the mutual ontological dependence of subject and object. Neither intention nor fulfillment can be given the edge over the other if the intending interpretation of the subject and the fulfilling presence of the object are both essentially "moments" of a putative whole. The delicate balancing of intention and fulfillment must, in other words, be seen as the actual "fitting in" of both subject and object into this whole. Only within it is consciousness properly consciousness of something and the object an object for consciousness. This, of course, does not mean that their being is dependent on their actual fitting in but only on the essential possibility of this.

Now, the *intended result* of the above may be expressed in a quotation from the *Ideen*: "To every object that truly is there corresponds in principle (in the *a priori* of unconditioned essential generality) the idea of a possible consciousness in which the object itself can be grasped originally and perfectly adequately. Conversely, if this possibility is guaranteed, *eo ipso* is the object one that truly is" (*Ideen I*, §142; Biemel ed., p. 349). As Husserl explains this, interpretative categories (*Auffassungskategorien*) are correlated to objective categories (*Gegenstandskategorien*). The condition of the possibility of the latter is correlated to the condition of the possibility of the former. The same assertions are made in the *Logische Untersuchungen*. The two works, however, distinguish themselves by the fact that the *Logische Untersuchungen* bases its assertion of a subject-object correlation on the above described schema of mutual dependence, while this schema is not at all present in the *Ideen*. The reason for this is relatively easy to observe. It is the presence in the *Ideen* — but *not* in the *Logische Untersuchungen* — of the epochè and phenomenological reduction. This reduction, as we recall, places the subject as an "absolute sphere of being" and the object as a dependent being. The result is the replacement of a mutual dependence by a one-sided dependence. The correlation, in other words, is itself the result of the ontological dependence of the object on the subject.

The question is whether or not this correlation can be grounded by the one reduction that is present in the *Logische Untersuchungen*: the eidetic reduction. Is this reduction sufficient for us to see the interpretative categories as essentially correlated with the objective categories — the former defining the subjective pole of the relation, the latter, its objective pole? The question here is essentially one of a method of determination.

In what way would the eidetic reduction allow us to establish this correlation? To only sketch the barest outline of an answer, which must be gone through in detail in our next chapter, the following may be noted. The eidetic reduction reveals an eidos or species. The latter, in its own being, is a pure possibility. This means that to demonstrate an eidos or species is to demonstrate a pure possibility, and *vice versa*. Thus, what the eidetic reduction can demonstrate is a possibility and this in terms of a unitary species. The conclusion, then, is that we must, in this method, demonstrate the *possibility* of the above correlation and this in terms of the compatibility of its component parts in a unitary, if complex, species.

We may pause for a moment and observe the reasons why Husserl must proceed in this manner rather than using the much more direct method of the phenomenological reduction. The reasons are all rooted in the guiding motivation of the *Logische*

Untersuchungen and the interpretation Husserl places on it. The motivation is that of securing the possibility of objective knowledge, and this knowledge is interpreted as *knowledge of objects.* This interpretation prefigures the satisfaction of the motivation in the *Logische Untersuchungen.* For, if being is to be correlated with knowability and if knowledge is to be interpreted as knowledge of objects, then we have here a *prior ontological interpretation* of being: beings must be regarded as objects. The effect of this on the conception of the subject is that it too must be regarded as an object. Otherwise, it could not be, i.e., be an object of knowledge. It would, in other words, be *unknowable.*

That Husserl is faithful to this interpretation of his motivation may be seen in his reply to Paul Natorp. Natorp, as Husserl quotes him, advances the following:

> The ego as subjective center of relations for my conscious contents has an asymmetrical relation to these contents. It does not have the same sort of relation to them as they have to it. It is not consciously present to its contents as they are to it. It thus shows itself to be *sui generis* in that others can be present to it, but it itself cannot be consciously present to another. It itself cannot be a content and is not similar to anything that would be a content of consciousness. . . . Otherwise put, every *presentation* that we could make of the ego would turn it into an object; but we have already stopped thinking of it when we think of it as an object. To be an ego is not to be an object but to be that which is over against all objects; it is to be that for which something is an object. The same holds for the object's relation to an ego. To be consciously known is to be an object for the ego. This being-an-object does not in turn allow itself to be made into an object (*LU*, Tüb. ed., II/1, 359-60; F., 548-49).

Husserl's reply to this is to ask how we can assert the above "if we cannot think it, and how should we think it without 'making' the ego and consciousness, as objects of our statements, 'into objects' " (*Ibid.*, II/1, 360; F., p. 549). The correlation here is between object and knowledge: what cannot be an object cannot be asserted, thought or known. Further, it cannot even be, given the identification between the sense of object and being.

There is here, as Husserl was later to realize, a basic inconsistency. We have, on the one hand, the subject-object dichotomy as basic to the intentional relationship. On the other hand, we have an ontology that in some sense denies this dichotomy. It states that all being, whether it be real or ideal, is an object.[8] The reason that Husserl must remain with this inconsistency is to be found in what would be required to overcome it. We would have to think the subject as other than object; and in his context, this means thinking the subject as other than real or ideal being, the two categories of being as object. Now, this is, in fact, the way in which the phenomenological reduction makes us think the subject. Its correlation of subjective and objective categories is based, as we said, on the dependence of the object on the subject. The subject is conceived, not as an object, but as a ground for objects. This implies, as we shall later see, that as a ground it has a fundamentally different nature than what it grounds. The method of the reduction for uncovering this nature is, in the first instance, that of "reducing" the subject — i.e., taking it out of the world. Since the world is understood as comprising both categories of objective being — i.e., real being and its ideal objective forms — this reduction opens the way for a third category of being. This is the being that is temporal and yet not real. It is the category of the *irreal* that we mentioned in the Introduction.

This solution is not possible in the *Logische Untersuchungen*. If we propose it, the question for Husserl arises: how can the subject be known? Within the interpretation of objective knowledge as knowledge of objects, the question is unanswerable. For an answer to appear, we must shift the interpretation of the problematic of objective knowledge. This implies not just a shift in its underlying ontology but also a reinterpretation of the whole process of knowing.

CHAPTER VI

THE SUBJECT-OBJECT CORRELATION

Carefully regarded, the last chapter presented two theories of the ideal vis-à-vis its role in the intentional relationship. The first has its basis in the Fregean distinction between concept and object. The properties of objects are not the properties of the species which define what properties objects must have in order to be subsumed under them. Thus, the concept *square* is not a square concept. The distinction in predication that is implied in this is taken by Husserl to apply generally to the whole ontological realm of the ideal. It is thus taken to apply to the perceptually embodied sense which, as ideal, cannot be considered as having the same predicates as our real conscious processes. We, thus, have the doctrine that "there dwells an ideal intentional content next to an inherent, actual content" of our psychological processes. The fact that the predicates of the one are not those of the other establishes what we called the "ontological transcendence" that specifically defines the intentional relationship. This is the transcendence of the ideal with regard to the real. It is a transcendence designed to avoid the psychological relativism that attempts to reduce the perceptual sense of the object to the psychological process involved in its apprehension.

How seriously Husserl takes this distinction of predication can be seen by the use he makes of it. He takes it as the principle by which the sciences of the ideal are separated from the empirical sciences of the real. Speaking of the range of the predicability of the concepts involved in each, he writes:

> The range of general concepts in the former is one of lowest specific differences. In the latter, the range is one of individual, temporally determined particulars. The ultimate objects of the range are, thus, in one case ideal species, in the other, empirical facts (*LU*, Tüb. ed., I, 178; F., p. 185).

It is this distinction in the range of predicability of these concepts which originally separates the types of science. In Husserl's words:

> Pure logic and arithmetic as sciences of ideal instances of particular genera (or of what is *a priori* grounded in the ideal essence of these genera) separate themselves from psychology as the science of individual instances of particular empirical classes (*LU*, Tüb. ed., I, 177; F., p. 185).[1]

Here, the doctrine is that the ideal can only be predicated of the ideal. This means, with regard to the logical laws, "*... the concepts making up these and other similar laws can have no empirical range*" (*LU*, Tüb. ed., I, 173; F., p. 181). In other words, "the pure laws of logic, when seen in their original content, relate only to that which is ideal ..." (*LU*, Tüb. ed., I, 159; F., p. 171). The intended result of this doctrine, as should be readily apparent, is to strip the logical law of any supposed psychological meaning. To quote Husserl once more, "No logical law, according to its genuine sense, is a law for the facticities of mental life. It is, therefore, neither a law for presentations (i.e., experiences of presentations) nor for judgements (i.e., experiences of judgements) nor for any other mental experience" (*LU*, Tüb. ed., I, 69; F., p. 104).

In this context, we may speak with Husserl of "... the basic, essential, never-to-be-bridged difference between ideal laws and real laws ...". Given the differences in predication, "no conceivable gradation could mediate between the ideal and the real" (*LU*, Tüb. ed., I, 68; F., p. 104). The result of this position may be seen in Husserl's discussion of the law of non-contradiction. The law, he observes, may be formulated as a natural law concerning "matters in time" — i.e., mental acts. It may also be formulated as a law concerning "timeless matters." These last are the pure contents of propositions, i.e., their ideal meaning units. Husserl, at this point, goes on to deny the possibility of "a single law which, with unchanged sense, merely functions differently or has a different sphere of application." Given his reference to the "unbridgeable difference" between the ideal and the real, Husserl feels compelled to say that it is "vain to seek a unitary conception" (*LU*, Tüb. ed., I, 99; F., pp. 126-27).

The difficulties with this were indicated in our last chapter. In some sense, the ideal and the real cannot remain unrelated once we place them in the dichotomy: real subjective act, ideal perceptual sense. The function of this act is, after all, to grasp this sense. There must, then, be some unity relating the two, a unity involved in the act of knowing. Otherwise, once we place the laws of the real on the side of the subject, we come to the conclusion that consciousness, as real, is causally determined. If the act of interpretation is causally determined, how are we to conceive the subject-object correlation? Would not the sense of the object, as grasped by a causally determined act, itself be causally — and *not* ideally — determined? Husserl's reply to this is to assert "that a form of thought *dwells within* all thinking, a form which stands under ideal laws that circumscribe the objectivity or ideality of knowledge as such" (*LU*, Tüb. ed., II/1, 8; F., p. 254, italics added). In this second theory, the form is considered to be ideal, and the ideal is seen to be immanent, rather than transcendent to the real. There is a corresponding shift in the role the ideal plays. It is not that of establishing the ontological transcendence of the intentional object with respect to the real subject. It is one of placing both within a defining correlation, a correlation that is to result in objective knowledge. The ideal form in question is that of the intentional or subject-object relation. Our remark in the last chapter that the laws which govern the relation are taken as definitive of the possibility of their being at all subjects and objects points to the understanding of this form as a defining one. As we shall see, the role of the ideal is here taken as that of being an *a priori* limiting structure of the real. As opposed to the first theory, the notion of this limitation demands a certain formal or conceptual identity between ideal relations and real relations (relations of empirical coexistence and succession). This follows insofar as the second theory maintains that the limitations of the latter are set by the former relations.

The proper level to express this second position is that of the world. The ideal, here, is understood as expressing the ontological sense and, by virtue of this, the ontological function of the world. The ontological sense of the world is that which is given by the ideal essences or species that define its formal structure. Its ontological function is that of providing, through this structure, a horizon of essential relationships in which subjects and objects find the defining conditions for their intentional relation. Here, we have to say that it is the world which, by virtue of its defining formal structure, is the *a priori* form of the intentional or knowing relationship. The ideal form of the relationship is, in other words, understood as a world-form. As a consequence of its ontological function, the world-form grounds a pre-established harmony between subjects and objects. In such a harmony, as Husserl puts it, "It is absurd . . . to doubt whether the actual course of the world, the real conditions of the world in itself, could come into conflict with the forms of thought" (*LU*, Tüb. ed., II/2, 200; F., p. 831). Since the forms of thought are the forms of the world, this would make the forms contradict themselves. The essential position here is that the laws that govern the forms of thought — what Husserl terms the "genuine logical *a priori*" — "tell us what pertains to the essential endowment of what is (*des Seienden*)." They transcend "all limitations according to spheres of reality . . ." (*LU*, Tüb. ed., II/2, 198; F., p. 829). As such they apply to both subjects and objects understood as worldly existents. They are understood as determining forms which limit the "empirical possibilities" of both (*Ibid.*).

The question that arises when we consider these theories together is whether the ideal can consistently be taken in the ways demanded by both. According to the understanding of the first it is what, by virtue of its non-predicability with respect to the real, establishes the specifically intentional relation. This is based, as we said, on an ontological distinction between, on the one hand, the *process of appearing* — the process involving a real act and a real presence of sense contents — and, on the other, the *appearance*. The latter is the ideal, perceptually embodied sense. In the second theory, the ideal is taken as that which, by virtue of its defining applicability with respect to the real, limits the latter's empirical possibilities. It is what assures us that the intentional relation can achieve objective knowledge and this, by placing both subjects and objects in a pre-established harmony.

This question will concern us in later chapters. For the present our task is to present the second theory in some detail. Here, we must stress the particular point of view which guides the descriptions we are about to undertake. The descriptions, when eidetically conceived as showing the compatibility of the elements of the intentional relationship, are to be taken as eidetically demonstrative of this relation. That which is to be demonstrated is the form of the relation conceived of as an ideal world-form. As ideal, it has the being of a possibility. This means that its being is grounded in its unity or in the compatibility of the elements that make it up. The elements in question are the intentions of thought, the perception of the object and the object itself in its own being. If, essentially regarded, the intentions of thinking — the predicative judgements by which we frame our knowledge — had nothing to do with perception, if, again, perception had nothing to do with the actual being of the states of affairs that are its objects, there would not be a compatible idea of the intentional relation as involving these elements. The species of the relationship would be impossible. Conversely, demonstrating the pure possibility, and, thus, the ideal being of this species involves just such a description of this compatibility.

This demonstration, of course, does *not* mean that the *actuality* of our objective knowledge has been shown. The latter is in some sense a question of subjective acts. We can put this more concretely by saying that the second theory demands, in order to correlate thought, perception and being, the performability of certain acts. These are the acts, conceived according to its descriptions, of straightforward, eidetic and categorial perception. In this sense, to demonstrate the actuality of objective knowledge is to show the performability by subjects of the acts that would allow the theory's correlation of the elements of the intentional relation to be applicable to these subjects' activity. This, of course, does not mean that the question of the applicability of the theory can be separated from that of the compatibility of the essence it describes. Subjective performance must be in accord with the essence. If the essence places conflicting demands on the subject's performance, then not just the inapplicability of the theory is shown. The essence it describes will itself have to be considered as incompatible. These issues we are raising will be considered in our next chapter. For the present, let us consider the first correlation demanded by the theory. This is:

The Correlation of Thought to Perception

The correlation of thought to perception is essentially an elaboration of a single notion. This is the notion of thought as an objective intending, an intending of objects that can be fulfilled in intuitive presence. If we ask how much fulfillment is possible, we come to the primary assertion of this doctrine. It is that the intending of sense by thought can, in the face of intuitive presence, become objectively interpretative of what we perceptually experience. In other words, the signative sense meant by an intention of thought can become the interpretative sense that an intuitive, objectifying act attempts to realize. Here, we must note that the intentions of thought can direct themselves either to individual objects or to "states of affairs" composed by them. In both cases, the assertion holds that the sense intended by thought can become perceptually embodied through an intuitive interpretation. The result in the former case is a straightforward perception of an individual object. In the latter, it is what Husserl calls a "categorial" perception of a state of affairs.

The correlation in terms of straightforward perception has already, in some sense, been discussed by us. We are referring to our discussion, in Chapter IV, of Husserl's "synthetic" logic of content. We shall, however, briefly review its conclusions as these can be taken as a model for the correlation of thought to categorial perception. The dominant notions in such a logic are of a nonindependent content and of an independent whole formed by such contents. The latter is defined as "a sum of contents covered by a unitary foundation without the help of any further contents" (*LU*, Tüb. ed., II/1, 275; F., p. 475). Now, this logic of perceptual contents, on the one hand, extends to the intentions of thought; for it tells us how the meanings meant by these intentions can be variously combined while preserving the possibility of an "intuitive illustration" in a straightforward perception. On the other hand, it extends beyond the correlation of thought to perception and embraces the correlation of perception to being. Thus, as we quoted Husserl, the distinction between non-independent contents and wholes formed of them "transcends the sphere of contents of consciousness and becomes a highly important distinction in the area of objects as such." The distinction becomes a part of "formal ontology" (*LU*, Tüb. ed., II/1, 225; F., p. 435). The reference to formal ontology means, first of all that perceptual senses cannot conflict if we are to posit being. Thus, the laws of the logic of content can be understood as specifying the basic conditions for the possibility of the perceptual presence of an object. They specify the possibility of its bearing a unifiable, non-contradictory set of senses. If we interpret being as the possibility of this perceptual presence, then its laws can be considered as extended to being. The deeper meaning of the reference to formal ontology concerns the notion of the species as expressing prior possibilities. In Husserl's words:

> The original possibility (or reality) is the validity, the ideal existence of a species; at least it is fully guaranteed by this. Next the intuition of an individual corresponding to the species and the intuitable individual itself are called possible. Finally, the meaning that fulfills itself with objective clarity in such an intuition is said to be possible (*LU*, Tüb. ed., II/2, 106-107; F., p. 752).

Here, the ideal existence of a complex, but compatible species guarantees and correlates the possibilities of the elements that make up the intentional relation, namely, the meaning intended by the thought that directs itself towards intuition, the intuition that fulfills it and the being of the intuitable individual itself.

According to Husserl, the same schema of possibilities applies to the case of categorial intuition. The ideal existence of a species is mirrored in a relation of logical lawfulness. The laws of this logic specify the prior possibilities of the being of categorial objects; they also specify the correlative possibilities of the intentions of thought and intuitions directed towards them. The advantages Husserl sees in this schema can be found in the following assertion:

> The relation between thought and intuition, which has previously never been brought to tolerable clarity by a criticism of knowledge, first becomes really transparent through the interpretation of categorial acts as intuitions. With this interpretation, knowledge itself in its essence and achievement becomes understandable (*LU*, Tüb. ed., II/2, 166; F., p. 804).

The key to this statement is the double correlation of thought to perception and perception to being. The "essence" of knowledge referred to in this passage is perception, intuitive self-givenness being the guarantee that the knowing relation has been brought about. The "achievement" of knowledge — which cannot be other than knowing entities — is guaranteed by the correlation of perception to being. Within this schema, we can say that the "interpretation of categorial acts as intuitions" clarifies "the relationship between thought and intuition" by making thought, which is taken by Husserl as a categorial activity, capable of intuition and, therefore, capable of exercising a knowing function with respect to entities.

In a moment, we shall examine more closely the relation of thought to perception. First, however, we should make a remark on Husserl's terminology. For Husserl, only "merely signative" thought (the thought of "merely thinking" about something, i.e., thought taken apart from any attempt at verification) is opposed to intuition. "Authentic thought" on the other hand is defined as the thought that directs itself to reality and whose sense can function as a successful perceptual interpretation. When this functioning occurs, thought, understood as categorial activity, becomes categorially intuitive. Husserl writes, "the founded acts that characterize categorial intuition count as the 'thought' that intellectualizes sensible intuition" (*LU*, Tüb. ed., II/2, 202; F., p. 832). Now, the meaning of this intellectualization can be seen by noting that Husserl equates authentic thought — i.e., the capacity for categorial acts — with the understanding (See *LU*, Tüb. ed., II/2, 197; F., p. 828). The thrust of the doctrine of authentic thought is, then, that of making the faculty of understanding intuitive. It is in some sense to be judged as an alliance with Plato and against Kant, the latter having declared that understanding is *not* intuitive (See *LU*, Tüb. ed., II/2, 202-203; F., p. 833). More precisely put, it can be seen as an attempt to give an account of rational inference, and this on the basis of an intuition which, while based on sensible perception, is itself intellectual.

The details of this doctrine can best be introduced by citing a passage from William James:

> There is not a conjunction or a preposition, and hardly an adverbial phrase, syntactic form, or inflection of the voice, in human speech, that does not express some shading or other of relation which we at some moment actually feel to exist between the larger objects of our thought. If we speak objectively, it is the real relations that appear revealed; if we speak subjectively, it is the stream of consciousness that matches each of them by an inward coloring of its own (*Psychology, Briefer Course*, Cleveland, 1948, p. 162).[2]

This passage may be interpreted in the light of Husserl's assertion, "All thinking, particularly all theoretical thinking and knowing, is accomplished by means of certain 'acts', acts which appear in the context of expressive speech" (*LU*, Tüb. ed., II/2, 1; F., p. 667). The preposition, conjunction, syntactic form mentioned by William James are termed by Husserl the "categorial elements" of speech. They do not themselves refer to sensible objects. They do, however, bind together the various referring names of our speech so as to give them a reference to what shows itself through the relation "between the larger objects of our thought." This is a state of affairs composed of a number of sensible objects. As James points out, in some sense, these linking elements (or, rather, the relations they point to) are felt to objectively exist. This is the case even though the relations specified by such words as *to, for, and, or, is, with*, etc. are not *per se* sensibly perceivable. Inwardly the stream of consciousness matches them with a "coloring of its own." In Husserl's doctrine, this match is caused by the fact of there being certain "categorial acts," acts which bring about our apprehension of the relations signified by the categorial elements of our speech. Thus, the *and* points to an act of conjunction, the *or* to one of disjunction and the *is* to an act of predication. With this, we have the definition of what Husserl calls the *categorial activity of authentic thought* or *understanding*. It is the bringing into play of those act moments which allow the formation of an interpretative intention directed towards the relationally articulated whole that we term a *state of affairs*.

The underlying basis for this definition is the point we stressed at the beginning of our discussion of the first correlation. It is that the significant sense of an assertion can become, in an act of knowing, the interpretative sense of a perceptual experience. In the present context, this means that we can consider our actual spoken and written expressions as expressive of the actual formative or shaping intentions of the perceptual experience. Here, of course, the doctrine of sense and reference enters in. The categorial elements of our discourse serve to give our assertions a unified sense and, therefore, a unified reference to some objective correlate. The same thing happens when the act moments behind these elements become perceptually interpretative. They work together to form a "unity of consciousness," one that is perceptually directed towards a single correlate. We can take as an example of this the assertion, "A is brighter than B." The act of intuition that can confirm such an assertion (or, indeed, any categorially structured assertion) is, according to Husserl, *based upon but not equivalent to* the intuitions of the individual objects that are part of its referent (See *LU*, VI, §46). Thus, the intuitions of A and B can by themselves be taken to ground any number of relations – e.g., A and B, A or B, A not B, etc. The non-perceivability of the relation in a sensuous, straightforward sense is indicated by Husserl in dealing with the example of a conjunction: "I can paint A and I can paint B. I can also paint them both on the same canvas; but I cannot paint the *both,* the A *and* the B" – as opposed, say, to painting the A *or* the B (*LU*, Tüb. ed., II/2, 160; F., p. 798). The perception of the *or*, or for that matter, the perception of the *is brighter than*, is something beyond the individual perceptions. This does not, however, make it something arbitrary. This follows, at least, if we are to assume that a knowledge of relations can advance an objective claim.

Now, in Husserl's view, the specifically *categorial* perception verifying the assertion, "A is brighter than B," is a function of separate act moments that unite perceptions of separate objects. The result of this is a unitary, perceptually interpretative intention which has a unitary objectivity as its referent. As Husserl expresses this, "That we speak of an act which unites these perceptions, and not of some conjoining or even of a being together of these perceptions in consciousness, naturally lies in the fact that there is here given a *unitary* intentional relationship and, corresponding to this, a unitary object . . ." (*LU*, Tüb. ed., II/2,

160; F., p. 798). The basis of this unity is, as we indicated, the unity of sense. A sense that unifies various elements allows us to propositionally refer to and perceptually intend a unified correlate. Here, we may mention once again the fact that in actual perception, the theses of being and sense are the same. We posit being when, in an act of objectifying interpretation, we "make sense" out of our perceptions. This making sense comes down to seeing whether a single objective sense with a single referent can be gathered from our various perceptual experiences. In this, it is the perceptually embodied presence of a unitary or a self-compatible sense that allows us to posit "a unitary intentional object," be this an individual object or a state of affairs.

The presence of this sense can be led back to those subjective act moments that come together to form a complex, though unitary, act of categorial intending. There is, however, a deeper grounding apparent when we inquire with Husserl into the formal possibility of the complex act. The act, as perceptually interpretative, takes place in a context of the dialectic of intention and fulfillment. As we mentioned in the last chapter, there is an attempt, one that forms the heart of the second theory, to provide a structuring ontological ground for the mutuality of intention and fulfillment. As in straightforward perception, this basis is provided by the species of complex meanings or senses. The ideal existence of these is grounded in the compatibility of their elements. As for the species themselves, they express in their being the prior possibility of such compatibility. In Husserl's words, "What is seen to be incompatible in species cannot be united or made compatible in empirical instances" (*LU*, Tüb. ed., II/2, 198; F., p. 829). Thus, in terms of the dialectic of intention and fulfillment, we may speak of an adjustment of the interpretative sense of an intending subject to the possibilities represented by the species. Only those categorial intentions that conform to the prior possibilities represented by the species have a chance of fulfillment. This follows, insofar as only those have a possibility of an intuitive embodiment or "illustration" by an empirical instance. We can also put this in terms of the identity in actual perception of the theses of sense and being. The formal ground for this identity is found in the fact that both the perceptually embodied sense and the posited being correlatively instantiate a set of possibilities whose original representatives are found within the ideal existence of the species.

An alternate way of expressing this ground is in terms of a relation of lawfulness. When Husserl advances the doctrine of the species as prior or "pure" possibilities, this occurs, as we saw, with the thesis, "Unity as such grounds possibility" (*LU*, Tüb. ed., II/2, 109; F., p. 754). This unity can be seen as itself grounded in certain laws, the laws of the compatibility of meanings. Insofar as these laws govern prior possibilities of unity, they can be seen as "running parallel" to the laws governing the compatibility of intuitions in an extended categorial intuition (See *LU*, Tüb. ed., II/2, 194; F., p. 826). Here, the fitting in or adjustment of intention and fulfillment can be seen as occurring within the framework of these laws. It is actually an adjustment to the relation of lawfulness specified by the laws.

To make our discussion somewhat more concrete, let us take a few pages and describe the character of these laws. The first set of laws are grammatical. Husserl attempts to revive "the old doctrine of a *grammaire générale et raisonée*, the doctrine of a philosophical grammar" (*LU*, Tüb. ed., II/1, 338; F., p. 525). In Husserl's view, this is a "pure grammar of the categorial forms." The laws of such grammar concern the formation of categorially structured senses and are, accordingly, referred to as the laws of sense. Husserl writes of them:

> The *laws of sense*, or normatively speaking, *the laws of the avoidance of nonsense (Unsinn) introduce into logic the generally possible forms of meaning, forms whose objective worth logic has first to determine.* This logic does by setting up *quite different laws* which separate formally consistent sense from formally inconsistent or contradictory sense" (*LU*, Tüb. ed., II/1, 334; F., pp. 522-23).

As Husserl explains this, a random collection of words cannot be considered a contradictory expression. Equally, it cannot be considered to be in a relation of contradiction to some other expression. Contradiction, in other words, presupposes senses in conflict. As such it presupposes that senses on some level are already given.

To clarify this, we may mention one of the laws that Husserl presents. It is the law of substitution. It asserts that in any given propositional sense, meanings in one grammatical category can be substituted only for meanings in the same grammatical category. In other words, names (or, generally, nominative material) must replace names. Adjectives must replace adjectives and relational terms, relational terms. If we violate this law, then according to Husserl, ". . . we only get a series of words in which each word has a sense or points to a complete context of sense; but we do not get what in principle is a closed unity of sense" (*LU*, Tüb. ed., II/1, 320; F., p. 512). Some examples of inappropriate substitution are the transformations "A resembles B" to "A horse B"; "This tree is green" to "This careless is green" to "This careless is more than" to "This careless but more than." In each case, we have replaced a term from one grammatical category by a term from another with the resulting disruption of the unity of sense.

Given that the grammatical laws, such as the one just mentioned, state essential conditions for the unity of species of complex senses, and given that such species represent prior possibilities for the actual intuitive illustration of these senses, the conclusion stated above follows. The grammatical laws are mirrored in the intuitive sphere by laws governing the possibilities of categorial intuitions. It is because of this that we can say that the syntactical, categorial forms of our discourse express, in a completely adequate language, the possibilities of the formative, categorial activity of our consciousness. It is also because of this that we can make our original and primary assertion, the assertion that the well-formed significant sense of a statement can become the sense yielded by intuitive categorial activity. We thus have the mirroring parallelity of the forms of discourse and the forms of categorial intuition. The effect of this parallelity may be put in terms of a unitary sense specifying a unitary reference. The parallelity implies that the grammatical laws, by which we unify the meanings of individual objects (or features thereof) into *one* propositional affirmation, express the laws of categorial intuition by which we achieve the unified grasp of a state of affairs corresponding to the affirmation.

The point may be put in terms of Husserl's goal in speaking of the correlation of thought to intuition. It is, as we said, one of specifying a compatible essence. Such an essence, broadly speaking, is one in which intuition can be reported in terms of a propositional thought and can itself confirm such a thought. This demands in Husserl's view, that intuition have the same structure as propositional thought does. The implication of this is that the appearing state of affairs is a linguistically structured entity. Both as intended and perceived it can, with a certain proviso, be understood as the correlate of a unified propositional thought. One may note here the closeness of this doctrine to the Anglo-Saxon forms of the philosophy of language. A dominant interest in such philosophizing is the attempt to match language, thought and perception into a compatible whole. In this, the "grammar" of a language — the term being understood in an extremely wide sense — is looked upon as determinative of both thought and perception. Husserl dissociates himself from the linguistic relativism inherent in this determination in two ways. The first is his insistence on the primacy of perception with respect to language. Thus, the proviso mentioned above can be put as follows: a state of affairs can be considered as linguistically structured only insofar as these structures express the parallel forms of categorial activity. The reference in this direction is to "an ideal and *a priori* system of performable acts." Thus the second way of avoiding relativism proceeds by way of an ultimate reference of the grammatical forms. The grammatical laws are not conceived as contingent laws of an empirically given language. They represent the laws that every language must have to give expression to this system of acts. The system itself, as should be clear from the above, has a final reference to the laws of compatibility which specify the prior possibility of complex meanings. This prior possibility correlates, not just thought and perception, but also perception and being, according to the inherent possibilities of each. Insofar as this second correlation is understood to deny relativism, the goal of this procedure is attained.

This understanding of the second correlation will be discussed by us later. For the present, let us speak of a second set of laws that enter into the first correlation insofar as it concerns categorial intuition. These are the laws of an analytic or formal logic. The distinction between these laws and those of the synthetic logic of content is readily apparent. The latter concern the compatibility of perceptual contents in the straightforward intuition of an individual object. The former laws abstract from all content, symbolizing objects with letters. Their concern is with the analytically derivable compatibility of objects within a state of affairs. According to Husserl, such laws can take the form, "If it is true that there is an A which is a B, then it is also true that a certain A is B or that not all A's are not B's, etc." (*LU*, Tüb. ed., II/2, 195; F., pp. 826-27). The "etc." refers to all the possible statements that can be analytically derived from the original assertion. Husserl's reference, as is clear from his examples, is to what are called laws of truth functional equivalence. By virtue of them, we can derive a circle of equivalent assertions, all of which are true if the original statement is true.

The features of these laws are mirrored in the laws of intuitive categorial activity. The latter, too, "are of an entirely pure and analytic character, and quite independent of the peculiarity of their matter" (*LU*, Tüb. ed., II/2, 189; F., p. 822). The laws specifying the possibilities of performable acts are, in other words, laws "of categorial intuitions in virtue of their purely categorial forms" — e.g., the forms of acts corresponding to the *is, is not, and, or,* of our logical discourse (*Ibid.*, II/2, 191; F., p. 823).[3] "They determine," Husserl says, "what variations of any supposed categorial form are possible with respect to some definite but arbitrarily chosen material which is held identical" (*Ibid.*, II/2, 189; F., p. 822). Corresponding to the laws of truth functional equivalence, we have here "an ideally closed circle of possible transformations of a functioning form into ever new forms" (*Ibid.*, II/2, 190; F., p. 823).

Given that the laws of logic, like those of grammar, are mirrored in the intuitive sphere, the assertions made about grammar can *mutatis mutandis* be repeated in the case of logic. The logical laws can be taken as "the pure laws of the validity of meanings, the laws of the ideal possibility of their intuitive illustration." In this, they are understood as specifying "the possibilities of combination and transformation of meaning which, in any given case, can be undertaken *salva veritate*, i.e., without prejudicing the possibility of a fulfillment of meaning to the extent that this previously existed" (*LU*, Tùb. ed., II/2, 194-95; F., p. 826). The basis for this assertion is the truism that the conditions for the possibility of meanings being fulfilled depend upon the conditions of the performability of the intuitions that would fulfill them. Once we state that the logical laws give us the former conditions, then they are also expressive of the latter conditions. This can be more precisely stated by saying that the logical and grammatical laws are so interpreted that they must run parallel to and, thus, express the laws governing the structure of intuitive fulfillment.

The point of this can be seen by noting that verification only concerns statements that are grammatically well formed, i.e., those that have, in grammatical terms, a "closed unity of sense." When we do have such senses, then we also can have the role of logic as providing rules for testing assertions. Thus, we assume that contradictory assertions with the same referent cannot both be confirmed by the same intuitional data. Growing out of this, we also have the predictive function of logic. This function is particularly apparent when logic becomes transformed into the mathematical inferences of modern science. As we reason from one set of observational data to another, such mathematical inferences can allow us to predict what will be observed with relatively great precision. All of this can be at least partially explained by saying that intuition is not just grammatically, but also logically structured. In Husserl's terms, we can say that logic is indicative of the structuring activity of perceptual interpretation.

This leads us to mention one of Husserl's aims in detailing the first correlation. This is the goal of providing a "theory of theories" — i.e., an account of how theories come to be formed and how, *as theories*, they can be confirmed by observational data. With regard to their formation, there is, according to Husserl, a "ladder of foundations." In terms of its materials, the bottom rung of the ladder is given by the straightforward perception of individual objects. Categorial activity relates these objects into simple states of affairs. It also relates relations just as the categorial elements of discourse relate statements of relations. What we have, then, is a ladder of founding and founded acts in which every relation can serve as "material" for relating acts of a higher level. Given that the structure of this ascent is that of categorially formed discourse, we can say with Husserl, "The possibility of unlimited complication is both *a priori* and evident" (*LU*, Tüb., ed., II/2, 181; F., p. 816).

This does not mean that there are not formal limits to this complication. There is, first of all, the requirement that no "rung" or level of the ladder of foundations be illegitimately skipped — which means, first and foremost, that at the basis of even the most involved theoretical discourse there must be the ultimate level of sensuous perception. At this level, the laws of synthetic logic apply to our perceptual predicates. Beyond this level, there are also the limitations imposed by the grammatical and logical laws. The purpose of these limitations should be readily apparent. It is to assure us that at each level of the ladder there is present a unity of sense. With this there is also a unitary referent pointing to a perception that can confirm the theory at that level.

As an example of this last point, we may take the grammatical law of substitution discussed by us above. The law demands that only names (or, more generally, nominal material) can be substituted for names. This implies that when we wish to relate one judgement to another by making it the second judgement's nominal subject, the first must be transformed into a name. Such transformations often occur with a shortening or abbreviation of the nominalized judgement. As such they are a part of every theory that attempts to keep its propositional assertions to a manageable length. The shortening can proceed to a point where a whole theory involving countless judgements and relations of these can be referred to by a single name, e.g., "the theory of evolution." The primary aim of such transformations is not, however, mere convenience in length of statement. It is to assure us that when we do relate judgements, we are making only a single assertion. This is a statement that has an assertive reference to a single relation, one that can be confirmed in a single intuitive act.

The technical doctrine behind this can only be briefly indicated. On the grammatical side, its essential position is that in transforming a judgement into an enriched name, we have robbed it of its power to grammatically make an independent assertion (See *LU*, Tüb. ed., II/1, 464; F., pp. 625-26; *Ibid.*, II/1, 475; F., pp. 633-34). The enriched name has its assertive or "positing" force only in the context of a new judgement. The judgement, in other words, includes in its content the content of the name. The name becomes *part* of the referent that the judgement asserts. The truth value of the judgement thus depends upon there being something corresponding to the name, though the name itself does not include the *independent* assertion of this correspondence. If it did, then the judgement that included it would make two *separate* assertions. It would not have as its correlate a unitary — if extended — state of affairs. This point may be put in terms of the ladder of foundations. As a correlate to this extended but unitary state of affairs, the judgement in question is a founded one. If we wish to make the enriched name it includes into an independent assertion, then we must descend a level on this ladder. Linguistically, this means transforming the name back into a proposition. It is at this point that it becomes an intention which can structure an independent state of affairs.

This movement is mirrored, on the side of subjective performance, by a doctrine of presentation and judgement (See *LU*, Tüb. ed., II/1, 467-74; F., pp. 628-33). Propositional affirmation is a function of the latter which is regarded as a synthetic "many-rayed" thesis. In judgement, we actively constitute a "unity of consciousness" by synthetically binding together a number of separate theses. The correlate of this unity is a state of affairs; the individual objects making up this state are the correlates of the separate theses. In judgement, then, we synthetically constitute a perceptual interpretation and, if this is fulfilled, also affirm it. Presentation, in distinction to this, is not a constitutive act. It is a "single-rayed" thesis in which we reflectively regard the result of our judging. This may be for the purpose of calling it into question, asking of its content is really so. It also may be for the purpose of including its content as an element of a new judgement. In neither case is the content *by itself* judgementally affirmed. From the above, it should be clear that grammatical nominalization corresponds to subjectively moving from judgement to presentation. Only as nominalized can a judgement enter as a "founding" rung in the ladder of foundations. In other words, the ascent up the ladder consists of transforming judgements into single-rayed presentations and making them elements in the many-rayed relational act of a new judgement.

Here, we should mention a point about Frege, against whose doctrine Husserl's position on grammatical nominalization is implicitly directed. Frege, in considering the sentence, "Whoever discovered the elliptical form of planetary orbits died in misery," notes that the first part of the sentence does not contain what he calls a "complete thought." It has not a complete propositional sense and, thus, cannot be assigned a truth value. In this, Frege claims to have discovered a "fault" of language. It permits the formation of enriched names which, while dependent upon an assertion for the thought of an actual referent, do not themselves assert this referent. They, thus, "seem to stand for something," but have — assertively at least — "no reference." ("On Sense and Reference," *Trans. from the Phil. Writings of G. Frege,* ed. cit., pp. 68-70). For Husserl, this "fault" is precisely what makes theoretical discourse possible. The fact that a judgement can become an enriched name, which cannot independently assert its referent, allows it to function in a wider assertion that has but a single, if complex referent. This points back to a subjective fact that makes extended theoretical discourse possible in the first place. One does not have to re-enact a judgement when making it a component in a new judgement. It can be held presentationally — i.e., in a single-rayed thesis — and, as such, enter in with other presentations in a many-rayed judgemental thesis.

With respect to the intuitive confirmation of a theory, this means that such confirmation can proceed step-wise. The underlying judgements need not be synthetically re-enacted, each demanding its own intuitive fulfillment. Only the relation on the level to be grasped stands in need of intuitive fullness. We, thus, have the possibility of a crucial experiment providing evidence for the relation in question and, thus, confirming the theory as a whole. Here, of course, the observational data cannot be seen as confirmatory apart from the theoretical context which made us search for them. They confirm a theory as a theory only insofar as they are categorially regarded within their position on the ladder of foundations.

Before we conclude our discussion fo the first correlation we must mention an essential condition for the categorial forms of our discourse expressing the categorial activity of our consciousness. This condition grounds the possibility of what Husserl calls a "logically adequate language." As Husserl defines this,

> The ideal of a logically adequate language is that of a language that would obtain, for every possible material and every

possible categorial form, an unambiguous expression. Certain significant intentions would unambiguously belong to its words, the intentions being able to come alive even in the absence of the "corresponding" — i.e., the fulfilling — intuition. There would, then, run parallel to all possible primary and founded intuitions a system of primary and founded meanings which would (in the sense of possibility) express them (*LU*, Tüb. ed., II/2, 191-92; F., p. 824).

The essential element in this ideal is that of the possibility of unambiguous expression. "Every possible material and every possible categorial form" would permit "unambiguous expression" only if they themselves were unambiguous. Given that the object of intuition is either an individual entity or a state of affairs composed of these, this demand naturally extends to them. It may be put in terms of a point we made above in discussing Husserl's assertion that an objective expression has the possibility of replacing a subjectively occasional one. The condition for this possibility — as well as for the possibility of a logically adequate language — is a notion of being demanded by epistemology. This is being conceived of as inherently unambiguous and, thus, as permitting a definite description of its content. It is, as we pointed out, a notion that is essential if we are to conceive the law of non-contradiction as applicable to entitities. It is, thus, also essential if we are to conceive this law (as well as the other logical laws) as giving the structure of our intuitive positing of entities. Such positing occurs in what we may call the *epistemological context* — the context of positing on the basis of truth. Here, we have to say that insofar as the descriptions of the first correlation have relied on the possibility of unambiguous expression, they have also relied on a notion of being as unambiguously expressible. More generally, they have relied on a notion which conceives being as having just those possibilities that are demanded by the epistemological context. To discuss this properly, we must consider Husserl's second correlation:

The Correlation of Perception to Being

The first correlation, as we noted, is essentially an elaboration of a single notion, the notion of thought as intuitively interpretative.

At the basis of the second correlation, there is also a single notion which becomes elaborated in some detail. This is the notion of the essential primacy of the epistemological standpoint. The standpoint itself is one that begins with the knowing relationship and takes it as its basis. As we remarked at the end of our second chapter, scepticism and relativism arise when some other relation — e.g., that of history — is considered as prior to and determinative of the content of knowledge. When we consider it as *other*, in the sense of *outside* of the relationship of knowledge, then we consider its determinations of this relationship to be unknowable. The theory that attempts to present them, thus, does *not* have the possibility of having its findings justified as items of knowledge. Only when the knowing relation is prior in the sense of setting its own standards would this be the case. Now, the double correlation of thought to perception and perception to being is an attempt to describe, on an eidetic level, the relation of knowing conceived within this priority. It is, thus, a description of the intentional, or knowing relation such that its result can be objectively valid knowledge. Here, we have the understanding, mentioned above, that sees the correlation of being to perception as a denial of relativism. The understanding takes the correlation as part of an account of the priority of the knowing relationship.

We can put the above in terms of Husserl's goal of establishing the eidos of an objectively valid, knowing relationship. Such an establishment involves showing the possibility of the eidos and, thus, also its compatibility. What the above indicates is that if the eidos did not involve priority, it would not be possible. Its notion as a relation that is posterior to and dependent upon some external relation is *incompatible* with its notion as resulting in objectively valid knowledge. Given that the very possibility of the knowing or epistemological relation demands its priority, we have, as corresponding to this, Husserl's assertion of the priority of epistemology: "Naturally epistemology must not be understood as a discipline that follows metaphysics or even coincides with it, but rather as one which precedes metaphysics just as it precedes psychology and all other disciplines" (*LU*, Tüb. ed., I, 224; F., p. 221). If we understand *priority* in the usual sense according to which one science is called "prior" to another when the other takes its principles from the first,[4] two conclusions immediately follow. The first is that epistemology cannot draw its principles from any other science since all other sciences are in their principles *posterior* to it. The second, which follows from this, is that it cannot derive its notion of being from any other science. As a first or prior science, epistemology must hold as absolutely prior the notion of being that it establishes in its own context.

The context is one of positing on the basis of truth. It is within this context that we can say that truth and being are "correlative" categories and that we can move from one to the other. As should be readily apparent, such positing only works within the priority of the epistemological standpoint. Only within this standpoint can we say that knowing (truth being its claim) is the guarantee of actual objective being. As for being itself, its correlation to perceivability directly follows. Given that, for Husserl, the context of truth is intuitive givenness, that which is posited must involve the possibility of such givenness. Since what is posited is being, the account of positing on the basis of truth assumes that this must inherently have the possibility of being perceived.

The same point can be made by defining epistemology as the study of our access to being. Given this definition and given the priority of the epistemological standpoint, the principles governing the possibility of being are to be drawn from those governing its accessibility to consciousness. Possibility, here, means the possibility of presence. Since knowing takes place in the context of presence, we must say that presence is definitive, in an epistemological context, of the notion of being. This can be made more precise by noting that Husserl, after having gone on for some length to declare that being is nothing perceivable in the object, asserts that "the notion of being can arise only when some being, actual or imaginary, is set before our eyes" (*LU*, Tüb. ed., II/2, 141; F., p. 784). These assertions can receive a satisfactory interpretation once we say that the notion of being does not refer to *what* is presented, but rather to the *presence* of that which is presented. It is intuitive presence itself rather than any particular feature of the object that first grounds our notion of being. The reason why the being must be "set before our eyes" — i.e., be *intuitively* present — can be taken from a point described above (See p. 52). Perception, as we said, contains an inherent standard of its own adequacy. Now, the epistemological or knowing relation must, as independent and prior, set its own *inherent standards* for its adequacy. Given this, it becomes an axiom that perceptual presence must be taken as the form of the presence of being. It is that which the relationship, as directed towards being, attempts to accomplish in "fulfilling" itself.

We may now turn to Husserl's explicit assertions of the second correlation. The most general of these occurs when Husserl considers the "doubt whether the actual course of the world, the real structure of the world in itself, could conflict with the forms of thought." Husserl replies with a double assertion, namely ". . . that a correlation to perceivability (*Wahrgenommen-werden-können*), intuitability, meanability and knowability is inseparable from the sense of being in general and that, therefore, the ideal laws that *in specie* pertain to these possibilities can never be suspended by the contingent content of a being existing at the moment" (*LU*, Tüb. ed., II/2, 201; F., p. 831).[5] The first assertion made is that it is the sense of being in general which demands perceivability.[6] Since perception and thought are themselves correlated, the correlation of being to perceivability extends as well to meanability (the intending of the object in thought) and to knowability (the fulfillment of this intention by intuition). We have, secondly, the assertion of a set of "ideal laws that *in specie* pertain to these possibilities" — the correlative possibilities of being, perception and thought. According to the first correlation, the laws which pertain to the thought that has the possibility of intuitive fulfillment are formally identical to the laws which govern intuitive categorial activity. The same formal laws are here asserted as pertaining to the sense of being in general (*Sinn des Seins überhaupt*). An individual being cannot set them aside.

What this means in terms of the objects of categorial intuition may be gathered from another of Husserl's statements. He writes:

> *The ideal conditions of the possibility of categorial intuition in general are, correlatively, the conditions of the possibility of objects of categorial intuition and of the possibility of categorial objects per se* (*schlechthin*) (*LU*, Tüb. ed., II/2, 189; F., p. 822).

The former conditions are, as we saw, given by the logical and grammatical laws. These laws are now seen to have, through the correlation of the conditions of intuition and being, a formal ontological force. In other words, the sense of grammatical-logical possibility becomes, in the second correlation, one of *ontological possibility* (possibility to be). In this, it achieves the same status as the possibilities determined by the laws of the logic of content. As we cited Husserl above, the distinctions formed by those laws become a part of "formal ontology."

This conclusion should not surprise us. The ontological force of the laws of analytical logic is just what is demanded by the priority of the epistemological context — the context of positing on the basis of truth. Such a context demands that being be unambiguously expressible. Only then can we correlate truth and being in such a way that a truth can be seen as having the possibility of pointing unambiguously to a being. As emphasized above, the possibility of unambiguous expression is governened by the laws of non-contradiction and excluded middle. The laws, therefore, must have a formal ontological force — i.e., govern in a limiting way the possibilities of being — for the correlation to hold.

To bring out more explicitly the role of this context in defining the notion of being, let us cite one further passage from the *Investigations:*

> But certainly there is nothing that *can*not be perceived. This however, means that the actual performance of the actual acts on the basis of these materials or, more exactly, on the basis of these straightforward intuitions, is in an ideal sense *possible*. And these possibilities in general are limited by laws insofar as certain impossibilities, ideal incompatibilities, are lawfully arranged beside them (*LU*, Tüb. ed., II/2, 188; F., p. 822).

As the context of this quote makes clear, the word "*kann*" is emphasized in order to set it in opposition to the word "*muß*". Husserl, then, is not asserting that everything that exists *must* be perceived. He is asserting only that it *can* be perceived, perceivability (*Wahrgenommen-werden-können*) being, in fact, inseparable from the sense of being *überhaupt*. We can penetrate the sense of this "can" by examining what is meant by the claim that the acts in question are in "an ideal sense possible." The immediate reference here is to positing on the basis of truth. As we recall, such positing does not make actual existence dependent on the actuality of our apprehension of it (See above, pp. 69-70). It does not demand that "there is nothing that is not perceived and that everything must be perceived." It correlates the actuality of being to the possibility of its perception. As we said, the intended result of this doctrine is to give being an objectively independent status without violating the notion of its inherent relation to consciousness. Thus, although the actuality of being does not depend upon the actuality of our grasp of it, it is understood as equivalent to the possibility of its being in relation to consciousness. The key point here is that *truth is an ideal species* whose subjective instances are "inwardly evident judgements" into the state of affairs that forms the truth's content. For Husserl, we may recall, the ideal existence of a species demands only the possibility of its instances. Thus, as defined within the context of truth, being, as such a state of affairs, demands only the possibility of the acts of intuitive judgement that apprehend it.

This leads us to make a further, if subsidiary, remark. This is that the apprehension of being in the context of truth must be an apprehension of it in its ideal character. Only so can it be acknowledged as objective – i.e., as independent of our momentary subjective grasp of it. Since truth is apprehended through the intuition of a state of affairs and since such states are *objects of categorial* intuition, these last must be regarded as being ideal. We, thus, have the doctrine put forward by Husserl: "We shall be able to characterize sensible or *real* objects as *objects of the lowest level of possible intuition and categorial* or ideal *objects as objects of higher levels*" (*LU*, Tüb. ed., II/2, 145; F., p. 787). The latter are apprehended as objects of intentions that can be expressed in propositions, having an objective and, therefore, universal claim to validity. The fulfillments of these intentions must, therefore, allow an apprehension of being with an ideal character corresponding to this claim. This point can also be put in terms of the epistemological notion of being as presence. According to this, the principles governing the possibility of being are drawn from those governing the possibility of its presence. Now, categorial objects have not the same possibilities of presence as real or sensuously apprehendable objects. They can only be apprehended in "founded" acts. This means that the principles governing their ontological possibility are correspondingly different. They express a different sense of being, one that, in distinction to the real, is ideal.

As a final observation in the passage cited on page 118, we may remark that, for Husserl, the ideal possibilities of intuitive acts are "limited by laws" because they can be set alongside of "ideal impossibilities" — i.e., "ideal incompatibilities." The equation of impossibility with incompatibility should remind us that the ultimate reference of this passage is to the existence of complex, though compatible species expressing prior possibilities. More precisely, it is to the laws governing compatibility, the laws of specific unity that ground the existence of complex species. Insofar as they give the prior possibilities of valid thought, intuition and being, we have a key to understanding Husserl's remarks on

The Source of the Ideas

In his "Forward" to the Sixth Investigation Husserl writes that its chapter, "The Laws of Authentic and Inauthentic Thinking," "offers a blueprint for the first radical overcoming of psychologism in the theory of reason." He thus considers it particularly "grotesque" that the Investigation should be considered one where he "fell back into psychologism" (*LU*, Tüb. ed., II/2, v; F., p. 622). In fact, the origin of this often repeated reproach can be found right in the "Introduction" to the Investigation. It occurs in a passage we have already quoted in part. Husserl writes:

> All thinking and especially all theoretical thinking and knowing is accomplished in certain "acts" that appear in connection with expressive speech. In these acts lies the source of all unities of validity which confront the speaker as objects of thought and knowledge or as the explanatory grounds and laws of these, as their theories or sciences. Thus, in these acts also lies the source for the corresponding pure and universal ideas whose ideal and lawful connections pure logic attempts to set forth, and whose classification epistemological criticism takes as its task (*LU*, Tüb. ed., II/2, 1; F., p. 667).

The proper way to understand these remarks is given by the chapter on authentic thinking. It is this chapter that directly engages in the correlation of thought, perception and being. In the light of this correlation, we cannot say that the acts of a real psychological subject are the source — in the sense of the *independent* origin — of the pure ideas. They can only be regarded as the subjective origin of our *knowledge* of this source. The distinction here is one between the *ratio cognicendi* and the *ratio essendi* of the origin of the "unities of validity" that confront us. The acts "that appear in the context of expressive speech" reveal to us the grammatical and logical laws that regulate such speech. Insofar as these mirror the laws of specific unity, such acts of discourse can be regarded as *the principle by which we know* of these laws. As for the latter laws, they are the objective origin of the unities of validity. In other words, they embody the principle by which the unities of validity that confront us *are*.

The essential point here is that source — in the sense of objective origin — must be understood in terms of Husserl's definition of "the pure and universal ideas." Such ideas, in their being, represent pure possibilities. The doctrine that accompanies this position is: "Unity as such grounds possibility" (*LU*, Tüb. ed., II/2, 109; F., p. 754). Thus, to talk of the origin of the *being* of the ideas, we must talk of the origin — in the sense of the ground — of their possibility. Such an origin can only be given by the laws of specific unity which ground the possibility and, thus, the "ideal existence" of the species. To put this in a slightly different way, we assert that source cannot in this case be understood *subjectively* in the sense of a real psychological source. It must rather be understood objectively in the sense of a relation of lawfulness that functions as a specifying ground for the possibility — and, thus, the being — of the ideas considered as species.

A few quotations from Husserl should make this point clear. The "genuine logical *a priori*" is for Husserl a title for the logical laws that define specific unity. In discussing the *a priori*, Husserl writes: "A relation to 'our' mental organization or to 'consciousness in general' (understood as the *universally human* aspects of consciousness) does not define the pure and genuine *a priori*, but rather a grossly falsified one" (*LU*, Tüb. ed., II/2, 197-98; F., p. 829). Rather than being defined by a relation to a species of judging beings, the laws of the *a priori* "pertain to the *essential* endowment of being (*zur essentiellen Ausstattung des Seienden*)" (*Ibid.*, II/2, 198; F., p. 829). This, we should point out, does not mean that these laws have no reference to the "act types and

and forms" that define the understanding in its categorial activity. The *a priori* does concern these insofar as the laws of logic are understood as giving the structure of such activity. Yet, when they are so understood, they do not just apply to the understanding's possibilities of valid or authentic thought; for they correlate these to the possibilities of intuition and being which they *also* express.

We may put this in terms of a remark that the *Investigations* repeats a number of times about the intentions of thought. Husserl states that ". . . The forms of logic are nothing more than the forms of significant intentions which have been elevated in the consciousness of their unity to objective ideal species" (*LU*, Tüb. ed., II/1, 150; F., p. 353).[7] This equation between the forms of significant intentions and those of logic is not intended to subjectivize the latter. It is rather to given an objective status to the forms or conditions that govern adequate signification. A significant intention is defined as one that can become perceptually interpretative. It is, thus, one that had the possibility of intuitive fulfillment. This means that when we elevate its forms to "objective ideal species," we also have regard to ideal forms or conditions of categorial fulfillment. This is the doctrine of the first correlation. According to this teaching, ". . . *the pure conditions of the possibility of completely adequate signification in general* . . . refer back to the *pure conditions of the possibility of categorial intuition in general*" (*LU*, Tüb. ed., II/2, 195; F., p. 827). This may be set alongside the remark of Husserl's we cited a few pages above: "*The ideal conditions of the possibility of categorial intuition in general are, correlatively, the conditions of the possibility of objects of categorial intuitions* and the *possibility of categorial objects* per se" (*LU*, Tüb. ed., II/2, 189; F., p. 822). When we place these remarks together, they can have only one meaning. The forms or conditions governing the possibility of adequate signification are those governing, correlatively, the possibilities of intuition and being. The assertion that these forms, when considered *in specie*, are the forms of logic means that the logical laws do not just have a reference to the subjective (or merely psychological) capacities of the understanding. They correlate the possibilities of the significant intention of the understanding with those of perception and entities. They do this by being identically present in a defining way in each of these realms.

To approach more directly the notion of the "source" of the ideas, we have only to note that it is the pure "possibilities" of the elements of the intentional relationship that are correlated. According to Husserl, ". . . possibilities themselves are ideal objects" (*LU*, Tüb. ed., II/1, 115; F., p. 345). To bring ideal existence "back to the possibility of the corresponding individuals is not to reduce it to something other, but merely to express it through an equivalent phrase" (*Ibid.*, II/2, 103; F., pp. 749-50). This means that we are dealing with a correlation of thought, intuition and being on the level of ideal existence. It also implies that the same laws, which correlate these elements by specifying that the possibilities for each are the same, are to be understood as also specifying their being in terms of ideal existence. In other words, the laws do not just ground their correlation; they also, as a specifying ground, function as a source with respect to ideal existence. Thus, with regard to "the unities of validity which confront the thinker as objects of thought and knowledge," these may be regarded as the instantiations of complex species. They are instantiations that can be present in the categorial combinations of authentic thought and, correlatively to this, present in categorial intuitions and the categorial objects of knowledge. Their source, in the sense of the origin of their possibility, is found within the species that are instantiated in these and, ultimately, within the laws of specific unity that ground such species. An indication of this position is the fact that Husserl equates "the *objective possibility* of complex meanings" with "the possibility of their accommodation to a unitary intuition that fulfills them as wholes" (*LU*, Tüb. ed., II/2, 194; F., p. 826). On one level, this can be regarded as the assertion that the intentions of meaning can be validly unified only to the point that the intentions that fulfill them can be unified – i.e., held in a single perceptual regard. On another level, this points to the fact that the forms of unification for both are the same. They are those given by the laws of specific unity. Since ideal existence and possibility are equated by Husserl, the "objective possibility" here referred to is nothing other than the objective existence of the ideal species of the meaning. Its equation with the possibility of a unitary intuitive fulfillment refers us, on the one hand, to the laws of specific unity. On the other hand, it refers us to a doctrine we considered above. This is the teaching that the obtaining of the instantiation – i.e., the actual intuitive regard of an object that unites the components of meaning – guarantees the existence of its species as representing its prior possibility (See above, pp. 67-68).

Let us venture a brief comparison of the above with the corresponding position in *Ideen I*. As we mentioned in our last chapter, this latter work also correlates interpretative and objective categories. The basis of this correlation is the *dependence* of the latter on the former. The interpretative categories, as pertaining to the subject, pertain to a realm of "absolute being", a realm upon which "all other regions of being ... are essentially dependent" (*Ideen I*, S76; Biemel ed., p. 174). This means that, along with the objective categories that pertain to it, objective "reality essentially lacks independence." As Husserl also expresses this, "Reality and world are here simply titles for certain valid *unities of sense,* namely unities of 'sense' that are essentially related to certain definite connections of absolute pure consciousness, connections that yield both sense and its validity" (*Ibid.*, §55; p. 134). The position that consciousness assumes in this is given by Husserl's remark that "... pure consciousness ... conceals in itself all worldly transcendencies, 'constituting' them in itself ..." (*Ibid.*, S50; p. 119). It is a position of absolute independence, one where "it needs no thing in order to exist" (*Ibid.*, §49, p. 150).

This doctrine, as is obvious, is not found in the *Investigations*. As defined by its acts of thought and intuition, consciousness is dependent rather than independent. The reason for this is that the "weight of being," as we put it, falls on the intentional relationship itself. The laws of the relation are prior to the elements related insofar as they define their very possibilities. This leads us to make a point about constitution. In the context of Husserl's later work, we can say that the constituting acts of the subject are the source, in the sense of the *independent* origin, of the "unities of validity" confronting the subject. They can be conceived as dependent on the connections of a consciousness that is *per se* independent. In the *Investigations,* on the contrary, constitution is not an independent act. It is, insofar as it posits being, an act that attempts to make sense of an already given intuitive presence. It is, thus, an act correlated with the possibility of presence which is the possibility of the object's being. The essential dependence of the act within this correlation is seen from a fact stressed above. In order to be fulfilled, it must, in the dialectic of sense and presence, conform to the laws governing the intentional relation as a whole.

There is, we may note, a second difficulty for those who may wish to interpret Husserl's remarks about the "source" of the ideas as a constituting source. His reference to the "acts" which function as such a source is not to these as real temporal processes. As the *Investigations* make clear, the reference is to "the specific nature of the acts in question" or, more generally, to "*the ideas of sensibility and understanding in general*" (*LU*, Tüb. ed., II/2, 196-97; F., p. 821). Such ideas, as ideal, are defined in terms of their non-temporality. The reference is, thus, not to constitution which, as a real act, is a process temporal in nature. Here, in fact, we must say that the ideal species, rather than being the result of the act of constitution, are this real act's defining and empirically limiting forms. This leads to the final consideration of this chapter, that of

The Ideal as Limiting the Real

The position of the ideal as limiting the empirical possibilities of the real is in some sense demanded by the way Husserl conceives the priority of the epistemological standpoint. The standpoint must be prior if it is to be possible. This priority, of course, extends to the relationship that defines the standpoint — i.e., the knowing or intentional relation. Now, the way in which the *Investigations* assumes this priority must be expressed is *in terms of the world.* As we said in the beginning, the form of this relationship must ultimately be understood as a world-form. The laws of the relation extend to *being itself* and, thus, to the whole of reality. This follows by necessity once we define the relation as that which yields objective knowledge, i.e., a knowledge of being as it is in itself. As embodying the world-form, the relation also assumes the ontological function of the world in its essential structures. It places subjects and objects, understood as worldly realities, in a formal harmony in which interpretative and objective categories harmonize. In summing this up, we can say that for Husserl it is the notion of the intentional relation as resulting in objective knowledge that raises it ultimately to the priority of a functioning world-form.

It is easy to see how the very conception of this form demands that it limit the real. With respect to the acts of subjective constitution, the *a priori* expressing the form of the intentional relation states the conditions for such acts achieving objective knowledge. Now, if these conditions cannot be realized, this would be because the laws of the real, the causal laws governing the real acts of a real subject, were considered to be inherently incompatible with the laws of the *a priori*. This, however, implies that this *a priori* involves in its own notion an incompatibility. It implies that it is to be conceived of as an *a priori* of that which, through its own laws, is inherently contradictory to it. What we would have, then, would be a world-form without any possibility of the ontological function that made us posit the form. This means that the priority of the knowing relation would designate a necessarily empty notion. Now, the forms of knowledge — i.e., the ideal forms of acts that result in knowledge — cannot be said to know. They are a-temporal, and knowing for the *Investigations* is a process carried on by a real, temporally situated subject. If these forms, then, are *essentially* contradicted by the real nature of such a subject, they designate a species whose instances are essentially impossible. The null set of instances, in such a circumstance, must be understood as designating a species that is inconsistent with itself and, hence, impossible.

To this we may add that if the *a priori* did not limit the real in its contingency, it would also be unknowable. Its forms have been obtained through the eidetic reduction. In this process, as we quoted Husserl, "... the forms of significant intentions ... have been elevated in the consciousness of their unity to objective ideal species" (*LU*, Tüb. ed., II/1, 150; F., p. 373). If the forms of such intentions exhibited a pure, factually determined contingency, then the eidetic reduction, when turned upon them, would leave us with no definite result. In fact, regarded as an abstraction from everything factually contingent, it would leave us with nothing at all. Such a situation would, of course, make impossible Husserl's project of a "radical overcoming of relativism." The forms of logic, as equated with those of significant intentions, would be factually contingent and, thus, considered as somehow derivable from facts. We would then return to what Husserl calls "relativism in the widest sense of the word," this being defined "as a doctrine which in some fashion derives the pure principles of logic from facts" (*LU*, Tüb. ed., I, 122; F., p. 144).

The above may be considered as setting the context of Husserl's description of the genuine logical *a priori*. He distinguishes this from the anthropological interpretation of the same in the following words:

> The concept of a common mental organization, like that of a physical organization, has indeed only an "empirical" meaning, the meaning of a mere matter of fact. Pure laws, however, are precisely pure from *matter of fact*. They do not tell us what is the common occurrence (*allgemeiner Brauch*) in this or that province of the real. They tell us rather what is plainly beyond all generalization and all division according to spheres of reality. The reason for this is that what they tell us pertains to the essential endowment of being (*LU*, Tüb. ed., II/2, 197-48; F., p. 829).

This passage distinguishes the "pure laws" definitive of the intentional relation from those that are based on empirical generalizations. Its essential assertion is that those laws that are free from empirical grounding have a *universal* applicability — one that pertains to the "essential endowment" of what is. The motivation behind this statement should be relatively clear. An empirical generalization, as derived from matters of fact, has the contingency inherent in such facts. It may, in Aristotle's terminology, be called a "secondary substance" or a derived reality. The primary reality if made up of those entities whose ways of being have been generalized into empirically grounded formulations. Now, the position of the pure law of the logical *a priori* is exactly the reverse of this. The logical law cannot be considered as contingent — i.e., as derived from facts. This is a demand that is essential if we are to avoid "relativism in the widest sense." As not derived or dependent on facts, it must in its being be considered as independent of them. Insofar, however, as the laws of the *a priori* must bear a relation to the entities for which they serve as an *a priori*, the demand is that they be considered as prior to and definitive of them. This may also be put in terms of the fact that the *a priori* itself is only a title for the laws of the intentional relationship. It is, as we said, on this relationship that the weight of being falls. The relationship has independent being, the individual entities it relates have dependent being. They are only to the point that they can enter the relation. This is why the laws of the *a priori* pertain to the essential endowment of the *Seienden*. This essential endowment, *which is the relationship itself,* is what defines the possibilities of the *Seienden* being at all.

The above position cannot but impress us with the contrast it presents to the passages quoted at the beginning of this chapter. In the latter, Husserl asserted that the concepts making up the logical laws "can have no empirical range"; he asserted that "the laws of logic . . . relate only to what is ideal . . .". In distinction to this, the doctrine we have just considered gives the logical laws a universal applicability. This means an applicability to the real and, consequently, an empirical range. To draw this out, we note that, as applying to every sphere of reality, the logical laws must also pertain to the reality investigated by the psychologist. They must also have a psychological meaning. Husserl accepts this conclusion in the following words:

> It is, accordingly, at once clear how far the logical laws and, in the first instance, the ideal laws of "authentic" thinking also claim a *psychological* meaning and also regulate the course of factual mental events. Each genuine "pure" law, which expresses a compatibility or incompatibility grounded in the nature of particular species, limits, when it relates to a species of mentally realizable contents, the empirical possibilities of psychological (phenomenological) coexistence and succession. What is seen to be incompatible *in specie* cannot be united or made compatible in empirical instances (*LU*, Tüb. ed., II/2, 198; F., p. 829).

This passage is so apparent in its meaning, it requires practically no comment. The logical laws, although not demanding that we actually apprehend certain species of content, do factually regulate those that we can apprehend. This "psychological meaning" of the logical law may be contrasted with the position given when we began this chapter. As we quoted Husserl, "No logical law, according to its genuine sense, is a law for the facticities of mental life. It is, therefore, neither a law for presentations (i.e., experience of presentations) nor for judgements (i.e., experience of judgements) nor for any other mental experience."

The reason why Husserl originally denied a psychological import to the logical laws can be recalled from our first chapter. It is part of his attempt to prevent the metabasis of the logical law into a psychological and, ultimately, into a causal law. The attempt turns on his distinction between real subjective capacity (as given by the psychological-causal laws) and the possibility defined by the ideal laws of logic. Thus, the denial that the logical laws have a psychological import with respect to the facticities of mental life is meant to lead to the following principle:

> Logical impossibility, as the inconsistency of the ideal contents of judgement, and psychological impossibility, as the non-performability of the corresponding acts of judgement, are heterogeneous notions . . .

Granting this, we can distinguish between the logical and the causal law. We can say, when confronted by a logical error, "the proposition is inconsistent but the act of judgement is not causally ruled out" (*LU*, Tüb. ed., I, 141–42; F., p. 158).

The ultimate basis that Husserl posits for this distinction is, as we stressed, a distinction in what we can predicate of the ideal as opposed to the real. By virtue of this, the ideal is assigned a specific function with regard to the intentional relation. The ideal establishes between a real subject and its contents of judgement an *ontological transcendence.* Such transcendence means that the contents of judgement *have not the being* that would allow us to predicate of their relations the causal relations that are appropriate to the real subject with its psychologically determined capabilities. In other words, when describing this subject, we do not also describe the ideal content of its judgement; for as Husserl says of the latter, "In no case can it be regarded without absurdity as a part or side of a mental experience, and so as something real" (*LU*, Tüb. ed., I, 171; F., p. 180).

We also have, however, the function of the ideal that is given in the theory of the double correlation. This is one of establishing not transcendence, but ontological *correspondence*, a correspondence which, for reasons we have given, Husserl also sees as necessary in order for the intentional relation to achieve objective knowledge. The obvious question before us is whether these two functions can consistently be thought together. A legitimate doubt on this point arises insofar as the second demands the applicability and, hence, the predicability of the ideal with regard to the real, while the first seems to deny this.

We can set the special context of this question by returning to a theme we touched on at the beginning of this section. Let us grant that, in order to be intelligible, the concept of an ideal eidos must include in its notion the concept of its relation to the real. If the latter concept is contradictory, then so is the concept of the eidos *qua* ideal. This admission has an especial force with respect to Husserl's attempt to describe the ideal form of the intentional or subject-object relationship. It implies that if we cannot resolve this eidos' relation to the actual intentional relationship (conceived as involving a real subject), then the eidos must be looked upon as specifying a concept that is incompatible and, hence, impossible. In Husserl's terms, it means that it has no ideal existence at all. The more general context of the question is that of the unity of being. Such a unity is demanded by the epistemological context, the context of positing on the basis of truth. The notion of such positing requires a common sense to the predicate "truth." On the basis of this, we can have a common sense to the predicate "being" such that we can say that both real and ideal objects *truly are* (See above, p. 61). Now, if we grant that the notion of being is expressive of a unified concept and if we further grant that both real and ideal objects have being, then the real and the ideal must be related to form a conceptual unity. They must form a self-related, articulate whole. On this level, our question transforms itself into that concerning the formal compatibility of the elements which make up this whole.

This will be the underlying question when we consider in the next chapter Husserl's description of the *acts* of subjective accomplishment that are demanded by his theory of the double correlation. Our focus will be on the description of the acts of categorial and eidetic intuition. They involve both the real and the ideal. They are "founded" on the straightforward perception of sensuous or real objects. Their own proper objects, however, are taken as ideal. In this, the difficulties we have mentioned will appear once again, although this time their appearance will be in a limited and well-defined context.

CHAPTER VII

CATEGORIAL REPRESENTATION

We may begin by recalling our remark that a purely linguistic ontology is not possible for the *Logical Investigations* (See above, p. 58). Laws of sense and reference give us the possibilities of positing objects, but actual perceptual presence is needed for us actually to posit being. The focus, then, of Husserl's "Study on Categorial Representation" is the subjective accomplishment of categorial intuition. How does it carry out its task of bringing about an actual perceptual presence? The analogies of truth and being, by which we posit both real and categorial objects, demand certain similarities in the perceptual presence of each. This means that their intuitions must show "a genuine community of essential features." As Husserl also expresses this, in considering the acts directed to categorial or ideal objects, "We call these new acts intuitions because, with the single exception of a 'straightforward' relation to the object..., they have all the essential characteristics of intuition. We shall find in them the same essential divisions, as they also show themselves capable of essentially the same achievements of fulfillment" (*LU*, Tüb. ed., II/2, 165; F., p. 803).

The mention of "achievements of fulfillment" refers to the dialectic of sense and actual intuitive presence. Such a dialectic is essential to the notion of intuition. In Husserl's words:

> How could we talk of categorial perception and intuition if any given material allowed itself to be brought forward in any given form, the founding straightforward intuitions thus permitting themselves to be arbitrarily connected together by categorial characters?... Certainly, we can think of any relation between any set of terms and any form on the basis of any material — i.e. think them in the sense of empty signification. But we cannot *really carry out* these "foundings" on

every basis, we cannot *intuit* sensible material in every desired categorial form; we cannot *perceive* it and, especially, perceive it adequately (*LU*, Tüb. ed., II/2, 188; F., p. 821).

Husserl's point here is that even in categorial intuition, there must be a check of intuition on interpretation. In terms of our last chapter, we can say that this check is provided in a formal sense by the laws governing the dialectic of intention and fulfillment. The logical and grammatical laws governing the possibility of significant statements are also laws specifying the possibility of their intuitive fulfillments. In a more than formal sense, however, this is insufficient. The mere existence of a significant statement does not demand the actuality of its intuitive fulfillment. If this were true, then fictional works — consisting of logically and grammatically correct statements — would, as fiction, be impossible. The novelist could only write of what was actual (as opposed to the merely probable). The check, then, must come from actual intuition — i.e., the materials that it provides us.

We can clarify this by observing that the *Investigations* sees the doctrine of *perception as interpretation* as inherent in the dialectic. Interpretation demands sense contents which are *there to be interpreted*. Thus, not every significant intention results in perceptual fullness because either the appropriate contents are not present or, if contents are present, they are not such as to sustain its interpretation. One of the essential "characteristics" of actual intuition is, then, the presence of these contents. Husserl calls them by the general name, "contents of representation — *repräsentierende Inhalte.*" They are the actually experienced contents of consciousness which, by virtue of sustaining a particular interpretation, "point unambiguously to the corresponding contents of the object" (*LU*, Tüb. ed., II/2, 78; F., p. 730). They, thus, "make the difference between 'empty' signification and 'full' intuition" and "determine a sense of the word 'fullness' " (*Ibid.*, II/2, 171; F., p. 808). As Husserl also expresses this, what makes an act intuitive (be it straightforward or categorial) is the fact "that it places the object before us *in its content*, that it interprets experienced contents as representatives of the object meant" (*Ibid.*, II/2, 172; F., p. 808).

The other essential characteristic of actual intuition is, of course, the interpretation itself. Husserl refers here to the "intentional matter" or, equivalently, the "interpretive sense" of an act. He defines it as the aspect of an act which "first and foremost gives it its reference to an object" (*LU*, Tüb. ed., II/1, 415; F., p. 589). The reference is included in the sense, and so the reference is to the object as it is intended in its particular, objectively definable features (See *Ibid.*). Now, we must observe, along with René Schérer, an ambiguity in the term "intentional matter." There is, in Schérer's words, ". . . a contradiction arising from the fact that this matter, announced as composed of the intentional content (p. 204), appertains in the analysis of §20 to the real content of the act (p. 218)" (René Schérer, *La Phénoménologie des Recherches Logique de Husserl*, Paris, 1967, p. 271).[1] Such "matter," in other words, "remains a concept suspended between real content and intentional content, between the experience and the objectivity . . ." (*Ibid.*, p. 272). This ambiguity, which embraces the notion of interpretation *both* as a *real* act and as *ideal* intentional content — i.e., an embodied sense that is a result of the act — is absolutely fundamental. Its significance will be seen in the following pages.

Now, for Husserl, the crucial question is how we are to carry over the notion of representing contents to the categorial act. They are, in his opinion, the essential, if problematic, aspect of the act. They are essential insofar as without them, no act can have the "fullness" of intuition. They represent in a concrete way the check of intuition on interpretation. Their problematic feature comes from the fact that they must be understood as *sensuous* and yet they apparently can have none of the characteristics definitive of this notion. That they must be sensuously (or really) present to consciousness comes from the fact that consciousness as real can have an *immediate* relation only to what is real. Interpretation, as a perceptual act, has as its goal the transcending of this real presence. It cannot, however, dispense with it. The difficulty here is that contents of external sensation, in Husserl's view, allow the perception only of external, individual objects. Husserl writes, "All sensuous (real) unity is a unity founded in the types of sensuous contents . . .". From this, the following implication can be drawn: If the categorial act moment that corresponds to a categorial form "were an immediate connection between sensuous representing contents..., so the unity produced by this moment would be a sensuous unity, for example, like the spatial or qualitative configurations or other types of unity which the sensible contents in question can in other ways also ground" (*LU*, Tüb. ed., II/2, 174; F., p. 810). The fact that the categorial form of connection is not *per se* sensibly perceivable and, thus, cannot produce a sensuous, individual unity rules this supposition out.

A related difficulty involves the fact that each of the categorial forms is intended and grasped as the same whether we connect real or ideal objects, whether we connect objects given in perception or objects we merely imagine (See *LU*, VI, §54). This leads, according to Husserl, to "the important truth that in all change of founding acts and interpretative forms, the representing content for each *type* of founded act is a single one" (*LU*, Tüb. ed., II/2, 170; F., p. 807). In other words, the representing contents must be type specific. No matter what the objects of the founding acts are, there is, for example, one and the same representing content for the form *and*, another for the form *or* and so on. This conclusion immediately disqualifies the sensuous contents of the founding, straightforward acts from performing the required representative function. The contents differ from object to object, while the categorial forms (as well as the corresponding representing contents) of conjunction, disjunction, etc., remain the same for each type of connection, this being the case no matter what the objects are.

The question we are left with, then, is how the categorial contents can be sensuously present to the mind and yet not refer to the sensuous features of objects we sensuously perceive. Husserl's explicit answer will be given in a moment. First, however, to set its context, we will examine some descriptions he gives of founded acts. The most extensive description concerns the act by which we intuit the relation of part to whole — i.e., the act underlying the assertion, "*a* is in *A*." According to Husserl, we first have a perception that grasps the whole, *A*, "immediately and in a straightforward way." Then, in a second straightforward perception, "in an *independent* act, *a* becomes an independent object of perception" (*LU*, Tüb. ed., II/2, 153-54; F., p. 793). The result is that "... the perception of the whole, which continues to be active, coincides, in its implicit intention to the part, with the particular perception," i.e., the one independently directed toward the part, *a* (*Ibid*., II/2, 154; F., p. 793). We, thus, have a coincidence of intentions or, Husserl also says, "both interpretations coincide . . .". Now, with regard to the content of representation, we can say that the same sensuous content grounds both interpretative intentions — i.e., grounds them to the point that they coincide in interpreting a specific sensuous content. We can also say that their coincidence or unity can itself function as a *distinct representing content*. In Husserl's words, "This unity itself now takes on the function of a representative; it will count in its own right as the experienced union of acts; it will not itself be constituted as an object, rather it helps to constitute another object; it will act representatively and in such a way that *A* will now appear as having *a* in itself" (*Ibid*., II/2, 154; F., p. 794). With respect to the question we posed, the point of this should be clear. It is not the contents of the underlying acts which provide the experienced unity that functions as a categorial representative. The felt coincidence that so functions comes from the interpretations directed at these contents.

This doctrine is repeated when Husserl speaks of the act of identification, the act that allows us to say, "This is the same." The basis for this judgement cannot be the sensuous content of the object. This content changes as we view it from different perspectives. As Husserl says, ". . . the phenomenological form of identification is essentially grounded in the founding acts as such, i.e., grounded in what these are and contain over and beyond their representing contents" (*LU*, Tüb. ed., II/2, 174; F., p. 810). Beyond these contents, which are there for interpretation, these acts contain interpretative intentions. This means, in terms of our finding an unchanging content for our assertion, we must turn to *recurring elements* of the interpretative intentions of our various perceptions. Insofar as they recur, they can, when synthesized, provide us with an experienced coincidence that can represent the asserted identity. Husserl writes, "Identity, for example, is not an immediate form of unity of sense contents. It is rather a 'unity of consciousness,' a unity which is grounded in one or another consciousness (repeated or differing in contents) of the same object" (*Ibid*., II/2, 175; F., p. 811). We can also say that it is not founded on the differing contents of the object; rather, this "unity of consciousness" is made up of the coincident interpretations that the different apprehensions of the object present us with.

Eidetic perception offers us another example of a founded act. We begin by perceiving a number of objects of the same sort, say, a number of chairs. To focus on the type present in these examples, we cannot rely on the sensuous contents we individually derive from them. They differ from example to example, while the type must apply to all particular chairs with their particular contents. How, once again, the representing content must be provided by the synthesis of the recurring elements of our individual acts of perceptual interpretation. There must, as Husserl says, be "an overreaching act of identification," one that has its initial basis in the acts of straightforward perception (*LU*, Tüb. ed., II/2, 162; F., p. 800).[2]

The doctrine behind these examples should be obvious. It is that "what is categorial" does *not* pertain to objects "according to their sensible (real) content" (*LU*, Tüb. ed., II/2, 175; F., p. 811). As Husserl also puts this in discussing the synthesis of elements that results in a categorial representative ". . . the moment of synthesis does not establish any direct connection between the representing contents pertaining to the founding acts . . .". It connects and is founded in what the acts are "over and beyond their representing contents" (*Ibid.*, II/2, 174; F., p. 810). Since this is their character of being interpretations, Husserl can conclude, ". . . the categorial moment . . . unites in all circumstances their *intentional materials* and is in a true sense founded on them" (*Ibid.*, II/2, 175; F., p. 811).

With this, we may consider the "contradiction" Schérer noted in the term "intentional matter." It refers, on the one hand, to the real, immanent content of experience. On the other hand, it refers, under the title "interpretative sense," to the necessarily ideal, intentional content. Husserl, it is to be observed, avails himself of *both* significations. Thus, availing himself of the second, he mentions the difficulty that the categorial representative must be type-specific. According to Husserl, ". . . this only means that the categorial function is founded phenomenologically on what is universal in the objectifying acts or that it is essentially tied to the generic elements of the objectifying acts" (*LU*, Tüb. ed., II/2,

175; F., 811). This universal, or generic, element is sense *qua* sense. We, thus, have the identification of the intending, interpretative act with the result of its activity of "making sense" of sensations. Now, Husserl does not elaborate on how this solves the difficulty, but a solution can be guessed at. Given that sense is universal or generic, it can be understood as the same in different types of acts. Thus, the sense intended by a perception can be considered as generically the same as that intended in an act of imagination. This implies that the type of act — or, corresponding to this, the type of object — does not itself differentiate the synthesis that is formed of these senses. The categorial representative can be the same no matter what the types of objects are.

Another motive for taking intentional matter as interpretative sense is hinted at by Husserl when he adds to the just quoted remark, "Only experiences of this type" — i.e., those containing "generic elements" — "permit categorial syntheses...". The necessity for such elements can be obtained by recalling Husserl's statement that a categorial act has a "unitary intentional relationship" to a "unitary intentional object." This relationship cannot be spoken of simply in terms of a "being together" or a collection in consciousness of the perceptions the act unites (See above, p. 104). Now, the only thing possible, if we are to speak of a synthesis of perceptions in terms of their *real* content, is just such a collection. This follows when, with Husserl, we define the real in terms of its necessary spatial-temporal distinctness. Sense, however, as manifesting a generic character, has the ability to show itself as one in many. Its presence in a multiplicity of examples does not turn it into a collection. Thus, only sense has the ideal being that allows it to form, instead of a collection, a genuine "unity" of coincidence.

A further motive for focusing on "what is universal" in the underlying acts comes from the nature of the categorial object itself. Husserl classifies it as ideal. This means "... that the objective correlate of a founded act has a universal element, a form with which an object can only intuitively appear in a founded act..." (*LU*, Tüb. ed., II/2, 178; F., p. 813). This universality of the categorial form is, as we said, what makes it type-specific. It can appear as *one thing in many* different types of acts. If the representative must "point unambiguously" to what it represents, there arises the demand that the representative too must have a universal character. In other words, only a synthesis of what is universal can fulfill an intention to what is universal. The synthesis, thus, must be one of interpretative senses *qua* senses. This alone can give a corresponding "ideal" fulfillment to an act directed to an ideal or universal element.

To this we may add a point springing from the relation of sense to intuitive presence. Husserl calls the sensuous contents of individual objects the *"unessential elements of the founding acts"* (*LU*, Tüb. ed., II/2, 175; F., p. 811). His stress on the fact that such contents do *not* enter into the categorial synthesis is meant to avoid a criticism that recent scholars have leveled against his doctrine. This is that "... the performance of the synthesis is possible only in the sensuous presence of the founding objects" (Ernst Tungendhat, *Der Wahrheitsbegriff bei Husserl und Heidegger*, Berlin, 1967, p. 124). In other words, "... a categorial intention can operate *only* when the mind is in active perceptual contact with the objects ingredient in the categorial object" (Robert Sokolowski, *Husserlian Meditations*, Evanston, 1974, p. 55). Two things argue against this view. The first is that the sensuous contents of the founding objects are not conjoined by the categorial synthesis. The second is that, were the act to require an "active perceptual contact" with the objects it relates, the point of Husserl's "ladder of foundations" would be lost. In moving up the ladder, we "nominalize" our judgements, this either to question them or to use them as new elements for a new synthesis of judgement. By virtue of such nominalization, we need not, as we said, intuitively re-enact the founding judgements when placing them in relation to each other.[3] Now, behind this process, there is a fact about sense. It is that sense can be separated from intuitive presence and held in a presentative regard. Sense, in other words, can remain as a residuum after intuitive presence has passed away. This fact acts as a motive for Husserl to strip the underlying acts of their sensuous contents and to regard the categorial synthesis as one of interpretative *senses.*

In spite of these advantages, the notion of intentional matter as sense suffers from a crucial disadvantage. This is the fact that sense *per se* cannot provide sensuous contents. The presence of a perceptually embodied sense is the *result* of an interpretation directed to such contents. As we said above, consciousness can have an *intentional* relation to an ideal intentional content — i.e., a perceptually embodied sense. As real, however, it can have an *immediate* relation only to what is real, that is, only to what is really present to itself. Thus, the necessity arises for taking intentional matter in its alternate meaning. It must be understood as a content immanent or really present in experience. This means that the categorial representative has to be understood, *not* as a coincidence of senses, but as a coincidence of *acts* directed towards these senses. The acts, as real elements in a real unity of consciousness, can be straightforwardly perceived. The "moment" of their coincidence can thus be *sensuously* perceived. In Husserl's words, "We clearly have to say that the perception of an act moment or act complex of whatever sort is a sensuous perception because it is a *straightforward* perception" (*LU*, Tüb. ed., II/2, 177-8; F., p. 813).

Husserl's understanding of intentional matter as referring to an immanent mental content is implicit in the following assertion: "The complete synthetic intuition occurs ... when the mental content connecting the underlying acts becomes *interpreted* as the objective unity of the underlying founding objects, as their relation of identity, of part to whole, etc." (*LU*, Tüb. ed., II/2, 177; F., p. 812). It becomes explicit when he expresses it in terms of a distinction between "primary contents" and "contents of reflection." The former are the contents yielded by the individual objects of external perception. The latter are the contents that are present when we "reflect on" — i.e., inwardly perceive — the acts of consciousness.[4] Husserl writes, "Corresponding to the difference between purely sensuous and purely categorial objects, there is also a distinction of representing contents: *only contents of reflection can function as purely categorial representing contents*" (*Ibid.*, II/2, 180; F., p. 814). Since it is the intentional matters of the underlying acts that are supposed to provide this content, the conclusion is obvious. Such intentional matters can only be obtained by inwardly regarding our real acts. They refer, in other words, to their immanent content.

This reading, we may note, has some *but not all* of the advantages of taking intentional matter as sense. Thus, with regard to the difficulty that the categorial representing content must be type specific, i.e., a single content for a single type of categorial connections — we may put forward the following solution. We can assert that the act itself *maintains its character* while uniting different kinds of objects in one and the same way — e.g., the way that gives us a disjunction. Thus, the contents in question could be type specific by referring to the act itself. Another advantage is that in focusing on the contents springing from the act, once again we need not demand that the objects to be related be sensuously present. There is, we observed in Chapter V, a necessary distinction between the act of interpretation and the intuitive contents which are there for interpretation.[5] Husserl emphasizes this point by asserting that there is a "real lack of relation (*sachliche Beziehungslosigkeit*) of the categorial act forms to the sensible contents of their bases..." (*LU*, Tüb. ed., II/2, 174; F., pp. 810-11). This real lack of relation implies a lack of real necessity for the presence of such contents in order for the categorial act to occur. We can also put this in terms of the fact that the coincidence that functions as a categorial representative can be understood as a coincidence of the interpretative intentions of the underlying acts. The separation of act and its intuitive content means that these intentions can be understood as "being able to come alive even in the absence of the 'corresponding' — i.e., fulfilling — intuitions" (*Ibid.*, II/2, 192; F., p. 824). Thus, even without actual intuitive presence, we can re-enact these intentions and place them in a unity of coincidence.

The question that faces us is whether intentional matter can be taken in *both* of the two ways we have outlined. Can it be understood as a real "mental content," one that provides us with a sensuous representing content? Can it, consistently with this, be understood as interpretative sense? Sense, as we said, because of its universal character, can be understood as providing the possibility of a genuine coincidence — as opposed to a mere collection — of interpretations. Its synthesis, involving as it does "generic elements," can provide appropriate fulfillment for an act directed to "what is universal" — i.e., a species or a categorial element of form.

Husserl's whole procedure seems to be based on the premise of the consistency of these two ways of taking intentional matter. He writes, for example, of the "mental moments" that are the coincident intentions of founding acts:

The same mental moments which are sensuously given in inner perception (and thus function within it as sensuous representatives) could, in a founded act of the character of categorial perception (or imagination), constitute a categorial form. Thus, they could thereby sustain a totally different categorial representation (*LU*, Tüb. ed., II/2, 179; F., p. 814).

In other words, the moments as pertaining to real acts can be sensuously representative. As "sensuously given," they can allow through their contents the perception of a sensuous unity. This is a straightforward perception of the real coincidence of the acts. They can also, however, be categorially representative. Here, we may be understood as focusing on the "universal" or "generic" elements of the acts since only they, according to Husserl, "permit categorial synthesis." They are that upon which "the categorial function is founded phenomenologically." Their unity or coincidence can, thus, be taken as providing the "totally different categorial representation."

This twofold representative function of one and the same contents has a number of implications, each with its special difficulty. We may note, first of all, that it implies the immanence of sense in the real act. More precisely, it implies the immanence of generic and universal elements providing real contents of sensation. If we recall Husserl's doctrine of the transcendence of the ideal, such immanence is not really possible. To quote Husserl once again on this point, ideality "does not have the meaning of mental 'being in the mind,' indeed, with the genuine objectivity of . . . the ideal, all real being including subjective being is transcended" (*LU*, Tüb. ed., II/1, 95; F., p. 325). Husserl, we recall, also puts this distinction in terms of the different *Dasein* of the perceptually embodied sense and asserts that what we can predicate of it, we cannot predicate of the real act as part of the sense's process of appearing. In such a context, to search for what is universal or generic in the "mental moments" of real acts is to search for *what cannot be in them*. This follows insofar as its very definition as ideal involves a transcendence of these real moments. We may also express this in terms of the impossibility of attempting to immanently found the categorial act on the results of its underlying straightforward acts. The latter acts, when successful, have a result that is transcendent to them. They achieve the *intentional* presence of an embodied sense — i.e., the presence of an "ideal intentional content." This last, as ideal, cannot become immanent so as to found a new categorial act. We should here add a remark on Husserl's distinction between categorial and sensuous objects as being, respectively, ideal and real. This distinction, we may recall, is in part required by the fact that we grasp truth as ideal or universal through the categorial act. The act corresponds propositionally to a judgement of experience claiming universal validity. This being said, it must also be admitted that the distinction does not take into sufficient account the presence of the individual sensuous object. Insofar as this presence is intentional, it also involves a certain element of ideality.

Now, if we do ignore the distinction between the "truly immanent" and the "intentional" contents of consciousness, a further implication appears. The term "intentional matter," as Schérer first observed, embraces both types of content. It brings together both the content of the real act and the intentional content that is the transcendent *result* of the act. Thus, if we do attempt to make it express a unified concept, we must identify the act with its result. The consequence, here, is that the act can be understood as *fulfilling itself.* In other words, as somehow containing its result, the act can be taken as *independently responsible* for its successful accomplishment in obtaining its result. The same consequence holds for the categorial synthesis of its founding acts. Looked upon as a synthesis of act intentions, it can itself be seen as a categorial or synthetic meaning intention. Viewed as a synthesis of the *results* of these intentions, it need not be interpreted as their real coincidence, but rather as the ideal result that they synthetically intend.

This consequence, we note, is not entirely hypothetical. It is implicit in the notion of the contents of the coincidence of intentions being *both* sensuously and categorially representative. Husserl comes close to explicitly embracing it when he reflects on the fact that the coincidence or categorial connection is one between the underlying acts taken *in abstraction* from their primary contents. Since such contents "make the difference between 'empty' signification and 'full' intuition," the acts that are stripped of such contents may in some sense be regarded as significative. Their mental coincidence or connection can thus be understood as representing an act of meaning, an intention directed towards the fullness of intuition. Husserl accepts this in the following words:

> *The mental connection that establishes the synthesis is, thus, meaning and is as much more or less fulfilled.* It is merely a non-independent component of the total meaning, a significative component of a significative meaning, an intuitive component of an intuitive meaning, in each case, however, a component that shares in the character of meaning and, thus, also in its differences in fullness (*LU*, Tüb. ed., II/2, 173; p. 809).

He immediately adds, however, "We, accordingly, and not without justification interpret the situation in such a manner that this component can also exercise a representative function" (*Ibid.*). Now, if the component of meaning, understood as an act *directed towards fullness*, can exercise for itself a representative or fulfilling function, the implication is clear. It can, as an act, provide its own fullness. It can independently achieve its own result.

This problematic conclusion can be understood in terms of the ambiguous way in which the term "meaning" is used in the above passage. Like intentional matter, it can be taken as referring to the *act of meaning* or to the *meaning meant* by this act. In the latter signification, it refers to the *sense of the categorial object that the act intends*. Insofar as we identify these two, *the contents representing the former also "represent" the latter.* They can be taken as sensuous representatives permitting the presence of the act in a straightforward perception. They can also be taken as categorial representatives of the meaning that is meant. They, thus, can be interpreted so as to make present the sense of the object the act intends. That the same contents springing from the act itself can be interpreted in these two different ways implies that the act can *fulfill itself by interpreting itself.*

The difficulty of this implication is readily apparent. If an interpretative act provides its own fulfillment, then it can never be without fulfillment. We could, in other words, "intuit sensible material in every desired form" — a possibility which, as we quoted Husserl at the beginning of this chapter, rules out the possibility of speaking of categorial perception as a genuine form of intuition. To make this more concrete, we need only state again Husserl's position that the categorial representative is formed by a synthesis of acts abstracted from their primary contents. Abstracted from these contents, the acts are indistinguishable from completely empty intendings. This implies that a series of formally impossible intentions – intentions, say, to a red tone – could be brought into coincidence to form an intention to the species red tone. The coincidence itself could, then, be taken as the representing content of the species. Understood in this way, eidetic perception, irrespective of the nature of its founding intentions, would always be fulfilled. Here, we may observe that any insistence that the underlying acts must be adequate – i.e., possess actual fulfillment – has no theoretical ground to stand on. It is ruled out of court by the fact that the contents that would give the underlying acts the quality of intuitive "fullness" are explicitly said not to enter into the categorial synthesis.

This leads us to a final implication of making universal or generic elements immanent in the real act. Such violation of the transcendence of the ideal makes error impossible. The inability to err is inherent in the notion of an intention providing its own fulfillment. This follows insofar as the *validity* of an act is defined in terms of this fulfillment. On a more general level, we may note again that the function of the transcendence of the ideal is that of distinguishing the act of judgement from the ideal intentional content. Thus, when Husserl says that with the objectivity of the ideal, "all real being including subjective being is transcended," his reference is to "the objective validity of thoughts and connections of thoughts," which one "sees" rather than "makes." The distinction between seeing and making is between what is transcendent to the act of judgement and what can be totally described in terms of the immanent processes of this act. Now, by virtue of this distinction between immanent content and transcendent, ideal content, a further difference comes to the fore. This is the distinction between real subjective capacity (including the capacity to err) and ideal, logically defined possibility. As we quoted Husserl towards the end of the last chapter, the two are "heterogeneous notions." Granted that this heterogeneity is based on the distinction of the real and ideal, it is destroyed when we immanentize the latter and see it as somehow present in the real act. This conclusion does not just have a reference to the doctrine of categorial representation, it has a more general reference to the theory of the double correlation. The theory, as we said, sees the ideal as an *immanent* limitation of the real's coexistence and succession. In such a position logical possibility and subjective capacity coincide. We cannot subjectively intuit what is logically impossible. Here, we have to say that if the psychological possibilities of coexistence and succession suffer *a priori* limitation, and if this limitation is correlated to the possibilities of perception and being, error seems to be ruled out of court.

In the light of this consideration, we can make the following claim. The term "intentional matter" is *fundamentally ambiguous* insofar as it conceals two conflicting ontologies. It refers to both immanent and intentional contents without firmly identifying or distinguishing them. This requirement is, in fact, impossible for it. On the one hand, the ideal intentional content must be immanently identified with the real act if we are to speak of universal elements within the "moments" of consciousness, moments that can be sensuously grasped in reflective perception. On the other hand, such content must transcend the act if we are to speak of perception as grasping an objective sense, a sense whose embodied presence stands against perception as a criterion for the validity of its accomplishment. Now, the fact that such intentional matter must be taken as both immanent and transcendent points to the fact that the theory that employs it requires *contradictory ontological grounds*. In terms of the concluding remarks of our last chapter, this implies that the theory of the double correlation can never be realized. This follows insofar as the acts of subjective accomplishment it specifies — acts of categorial and eidetic perception — are now seen to be *formally impossible*.

Finally, we may note a guiding motivation arising from this situation. As we shall see in our next chapter, Husserl will attempt to rehabilitate the theory of the double correlation and, with this, the notion of intentional matter. Their basis, however, will be a radically different ontology.

CHAPTER VIII

ONTOLOGICAL DIFFICULTIES AND MOTIVATING CONNECTIONS

The goal of this final chapter is to show the ontological shift between the *Logische Untersuchungen* and the volumes of the *Ideen*. There is, as we shall see, a sort of Copernican transformation of the basic doctrines and concepts of the former work. In this, the position of the *Ideen* stands as the result of the transformation. Both the latter work and the transformation itself can be looked upon as a *motivated response* to the difficulties we have uncovered in our last two chapters.

Let us begin, then, by summing up these difficulties under a general heading. Essentially they concern the lack of resolution in the relations of the real and ideal. Thus, on the one hand, Husserl asserts that there is a conceptual unity of being, a unity embracing both the real and ideal. On the other hand, he asserts that there is within this unity a fundamental ontological difference between the two. Both assertions occur in the following passage:

> We do not deny, but rather emphasize the fact that within the conceptual unity of being (*des Seienden*) – or what is the same, the conceptual unity of object as such – there is a fundamental difference. We take account of this through the distinction between ideal being and real being, being as species and being as individual. The conceptual unity of predication likewise splits into two essentially different types according as properties are affirmed or denied of an individual, or general determinations are affirmed or denied of a species. This difference, however, does not dissolve the highest unity in the concept of an object nor, correlatively, the concept of a categorical propositional unity. In each case, something (a predicate) pertains or does not pertain to an object (a subject). The sense of this most universal pertaining (*Zukommen*) together with the laws belonging

to it determine the universal sense of being (*Sinn des Seins*), i.e., that of object in general. In the same way, the more special sense of generic predication with the laws belonging to it determines (or postulates) the sense of the ideal object (*LU*, Tüb. ed., II/1, 125; F., p. 353).

This passage states that the identity and difference between the real and ideal depends upon the identity and difference in the sense of predication attaching to each. Its essential assertion is that this sense of predication "determines" the sense of their being. Given this, we can say that the presence of a general sense of predication implies the presence of a general sense of being. We can also say that the absence of a general sense of being implies the absence of a general sense of predication. Can this schema allow us to speak of *both* the identity and difference of the real and ideal? Can we maintain both a general sense as well as special sense of predication attaching to each?

Let us begin with the necessity for assuming a general sense of predication. This necessity arises from the original argument for positing the ideal on the basis of our possession of truths about it. As we recall, the argument does not just depend upon asserting a correlation between being and truth. One must also grant that there is a common sense to the truths (or predicate judgements) that pertain to the real and the ideal. Without this, we cannot *unambiguously* assert that both types of objects "truly are" (See above, p. 61). This may also be expressed by noting that the argument for positing the ideal is one that has its basis in an analogy with our positing of the real. In this, the being of the ideal functions as a sort of fourth proportional, the first two terms being the truths about the real and ideal and the third being the existence of the real. Thus, we admit that the real exists and that we are in possession of truths about both the real and ideal. We also assume a correlation between truth and being — i.e., between predicative sense and ontological sense. It is, then, the analogy between the truths we have (their possession of something in common) that allows us, through the correlation, to say that the objects of these truths can, with a certain unambiguity, both be called being. This means that, given the real, we can posit the ideal only to the point that the sense of predication attaching to it has something in common with that attaching to the real.

Now, the passage we quoted occurs in the midst of Husserl's argument for the positing of the ideal. The assumption of a common element required for such positing can, thus, be identified with the passage's claim that there is a general logic of predication — i.e., its claim of a "most universal pertaining together with the laws belonging to it." What we have, then, is the assertion of a set of universal laws which defines the conceptual unity of predication, the unity which itself must serve as the basis for our analogous positing of the ideal with the real. In fact, we may compress this and say that such a logic is the general logic of such positing. Here, we can see how the general sense of predication, as given by this logic, can be thought of *as determining* the general sense of being. We said in our sixth chapter that the logical laws governing positing on the basis of truth express the laws of the double correlation — i.e., the laws of the "genuine logical *a priori.*" As such, they can be characterized as the laws which describe *in specie* the valid combinations of predicative meanings — i.e., those which are capable of being illustrated by a posited object. Their determinative character comes from the fact that the same laws give us the conditions of the object as such. In other words, as pertaining to being's "essential endowment," they express the logically determining conditions that allow a being to be.

We can draw from the above the conclusion that when we assert that the general sense of predication *determines* the general sense of being, we are asserting, in the context of the *Logische Untersuchungen*, the existence of the genuine logical *a priori.* The assertion of this latter is, by definition, the assertion of a universal sense of being, for the logical *a priori* states the laws of being's *essential* endowment. Given this context, the ontological sense of the species is relatively easy to delineate. To the point that there is a universal sense of being, we must say that the species express this sense. This fellows, first of all, because without this sense, there would be no way of positing the species by way of analogy. It is only insofar as their own sense expresses elements that are in common with the sense of the real that the analogy has a basis. In the second place, it is the general logic of predication — i.e., the logical *a priori* — which supplies this basis. Since the sense of predication determines the sense of being, the universality of the logical *a priori* requires that the sense of the species' being also be thought of as universal. To make this more precise, we need only observe that the laws of logical *a priori* are the laws determinative of specific unity. Since the existence of a species is also the existence of a specific unity, the universal sense of these laws carries over the the species they determine.

To sum this up, we can say that we are engaged here in a set of notions that mutually imply each other. The notion of predication *determining* the sense of being points to the doctrine of the logical *a priori* which is defined as expressing a universal sense of being. This in turn points to the species as expressing this sense. With this, we can return to the conclusion drawn from the doctrine of the double correlation. The fact that the species expresses a universal sense of being means that relations that are incompatible *in specie* are also incompatible in real empirical instances. In other words, we assert that the ideal species, as defined by the logical *a priori*, are universally applicable to or predicable of the real. This follows from the matching of the senses of the real and ideal, a matching whereby we say that the instance "has" the sense of the species. It is, after all, this community of senses that first allowed us to posit the ideal.

Let us engage in an historical comparison to bring out an implicit consequence of this doctrine. The doctrine, we can say, appears Platonic in its conception. It implies that to the point that the species or eidei are predicable of empirically appearing things — i.e., have predicable senses in common — to that point both must *be* in the same way. To put this in the negative, we can say that given a non-identity in the sense of their being, ideas in their relations are not predicable of things in their relations. Plato's *Parmenides* (133d–134e) contains a general statement of this principle. Its argument can be summarized as follows: If ideas *are what they are* solely by virtue of their relationships to each other, and if things *are what they are* solely with respect to their own mutual relations, then a complete non-identity of what it means *to be* an idea with what it means *to be* a thing leads necessarily to a complete non-identity of their respective sets of relations. In other words, since the sense of their being is specified by their relations, a non-identity in the sense of their being necessarily implies a non-identity in their relations. Thus, given this non-identity in the sense of their being, ideas or their relations cannot be predicated of things or their relations, and a knowledge of the former in no way implies a knowledge of the latter (or *vice versa*, if we wish to ascend from things to ideas).

The consequence of this doctrine is plain. It is that genuine predication requires a *genuine ontological identity* of species and instance. Plato may be seen as accepting this consequence insofar as he grounds the being of the ideas in their self-identity and goes on to refer to this latter as "the very essence of to be" (οὐσία αὕτη τοῦ εἶναι).[1] This means that the ideas, in their expressing self-identity, express a *universal* sense of being. Beyond this, it also implies that the instance has *not* a being whose sense is other than or independent of the being of the species. Rather, the species represents the very essence of the being through which the instance is. The nature of this ontological identity can be clarified by observing that, for Plato, the ability to predicate and the ability to ascribe being are one and the same. Thus, when we recognize an object as existent, we recognize it as maintaining some self-identity as it persists in time. The changes that it undergoes are understood as changes of a persisting being. Given this understanding, loss of all identity with what went before is not taken as change, but as annihilation, pure and simple. It is an individual's replacement by another individual, one whose persisting being is understood as undergoing its own changes. For Plato, this recognition of self-identity in granting existence is also a recognition that the existing individual has a specifically predicable sense. That which remains self-identical allows the possibility of applying a predicate that is itself self-identical. This is the species or eidos. Its relation to the ability to ascribe existence is given by the fact that it expresses in a conceptual predicate the same self-identity that is at the basis of ascribing existence. We may here observe that the ultimate Platonic consequence of this line of thinking is a reformulation and reaffirmation of Parmenides' doctrine that the ability to be conceptually thought (νοεῖν) and the ability to be (εἶναι) are one and the same. Once we grant that the same self-identity is required for both being and being thought, this can be reformulated as a doctrine of participation. We can say that to the point that individual realities participate in the self-identity of their ideas, to that point, they are.

Husserl, of course, does not carry his argument this far. In fact, he asserts "within the conceptual unity of being . . . a fundamental difference" between the real and ideal. Given that this fundamental difference is also supposed to spring from the notion of predication determining the sense of being, can we maintain it *along with maintaining a universal sense of being*? Let us recall the implication we drew from the notion of this determination. It is that if a general sense of predication implies a general sense of being, then a denial of the latter implies a denial of the former, i.e., a denial that there is any general sense to the predications made of the real and ideal. We can see the force of this implication in Husserl's arguments that the species, as pure *possibilities*, are fundamentally different from individual existents considered as *actualities*. Their basis is Frege's distinction between concept and object. As we said above, Frege can be understood as arguing that, in mathematics, definition specifies the range of a concept; but such specification involves only the *possibility*, not the actuality, of the objects of the range (see above, p. 63). It is from this position that Husserl draws his assertion that the thought of the species, as given by their definitions, involves only the notion of possible existence. As Husserl says of the existence of the species, "This 'it exists' has here the same ideal sense it has in mathematics. To bring it back to the possibility of the corresponding individuals is not to reduce it to something other, but merely to express it in an equivalent phrase" (*LU*, Tüb. ed., II/2, 103; F., pp. 749-50). Now, this position rests upon the assumption that the concept and object (or the species and instance) have *not* predicable senses in common. This is put by Frege in terms of the properties these senses designate. Thus, the concept *square* is not itself square, for it has not, as a concept, the property of rectangularity that would justify this predication. The general conclusion is that the properties of objects specified by concepts are not themselves properties of these concepts. When we think a concept by means of its definition, we, thus, do not think of any *actual* objects that have the properties specified by this concept. As Frege puts this, "Whether such objects exist is not immediately known by means of their definitions. . . . Neither has the concept defined got this property, nor is a definition a guarantee that the concept is realized" (*Trans. from the Phil. Writings of G. Frege*, ed. cit.,

p. 145). From such a position, we can arrive at the doctrine that the concepts (or species) do not contain the thought of the actuality of the objects of their range. They rather specify them in terms of their possibility, i.e., their possibility of receiving some definite predicate. In this, the essential point is that the species can express only possibilities — as opposed to actualities — because the predicates in question do not apply to them. If they did, then their own thought — as expressed in a definition — would contain the assertion that there was at least one entry, the species itself, that *actually* had the property specified by the predicate.

In the above context, then, the assertion of the species is coupled with a *denial* of a universal sense of being. The species have their own specific ontological sense of pure possibilities precisely insofar as they do not have predicative senses in common with their instances. In other words, we again have the implication drawn from the notion of the sense of predication determining the sense of being. The assertion that the species have a special ontological sense can only be made by undermining the assertion of a genuine community of predicative senses. We can also draw the conclusion that insofar as the species expresses a special — and not a universal — sense of being, they cannot be considered as predicable of their instances. Predication requires senses in common, but to the point that a species is considered as a pure possibility, it has not senses in common with its instances.

That Husserl can be seen as accepting this conclusion is apparent from the remarks we quoted in our sixth chapter. They assert that the ideal is genuinely predicable only of the ideal, that the concepts making up the ideal laws "have no empirical range" (see above, p. 96). Two statements particularly illustrate our point. In fact, they can be seen as paradigmatic examples of Plato's position that a non-identity in the being of species and instance implies a non-identity in the relations that can be predicated of them. The first is his remark-that "No conceivable gradation could mediate between the ideal and the real" (*LU*, Tüb. ed., I, 68; F., p. 104). This means, in Fregean terms, that there is no mediating element between concept and object. None of the senses predicated of the real object are also predicated of the ideal concept. Translated into the ideal and real relations that define the two, we have Husserl's statement, "There is an unbridgeable difference between ideal laws and real laws, between normative rules and causal rules, between logical and real necessity, between logical grounds and real grounds" (*Ibid.*). Given this non-identity in their respective relations, a non-identity implied by the distinction of their ontological senses, the argument of the *Parmenides* applies: Ideal objects in their relations cannot be predicated of real objects in their relations. A knowledge of the one does not lead to a knowledge of the other.

To draw a general conclusion from this, we note, on the one hand, that the tie of being to predication is demanded by the argument for positing the ideal on the basis of truth. It allows us to base the required general sense of being on an assumed general sense of predication. As for the argument for such positing, it is, as we earlier observed, an expression of the position that sees the epistemological standpoint as primary (see above, p. 157). On the other hand, this framework does not permit our making Husserl's ontological distinction between the real and ideal. To the point that such a distinction is posited, our evidence for the being of the ideal vanishes. According to our schema, a distinction in the sense of being implies a distinction in predicable senses. It is, however, an identity of such senses that allows us, through the argument by analogy, to posit the ideal. The general conclusion, then, is that the notion of predication determining being *does not* per se *give us a level on which we can assert both the identity and difference of the real and ideal.* The assertion of the one must occur at the expense of the other. Symptomatic of this fact is that *the notion of predication determining being* can here only be understood *in terms of the concept of the genuine logical a priori.* To tie the assertion of special senses of being to the former is thus to tie it to the latter. This, however, is inappropriate since the *a priori*, as expressing being's essential endowment, gives only being's *universal* sense.

We can strengthen our conclusion by examining the necessities for asserting that ideal being has the special sense of a pure possibility. As we shall see, these demands are frustrated once we do assert a general sense of being. First of all, we have the demand that the species in their independence be distinguished from empirical generalizations. The generalization, according to its concept, is dependent upon the observation of actual examples.

A contrary example changes its concept. Now, when we say that the species expresses only possibility — i.e., that it specifies its examples in terms of the possibility of their receiving a definite predicate — this dependence is reversed. A species is conceived as *defining* what can count as a member of its range of examples. It is not thought of as something defined in its content by those examples. As such, it is a matter of definition that no example contrary to its notion can be found in its range. What happens, then, when we say that a species expresses a universal sense of being — i.e., that it includes the thought of the actuality of its instances? At this point, its notion takes such instances as actual givens — i.e., as individuals actually given by experience. As Husserl says, "assertions with existential content are inseparable" from thoughts (or laws) "... drawn from experience and induction." The presence of the thought of the actuality of its instances, thus, implies for Husserl that the species is an empirical generalization. Otherwise put: by virtue of the notion of the origin of its examples, as implied by the thought of their actuality, the thought expressed by the species cannot, in this case, be considered as independent of empirical observation.[2]

The second necessity for considering the species as pure possibilities concerns their functioning as norms. By a norm we mean that which determines as a standard. Thus, a norm for arithmetical correctness imposes no real necessity upon the mind as it performs a calculation. It merely states the conditions that have to be fulfilled if the calculation is to be considered as correct. The thought of the species as pure possibilities contains this notion of normative determination. As expressing only possibility, it imposes *no real necessity* on any actual object. It merely defines what can count as an object of its range — i.e., it states the conditions that an object must fulfill in order to be such a member. We can transfer this distinction between real and specific determination to the corresponding concepts of real and specific unity. As we recall, Husserl makes an equation between real, temporal and causal unity. What is real endures through time. Its unity as enduring is a function of its present contents being necessarily determinative of the contents that follow them. This determination of contents according to the order of temporal succession is understood by Husserl as causal determination (See above, pp. 73–74). In distinction to this, specific unity is the form of ideal being. Its laws abstract from time and, thus, have an independence of the causal relations that necessarily pertain to temporal (or real) objects. The necessity of this distinction follows from the normative functioning of the species. If, in pertaining to matters in time, their laws expressed the causal necessity inherent in coexistence and succession, they could not tell us how we *ought* to think; they would only tell us how we are causally determined to think.

Here, we may observe a reason that Husserl cannot remain with this distinction, why he must, in advocating a general sense of being, in fact, collapse it. According to the above, every act of consciousness, as part of an extended temporal unity, is causally determined. This prompts Theodor De Boer to ask, "How can one combine the postulation of eternal norms with a naturalistic interpretation of consciousness?" (*De Ontwikklingsgang in het Denken van Husserl*, Assen, 1960, p. 582). The difficulty is that according to such an interpretation, every act of judgement, *whether correct or not*, is causally determined. Such determination is, in other words, no respecter of the norms for correctness. Thus, when Husserl writes, "My judging that $2 \times 2 = 4$ is certainly causally determined, but not the truth that $2 \times 2 = 4$," we may ask how this determined judging can avail itself of a norm for the validity of its act (*LU*, Tüb. ed., I, 119; F., p. 142).

The difficulty seems to require for its solution some mediating link between the real act and the ideal norm. It is partly for the purpose of providing this link that Husserl proposes that the species do have a universal sense of being. What *in specie* cannot be unified according to the laws of specific unity also cannot be unified in real empirical instances. This means, when we consider the real psychological subject, that the laws of specific unity determine the empirical possibilities of psychological coexistence and succession. Since Husserl continues to maintain the causal determination of coexistence and succession, we must assume that the two determinations coincide. In other words, the normative rules of the species, taken as pertaining to matters in time, now express the same empirical necessities that causal laws are stated to do. They no longer function as norms but as expressions of a real empirical determination. This returns us to our earlier point that when we give the genuine logical *a priori* an empirically determinative function, we seem to make error impossible (see above, pp. 145-147). The species as defined by the laws of this *a priori* have, indeed, a universal sense of being; but precisely on this account they cannot tell us how we *ought* to think.³

The above may be considered as a sufficient discussion of the general form of the ontological difficulty besetting the *Logische Untersuchungen*. Let us now turn to the ontological shift itself. Our guide for discussing the shift and the position it results in will be Husserl's remarks about his own work. As we quoted him in our Introduction:

> ... it simply concerns a motivated path which, starting from the problem of the possibility of objective knowledge, wins the necessary insight that the very sense of this problem leads back to the pure ego existing in and for itself, the insight that this ego, as a presupposition for knowledge of the world cannot be and cannot remain presupposed as a worldly being, the insight therefore that this ego must, through the phenomenological reduction and the epoché with respect to the being-for-me of the world, be brought to transcendental purity ("Nachwort," *Ideen III*, Biemel ed., p. 150).

Concretely speaking, the motivated path is *from* an understanding of the subject as a part of worldly being. This is the subject conceived of as suffering both real and ideal determination. Its *terminus* is an understanding of the subject as non-worldly. Here, as we said in our Introduction, the subject is conceived of as determinative, in the sense of an explanatory condition, of both real and ideal being.

This means that the realization which we have to ground – in the sense of showing its motivations – is that of the *phenomenological reduction*. This, according to Celms, is "... the leading back of objective (transcendent) being to the being of the corresponding modes of consciousness." "The reduction," as Celms also writes, "is the leading back of the conditioned to their conditions" (*Der phän. Idealismus Husserls*, ed. cit., pp. 309, 310). In summary, the *modes of consciousness*, by which objective being shows itself what it is, are, by virtue of the reduction, to be viewed as the *explanatory conditions* of objective being. They are to be understood as explaining the schema of species and instance which characterizes objective being.

This explanation, we may note in advance, involves not just a transformation of the notion of consciousness as given in the *Logische Untersuchungen*. It will also necessitate a reworking of many of its basic concepts and doctrines, e.g., constitution, transcendence, the subject-object correlation, the dialectic of intention and fulfillment, categorial representation and the position of the species as pure possibilities. The purpose of this reworking will be to explain these in such a way that the difficulties of the earlier work do not reoccur. It is also to preserve their inherent sense insofar as this is demanded by the general notion that serves as Husserl's goal, namely that of the objectivity of knowledge.

If we ask what are the elements which make up the motivation for adopting the phenomenological reduction, we come to the following reflections. The *first* stems from our general discussion of the difficulty confronting the *Logische Untersuchungen*. It is that the real and ideal, as conceived by this work, are ontologically insufficient to ground their own relation. To the point that they are considered to be distinct categories with distinct ontological senses, we cannot unambiguously call them "being." They lose that identity of predicable senses which is required for this and is required as well in order to predicate the species of the instances. A *second* reflection concerns the factual reality of consciousness. As is readily apparent in the exegesis given in our third through fifth chapters, it is Husserl's conception of this reality that motivates him first to make the ideal transcendent to the real, and then to conceive it as an *a priori* actually determinative of the real. It motivates him to distinguish what is in itself normatively possible and what is actual (i.e., real). It then motivates him with respect to the "authentic" act of logical thinking to collapse this distinction. The conflicting nature of this motivated response can, as we saw, be traced to the irreconcilable properties of the real and ideal. When conceived in terms of their distinguishing senses, they do not allow us genuinely to think causal and ideal (or normative) determination and think them as somehow combined. When subjectivity is conceived as a factual reality, i.e., a real causal unity — then a turn to subjectivity, as in the analysis of the logical act, results in the disappearance of the norm and in the apparent universality of causal explanation.

The *third* reflection concerns the subject-object distinction. It is that this distinction has been inadequately conceived. The basis for this difficulty is Husserl's conception of his guiding motivation, that of securing the objectivity of knowledge. In this, knowledge is interpreted as knowledge of objects. The result is that the subject, if it is to be known, must be conceived of as an object. The same result follows when we assume the priority of the epistemological standpoint and say that being is correlated to knowledge. The interpretation of knowledge as knowledge of objects demands the equation of the universal sense of being with that of object. If this is so, then we have to say that the subject, in order to be, must be an object. Ontologically regarded, then, the *subject-object correlation becomes reduced to an object-object correlation.* In fact, insofar as subjects and objects express the same type of being, we have the demand that the same ontological categories apply to both. Now, the inadequacy of this conception is shown by the fact that "object" in the *Logische Untersuchungen* is not an univocable concept. Objective being is divided into the real and ideal, each with their own special categories. The attempt, then, to specify the subject as an object cannot but be ambiguous. The unresolved issue in the *Logische Untersuchungen* is, indeed, how we are to conceive the subject. Are we to understand it according to the categories of real unity, or must we add to this the categories of specific unity — i.e., conceive the subject as suffering *both* real and ideal determination? The failure of this last conception simply points to the ambiguity of what we mean by "object."

Let us turn from these reflections to the motivations that can be drawn from them. By this we mean those motivations which can be seen as directly leading to the subject as defined by the phenomenological reduction. This is a subject that is not "presupposed as a worldly being" — i.e., as a part of the objective being of the world. It is a subject that is understood as a "presupposition" for knowledge of worldly (objective) being. Now, the content of the first reflection is that the real and ideal cannot, within their own terms, consistently specify their relation to one another. From this the motivation arises *not* to see these categories as ultimate. Positively expressed, it is a motivation to seek a relational *ground* of the two. It is to seek that which, beyond the special senses characterizing the two, expresses that *by virtue of which* both can be called being. Implied here is the thought that the ground cannot be defined as either real or ideal — i.e., be characterized by the special ontological sense of either. We may tie this to the sentiment of Fichte that "the ground lies, by virtue of the mere thought of the ground, outside of the grounded." In other words, if the ground were the same nature as the grounded (i.e., if it were either real or ideal), it too would show itself to be in need of a ground.

The second reflection can be viewed as giving rise to the motivation of removing the subject from the category of reality. To see this, let us restate it in terms of a chain of assumptions. Its content is that the *Logische Untersuchungen*'s ontology is determined by its conflicting attempts to come to terms with the reality of the subject. The primary assumption behind such attempts is the equation Husserl draws between real, causally determined being and being manifesting itself through time. When applied to the subject, the equation demands that this last, as a temporal unity, be considered as a causally determined reality. This leads to the problem of psychological relativism and, with this, to the motivation of overcoming this relativism. Thus, insofar as the statements on ideal being are guided by this motivation, they are motivated by an assumption of reality — the "worldly" reality of the subject. It is this, first of all, that makes one say that the whole of the *Logische Untersuchungen* proceeds on a "worldly" level.[4] The eidetic reduction, performed on this level, carries with it these assumptions. It is, it can be said, something performed with the prejudices of the "natural attitude."[5] Let us put this in terms of epistemology. Epistemology is the science of knowing and only individual subjects, taking time to perceive, reflect, etc., can, in a concrete sense, be said to know. The forms of the acts of knowledge are thus understood as presupposing the temporal reality of that which actually engages in these acts. This means that epistemology itself, according to the above, must assume the causal reality of the subject. But insofar as it does, it cannot really be described as presuppositionless. It cannot, without any ontological assumptions, ask what being must be in order that there be the possibility of objective knowledge. Since the primacy of epistemology depends on its not having assumptions given to it — i.e., on its not taking from some other science the principles of being — this primacy here, in a certain sense, is undermined (see above, p. 116).

This implies that, to establish a truly presuppositionless epistemology, we must dispense with assumption of the reality of the individual subject. This move is also necessary for epistemology to explore the level indicated by the motivation drawn from the first reflection. The level is that of the *ground* of the real and ideal; as a ground, it does not, by definition, presuppose either. In order to be an investigation appropriate to this level, epistemology itself must not assume as a given any such presuppositions. To make this more concrete, we note that Husserl, at the very beginning of *Ideen I*, characterizes the level of the phenomena uncovered by the phenomenological reduction as *das Irreal*. He writes, "It is just these irrealities which phenomenology investigates..." (*Ideen I*, "Einleitung," Biemel ed., p. 7). Now, the tie between the individual, temporally enduring subject and the notion of its reality can be broken only if we do not make the primary assumption behind it. We must not assume that the category of reality — i.e., of causally determined being — is coincident with that of individual temporal being. Thus, as Husserl announces in his "Introduction" to *Ideen I*, "It will become evident that the concept of reality is in need of a fundamental limitation by virtue of which a distinction must be made between real being and individual (simply temporal) being" (*Ibid.*). In other words, by virtue of this limitation, we can distinguish between real and temporal being; not all individual, temporal being must be classified as real.

The advantages of this move are readily apparent. In the *Logische Untersuchungen*, the naturalization of consciousness constantly threatens to result in the naturalization of the species. A correlation of the ideal relations holding between the species to the relations obtaining in what we assume is a real, causally describable consciousness seems to allow causality to invade the relations between the species. When, however, we say that "... the phenomena of transcendental subjectivity shall be characterized as irreal," then a turn to subjectivity does not have this result (*Ideen I*, Biemel ed., p. 6). In fact, it cannot be seen as a turn either to what is real and causal or what, in itself, is ideal.

To summarize, we can say that the first reflection leads us to search for a non-worldly ground of the real and ideal – i.e., a relational ground of worldly being. The second reflection motivates us to deprive the subject of its worldly being. It leads us to think of a subject that is not "presupposed as a worldly being." Now, it is the motivation arising from the third reflection that allows us to identify these two results. It motivates us to see the non-worldly being of the subject as the required relational ground. In this, the subject appears as a "presupposition" for knowledge of both the real and ideal.

The content of the third reflection is that we cannot equate the universal sense of being with that of object. If we do, then the subject-object correlation becomes reduced to an object-object correlation. We will not restate the impasse that this reflection focuses on. Rather, let us observe that the way out of this difficulty is provided by the thought that being an object is *being in relation to a subject,* and *not* simply having a relation to another object. Here, in fact, the universal sense of being, as embodying both the real and ideal, points to the subject as a common relational ground. The subject is *that in relation to which* an entity becomes an object and thus has the objective being that may further be specified as real or ideal. Another way of expressing this is to say that the subject is the ground of, in the sense of an indispensable condition for, objective presence (the presence of an entity as an object).

To this we may add two subsidiary thoughts, both following from the notion that presence can be equated with the general sense of being. The first concerns the fact that presence points to being in its quality of *not* being a predicate. As we said above, the epistemological notion of being does not refer to *what* is presented, but rather to the presence of what is presented (See p. 116). It is an intuitive presence, rather than any particular predicable feature of an object, that first grounds our notion of being. Given this, the subject can ground the real and ideal in terms of their objective presence without violating their specifically different predicable senses. In other words, the subject, through its grounding of such objective presence, can be thought of as that by virtue of which both the real and ideal can epistemologically be considered to be being.

The key point here is that objects do not have an epistemological presence to other objects. Real objects have to real objects only the spatial-temporal relations characterizing mere bodily things. Now, if presence to a subject does describe a unique relationship, then the subject cannot be considered as that which is specified by the categories of objective being. In other words, this unique fact demands that we make an ontological distinction between subjects and objects. We may also express this by saying that the thought of the subject as that which is required for objective presence — i.e., its thought as a necessary "presupposition" for the knowledge of such objective presence, be this the presence of real or ideal objects — demands that it not have the categories of the objects it allows to be present. Stated more explicitly, it is precisely the fact that the subject does not have either real or ideal being that allows it to be seen as a presupposition of the real or ideal.

This leads us to our second thought. This is that if presence is epistemologically definitive of being, then the distinction between subjective and objective being requires a distinction in their presence. Such a distinction, it is to be observed, is not on the same level as that which we drew between the real and ideal. The fact that real objects are present in straightforward acts, while ideal objects achieve their presence in founded acts, certainly points to a distinction in modes of presence; but these modes are identifiable insofar as they are both modes of *objective* presence. Here, however, we have a motivation to look upon the subject, not as something objectively present, but rather as present as a ground of objects — i.e., present in what we shall call a "preobjective" sense.

Let us summarize the above reflections by stating the essential elements of the motivated path whose course we are seeking to trace. We first have the thought that the real and ideal require a relational ground. Next comes the notion that the conflicting characteristics of the real and ideal — characteristics which show these categories' need for a ground — spring from the assumption that the subject must be understood in terms of such categories.

From this reflection alone, it may be observed, comes the presentiment that these conflicting characteristics can be eliminated with the elimination of the assumptions that motivate them. In other words, we have the suggestion that their conflict can be resolved once we deprive the subject of its real worldly being. Taken with the first reflection, it also suggests that the positing of a non-worldly subject gives us the required resolution — i.e., the required relational ground for the real and ideal. The thought springing from the third reflection provides the crucial confirming link in this motivated path. It states that the subject can be taken as the ground of objective presence — i.e., objective being — only when it is not understood in terms of the categories of real or ideal being. At that point, it can be seen as a presupposition of such presence and, thus, as a presupposition for the knowledge of the real and ideal being that is embodied by objective presence. With this, we have the subject as defined by the phenomenological reduction.

How does the ontological shift in the being of the subject resolve the difficulties in the *Logische Untersuchungen*? To answer this question, we must consider the transformation this shift occasions in the doctrines of this work.

Let us begin with a very general consideration of the doctrine of constitution. In *Ideen I*, as Husserl presents it, the argument for the non-worldly being of the subject is an argument for the constituiton of worldly being by this non-constituted subject. In other words, it is as non-constituted that the subject is seen to be non-worldly; it is as constituting that the subject is seen to be the epistemological ground of worldly being. This position may be understood as flowing from a number of premises. We first have the notion of constitution as the subjective act of making an object intuitively present. In terms of the epistemological equation of being and presence, it is seen as the primary act of the subject with regard to its attempt to relate itself to objective being. Now, the phenomenological reduction with its ontological shift implies that the ontology of the world is to be grounded — i.e., explained — by the activity of the subject. If this is true, then it is as constituting that the subject must be seen as the explanatory ground of the world in its presence (i.e., being). Similarly, it is non-constituted that the subject is to be seen as non-worldly — i.e., as not having a worldly, objective presence. A further implication, here, is that this act cannot be explained in terms of the ontology of the world, an ontology which it itself is supposed to explain. This would be to argue in a circle. Thus, insofar as constitution in the *Logische Untersuchungen* is expressed in terms that presuppose the objective world, it must be reinterpreted.

Let us take objective, wordly being as transcendent being. Expressed in such terms, the presupposition of the objective being of the world is equivalent to the presupposition of transcendence. In the *Logische Untersuchungen*, the act of constitution is understood as presupposing transcendence (and, thus, objective being) in at least two ways. In the first, we have the doctrine that contents of sensation are a *necessary* condition for the objectifying, interpretative act. With a respect to this act, these contents are understood *as a given*. They are not produced by the act, which consideration means that in external perception their source is understood as something transcendent to consciousness. If we ask why this must be so, we come to a fundamental assumption. It is that the world is given and, with it, transcendency. In other words, transcendency *precedes constitution by virtue of the fact that the given world precedes constitution interpreted as a real act taking place within it*. This "within" has here a spatial-temporal sense. We can, however, also speak of the presupposition of transcendence understood in its strictly epistemological sense. Epistemological transcendence is, we recall, based on the ideality of the perceptually embodied meaning. What allows the object in its inherent meaning to "stand against" the subject — i.e., stand as a criterion for the correctness of the subject's interpretative acts — is the ideality of this meaning. The meaning as ideal is *no real part* of the subjective act which grasps it. Here it is in a direct sense the ontology of the world that is presupposed. The objective categories of real and ideal being specify in advance what the act of constitution is supposed to accomplish. A real act of consciousness, acting on real contents of sensation, is supposed to constitute (i.e., make present) a perceptual sense that is no real part of itself.

The difficulty inherent in this picture concerns the notion of this transcendence. It is that the transcendence of the ideal seems to be the very opposite of what is required by a framework which sees the correlation of subjects and objects in terms of the limiting inherence of the ideal in the real. In other words, there is a conflict between the ontological requirements for a *correlation* of subjects and objects and the requirements for a *distinction* of the two.

How does the doctrine of constitution as presented in *Ideen I* resolve this conflict? Let us focus for a moment on its general character. As we said above, the subject as constituting is seen by the *Ideen* as the ground of worldly being. This means that constitution itself is taken as the act of grounding. It links the subject to the world in the relation of ground to grounded. Thus, insofar as transcendence is taken as the characteristic of objective, worldly being, transcendence itself, in the new view, is seen as something which is subjectively grounded. The concrete expression of this is the doctrine that transcendence is the grounded correlate of "specific *types*" of perceptual interconnections (See *Ideen I*, §47; Biemel ed., p. 111). The reference here is to the types of connections that order perceptions into perspectival series of views of an object. Given that such a series shows the possibility of an indefinite continuance — i.e., that views of one side of an object call forth the possibility of views of another side — we have the following contrast. On the one hand, we have to admit that the series of our actual perspectival views of an object is always *finite*. On the other hand, the interconnections through which the object appears give it the sense of something capable of manifesting itself in a potentially infinite series of perspectives. By virtue of this, the object is understood as something transcendent — i.e., as that which is not equatable with the sum of our actual views of it.[6]

To bring out the special features of this doctrine, let us observe where it diverges from the position of the *Logische Untersuchungen*. We note, first, that for both works, the epistemological presence of a real object is the presence of a sense. As the *Ideen I* expresses this, "All real unities are 'unities of sense'" (*Ideen I*, §55; Biemel ed., p. 134). For both, again, the transcendence of an object is understood in terms of its not being equatable with the sum of a subject's actual apprehensions of it. For the *Logische Untersuchungen*, however, this second position is tied directly to the first. Its teaching is that sense *per se* has an ideal character. As such — i.e., by virtue of its inherent *ideal* nature — it is correlated to an indefinite range of possible apprehensions (See above, pp. 68-69).

Now, we can see the *Ideen I* as both preserving and transforming this doctrine by speaking of the immanent grounding of the ideal character of sense. As in the *Logische Untersuchungen*, the sense of an object refers to the common element that is manifested in an indefinite range of the object's actual and possible apprehensions. This common element, however, is now seen to be immanently established by the way in which these apprehensions are connected to each other. It is a function of those types of interconnections which set up the possibility of an indefinite continuance of experiences while allowing a certain point of unification (a common element) to remain through this series.

This doctrine, whose character we have only lightly sketched, allows us to see sense as something which is *not per se* transcendent to consciousness. In fact, given that sense is a "one in many" that is immanently grounded by the interconnections of experience, the epistemological transcendence that is based upon sense becomes what can be called a *transcendence in immanence*. Such transcendence, as a character constituted by the interconnections of consciousness, cannot, in other words, be thought of as expressing an ontological opposition to consciousness. We, thus, have Husserl's radical assertion that ". . . pure consciousness in its own absolute being ... conceals and constitutes in itself all worldly transcendencies..." (*Ideen I*, §50, Biemel ed., pp. 118-19). For Husserl, this means that the presence of a transcendent object is only a grounded correlate of specific types of interconnection. The thesis of its transcendent being is that of the noematic X we mentioned in our Introduction (See above, p. 7). It is, in other words, the thesis that the experiences that do show the possibility of an indefinite continuance also have a continuing point of unification.

With regard to the difficulty we mentioned above, let us mention how this doctrine establishes, on an immanent basis, both a correlation and a distinction between subjects and objects. If we define subjective categories as categories of constitution, then they can be seen as immanently correlated to the categories of constituted objects. This, however, does not mean that the subject, as constituting, is placed in the category of objects – i.e., the category of what it constitutes. Constitution is a relation of ground and grounded, one involving an ontological distinction between the two. The correlation between being and presence allows us to see this as a distinction in presence. Thus, the subject, as we indicated above, does not have an objective presence. It appears, rather, as "pre-objective" – i.e., as a ground of objects. This can be made explicit by observing that the constitutive (or grounding) process is based on a distinction between perceptual experiences which, separately regarded, *have no perspectives* and objects which show themselves in perspectival views. By coming together in certain types of connections, the experiences constitute the object in each of its features. Thus, the way in which the subject is recognized as other than the object is that, as a field of experiences, its individual elements have a presence that excludes perspectives, yet every feature of the object, as something *there*, does show itself perspectivally (See *Ideen I*, §42; Biemel ed., pp. 94-95).

What we have here, in fact, is a concrete expression of Husserl's general assertion that the experiences of consciousness, though temporal, are *irreal*. To make them real, in a spatial-temporal sense, is to change their nature. It is to assume that, individually regarded, they could be capable of perspectival appearing. Now, if we grant that causal relations, as relations involving time and spatial location, do presuppose spatial-temporal objects as their subjects, then the above shows us that such relations cannot be applied to the field of conscious experiences. Such experiences, as non-perspectival, lack the spatial-temporal being that would permit the applicability of these relations. In other words, only the objects which these experiences in their connections constitute have a being that can be considered under the category of causality.

The conflict between the ontological requirements for transcendence and those for a correlation of subjects and objects can be expressed in terms of the dialectic of intention and fulfillment. The dialectic, as we pointed out, was not sufficient to establish a correlation between subjective and objective categories. Insofar as it took for granted the existence of a real act interpreting real contents of sensation, the relation between the act and its contents could be seen as a real or causal relation. In other words, both the act and the effect of its interpretation (i.e., the presence to the subject of the object) could be considered as based on contingent matters of fact (See above, p. 85). The attempt to remedy this situation by viewing the ideal as immanent in the real and as acting to inherently limit the contingency of the real brought about, indeed, a genuine subject-object correlation. Its effect, however, was to undermine the dialectic insofar as this did establish transcendence. The theory of the correlation, as we have stressed, undermines the very notion of error and, with this, the notion that the object is something epistemologically transcendent. Now, in a narrow sense, the resolution of this difficulty can be specified as one which preserves the goal of the dialectic — i.e., its goal of establishing transcendence — while overcoming its conflict with the demands for a subject-object correlation. In broader terms, we may note that the conflict is one within the worldly ontology that limits itself to the categories of the real and ideal. It springs from a notion of a subject-object correlation that takes the ontological transcendence based on these categories as a given. In these terms, the resolution pointed to is one which moves from a worldly to a "non-worldly" ontology — i.e., one that specifies a subject-object correlation such that transcendence, rather than being presupposed as a given, is taken as established by the correlation.

To bring this out, let us consider the dialectic first in the *Untersuchungen* and then in the *Ideen*. What is common in both works is the fact that a description of the dialectic is tantamount to a description of constitution. Thus, to the point that constitution is taken as assuming the givenness of transcendence, so must the dialectic. We have already mentioned how constitution in the *Logische Untersuchungen* presupposes transcendence. Primary sense contents are assumed to have a transcendent source. As for the result of the constitutive (or objectifying) act, as an *ideal* intentional content, this cannot be taken as an immanent part of the *real* act. Both transcendencies are crucial for the working of the dialectic. Thus, the assumption that sensuous contents have a source transcendent to the act which interprets them allows us to separate act and contents acted upon. It is by virtue of such a separation that the act cannot be said to provide its own sensuous fulfillment in attempting to ground its interpretation of these contents. If we speak of fulfillment in terms of the presence of a sense that fulfills an intention by corresponding to it, then it is the ideality of this sense (or intentional content) that prohibits any confusion between intention and fulfillment. It, thus, permits a dialectic — as opposed to a simple identification — between the real act and its intended result. In this context, we can say that epistemological transcendence is established on the basis of worldly transcendence. The objects' transcendence is shown by the fact that it can repel the interpretations that consciousness makes. Such interpretive activity can be described as an attempt to "make sense" of given sense contents — i.e., as an attempt to see within their multiplicity the presence of a unified objective sense. The *given* sense contents can fail to support the intuitive presence of the sense intended. They can also show the interpretation to be in error insofar as the sense whose presence they can support is seen to be other than that originally intended. We thus can have the doctrine that consciousness cannot, by virtue of its act of interpretation, inform the object with every possible sense. In other words, only those senses which are fulfilled or embodied by the intuitive being-there of the object — i.e., by its presence — can be taken to apply to it as such.

When we abandon the assumption of worldly transcendence, then this description must be transformed. If we are to fully affirm immanence, then we have to say that immanent within the acts of consciousness is to be found the fullness of a perceived presence. In other words, the possibility or impossibility of an intuition must be considered to have its sufficient conditions in the connections and immanent experiences of consciousness. We can also express this in terms of the position of consciousness as an ultimate ground of transcendence. Once we give the subject this position, we cannot, without arguing in a circle, consider it in its acts of constitution as depending on what is really transcendent to such acts. Thus, its achievement of apprehending a perceived presence cannot be taken as dependent on externally acquired contents of sensation. This would return us to the ontology of the *Untersuchungen* in describing the acts. Here, in fact, we have to say with De Boer, "Transcendental consciousness does not know an 'outside' in the sense that a world, existing in itself, had to press its way in $\theta \acute{v} \rho \alpha \theta \epsilon \nu$," i.e., "from outside" (*De Ontwikklingsgang*..., ed. cit., p. 595). The same point can be made about the senses of the world. The position of consciousness as an ultimate ground demands that they, along with their transcendence, be immanently grounded (See *Ideen I*, §55; Biemel ed., p. 134). What this means concretely is that, on this new level, perceptual experiences in their sense and intuitive presence cannot be understood as things which are transcendently given to the subject. They must be thought of as included within the subject, the subject being taken as a self-grounding field of experiences.[7]

This view allows us to establish on an immanent basis a correlation of subjects and objects. Does it also allow us to preserve the notion of a dialectic of intention and fulfillment? Can the notion of transcendence which this dialectic is supposed to establish be preserved and yet not be in conflict with the conception of the correlation? Two facts indicate that this is still possible. The first is that the individual experiences we have continue to manifest the phenomenon of fitting or not fitting together. The second is that this phenomenon gives rise first to an intention and then to a fulfillment. Thus, a series of views may arrange themselves in a perspectival series. Such a series gives rise to the intention, in the sense of an expectation, of seeing a spatial-temporal object. If the views which follow fit in with this, i.e., continue the perspectival series, then the intention is satisfied. A sense of the object appears which conforms with (or "fulfills") that of the expectation. We can also say that the sense's one-in-many character as a point of unification of the different views of the object shows itself as the same and, in fact, coincides with that which was manifested when the intention was originally set up. Similarly, if the views do not continue in this way to fit in, we have the situation of the frustration of the intention. The same point can be made when we take the notion of an intention as signifying an intuitive claim — i.e., a claim about what is intuitively there. It can, as a claim, be judged in terms of whether or not our actual experiences fit together in the way that our intention supposes.

Here consciousness itself serves as a final ground for the transcendence established by the dialectic. It is no longer the object, considered as something independent, which repels the interpretations of consciousness. This view of the object's independence is now considered as grounded in the connections that set up the object and, with this, establish the subject-object correlation.

In other words, it is now consciousness, with its types of interconnections, that grounds the object as both correlated to and transcendent to the subject. These types, we can say, *function as norms* for the fitting together (or not fitting together) of new perceptions with the series of perceptions we have already had. They, thus, also function as norms for the harmony (or lack thereof) of new perceptually based predicates with those that the object previously acquired.

The ontological implications of this normative functioning will be considered by us later. For the present let us observe that there is implicit in the above a transformation in the notion of an "intentional experience." For the *Logische Untersuchungen*, such experiences are viewed as component parts of the total experiental complex (See *LU*, Halle ed., II, 342). One can identify them with acts which act on other experiences — the latter being taken as experiential contents which are *distinct* from such acts. In *Ideen I*, by way of contrast, the intentional experience is no longer viewed as something alongside of other experiences. We have, instead, a doctrine of the constitution of the intentional experience from experiences that are not *per se* intentional. Thus, the new position is that no individual experience within the field of consciousness has *of itself* the character of being directed to a transcendent object. Such experiences achieve this character only when they form inherent moments within the intentional experience. The latter, in other words, is an *extended unity* constituted by the connections of the individual experiences (See *Ideen I*, §36). It appears when the experiences making it up exhibit a point of unification. Now, the correlate grounded by this one-in-many character is, as we said, a unity of sense. It is the intentional presence of an object as a sense. Here, in fact, we have to say that both the intentional experience and the object are constituted at one and the same time.[8] The frustration of the intentional experience — i.e., the fact that new perceptions do not fit in with the unity that has so far been established — is, then, at the same time, the undermining of the object's intentional presence.

The advantage of this reinterpretation of the dialectic of intention and fulfillment may be seen by considering the difficulties discussed in our previous chapter. The doctrine of categorial representation suffers, as we said, from essentially two objections.

The first concerns the ambiguity of its notion of intentional matter. In order to serve as a categorial representative, this "matter" must be viewed by the *Untersuchungen* as *both* immanent and transcendent. Transcendence is required in order for the matter to have the ideal characteristics pertaining to sense. Immanence is required for it to be directly available as material for the immanent categorial act. In other words, if the categorial act is to be possible, the ideal intentional correlate must somehow be considered as "within" consciousness. Only then is it possible to find elements within consciousness that, by virtue of their ideality, have a "universal" or "generic" character, a character allowing them to be taken as representatives of a universal form. As Schérer writes on this point:

> To treat of intentional content as "matter" (in Husserl's sense) is, in fact, to be already situated in the attitude of the reduction as the *Ideen* understands this. It is to assume, in effect, that one can speak of intentional correlates in the midst of intentional experiences or rather of components that are not inherently real (*reel*) still forming part of the conscious experience itself (René Schérer, *Le Phén. de R. L.*, ed. cit., p. 272).

We shall consider in a moment how the notion of transcendence in immanence, as yielded by the reduction, satisifes this assumption. First, however, let us mention the second objection. It concerns the fact that the doctrine of categorial representation gives us no theoretical basis to distinguish between intuitive and non-intuitive founding acts. It is their own sensuous contents that make such acts intuitive. Yet, as Husserl states, it is only when such acts are abstracted from these contents that they can enter into a categorial connection and serve as representatives for the founding act. In other words, insofar as they do serve as such representatives, they are indistinguishable from non-intuitive or merely signative acts. It, thus, seems possible that a connection of non-intuitive acts would also serve as the basis of an intuitive categorial act.

To meet this first objection, we must assume that the intentional content, while maintaining its identity, is *not* to be viewed as something ontologically transcendent to the individual experiences of consciousness. As indicated, the necessary assumption is one of transcendence *in* immanence. Its basis is given by the doctrine of the immanent grounding of sense in its ideal (or transcendent) character. This yields the notion that, immanently regarded, the presence of a sense of an object is the presence, within our perceptual experiences, of a persisting point of unification. Let us, for a moment, review this doctrine. The experiences of a given object have, we say, certain recurring elements. In addition, their connections manifest a perspectival ordering. The first fact allows us to say that these experiences, when synthesized, give us in their overlapping a certain immanent coincidence, i.e., a point of unification. The perspectival ordering of these experiences gives us the notion (or rather, the immanent intentional anticipation) that what has recurred will continue to recur. In other words, it adds to the point of unification the notion of persistence. Both coincidence and persistence immanently establish the presence of sense as that which can persist in an indefinite range of instances. The instances are individual experiences which by virtue of these two facts ground the presence of a sense and thus allow themselves to be taken as experiences of a single object.

It is, let us note, the irreality or pre-objectivity of individual experiences which permits us, without leaving the immanent sphere, to consider them as capable of genuine coincidence. Real entities, as spatial-temporally distinct, can only be gathered into a collection – not a coincidence (See above p. 139). This may also be put in terms of the *Untersuchungen*'s assumption that individual experiences are real events forming the real causal unity of consciousness. The content of what is caused is determined by what went before. It is temporally determined to exist at a specific moment in time. In this light, the assertion that experiences are irrealities can be seen as necessary to free them from positions in objective time – i.e., as necessary for their being brought into coincidence in an ongoing present.

In Husserl's terminology, the experiences can, through a series of "retentions," be considered as retained in the now, their availability in the now preserving their serial – i.e., perspectival – ordering and preserving as well their inherent content. It is by virtue of this that they have the possibility of being available for the ongoing synthesis of a persisting point of unification.[9]

If we grant that sense may, indeed, be immanently grounded, then the following account of categorial representation can be given. The basic doctrine of the *Logische Untersuchungen* is that the categorial representative is formed by a "categorial connection" involving a certain coincidence of the senses — the *Auffassungssinne* — of the underlying acts. Immanently regarded, this can now be understood as a coincidence of points of unification within the field of consciousness. Let us take as an example the intuition of a part-whole relation. Both the part and the whole, as spatial-temporal, show themselves perspectivally. They can, thus, be individually apprehended through the presence of points of unification in the perspectivally arranged series of apprehensions directed to each. Now, the fact that these points are themselves immanent allows them to be immanently connected. Just as the experiences making them up can be retained, so can these unities. They can be brought into a present coincidence. We can further say that just as the individual points "represent", in the sense of "ground", their transcendent correlates, so their connection represents a transcendent categorial correlate.

In this doctrine, the notion of "intentional matter" has been rehabilitated as a connection of points in unification. With this, the second of our objections has already been answered. According to what we said above, the establishment of a point of unification is also the establishment of both the adequate intentional experience and the presence of its objective correlate. Both are constituted at one and the same time through the coming together of experiences to form this point. This means that we no longer have the possibility of merely signative (or non-intuitive) acts founding an intuitive categorial act. The very fact that they function in the categorial connection as points of unification — i.e., as connected unities of experiences which are undergoing a further ("founded") categorial connection — rules this out. Such points, themselves, are the establishing of the intuitive character of the underlying acts.

To complete this account a further item should be mentioned. The original doctrine of categorial representation fails insofar as it cannot preserve in the categorial sphere the dialectic of intention and fulfillment. In the new doctrine, however, we can speak of a preservation of "the essential characteristics" of straightforward intuitions – i.e., their characteristics of being fulfillments. This, of course, depends upon the transcendental reinterpretation of the dialectic. In the case of straightforward intuitions, the dialectic is one of the fitting or not fitting together of individual experiences. Their fitting *fulfills*, their lack of fitting *frustrates* the claim of their being experiences of a single objective correlate. The same assertion can be carried over to the realm of categorial intuition. Here, however, it is not individual experiences, but rather their connected unities (their points of unification) that form the material for the dialectic. It is these that must harmoniously fit together – i.e., allow a categorial connection – in order for the categorial object to appear as a unity. As in the case of straightforward intuition, the representative function of immanent material is to be understood in terms of grounding. The categorial connection, in forming a new, "founded" point of unification grounds both the categorial intentional experience as something adequate and grounds as well the intellectually intuitive presence of its correlate.

When we reflect on the above view of constitution, two themes appear as essential to it. The first is that of the normative function exercised by the types of experiential connections. Talk of the "fitting together" or "not fitting together" of individual experiences receives its sense from the notion that such types determine what is required for an individual experience to connect harmoniously with experiences previously connected. Thus, a series of experiences perspectivally connected normatively demands that further experiences conform to this type if they are to enter into the ongoing synthesis that is resulting in a point of unification. The same can be said *mutatis mutandis* if the connections are categorial. Thus, our discussion in Chapter Six of the *a priori* of grammatical and logical laws can be seen as a discussion of norms of categorial connection. More precisely expressed, such laws can be seen as giving normative rules for connecting points of unification. Thus, the law that a whole is greater than its part expresses both a type of categorial connection and a norm for making connections of this type. Its denial, given that the part is defined as less than the whole, is not just logically contradictory. It also violates what is normatively required for the intuition of the part-whole relation. According to this requirement, an intuitive categorial connection of this type can only arise when the apprehensions of the whole and part — or, more precisely, the points of unification corresponding to these — definitely, yet only *partially*, coincide. Apprehensions whose relations do not have this feature frustrate the intention to see a part-whole connection.

The second theme is in some sense a premise for the new view of constitution. It is a premise that is embedded in all its results. It is the theme of the absolute independence of consciousness. Let us develop this to the point of its meeting with the theme of the normative functioning of the types of experience. Taken together, the two themes will allow us to resolve the difficulty with which we began this chapter. This is the reconciling of two apparently conflicting demands: first, the demand for the ontological identity between the real and ideal, secondly, the demand for their distinction. This latter, as we recall, is required for the species to assume a normative function.

We can begin by noting a crucial change brought about by the new interpretation of the dialectic of intention and fulfillment. In its old form, the dialectic can be considered as one between sense and presence. As originally noted, the effect of this dialectic is to separate as well as relate the theses of sense and being. Being is not a function of sense alone. The dialectic takes it as a function of the *confirmation* (or embodiment) of sense by intuitive presence.[10] Now, this doctrine obviously changes when we say that immanent within consciousness is the fullness of intuitive presence. The implication is that *sense* — understood on the transcendental level *as a point of unification* — *has within it such fullness*. We can also understand this in terms of the doctrine that the constitution of this point is the constitution of both the intentional experience and its intuitive correlate. As such, it is also the constitution of their confirmation. Insofar as such confirmation is understood as being, and insofar as sense is this point of unification, we have here a certain collapse of the theses of sense and being. As De Boer puts this, we must say that on the transcendental level, ". . . constituted sense is being itself . . ." (*De Ontwikklingsgang* . . . ed. cit., p. 597).

Husserl expresses this conclusion in the following way: "All real unities are unities of sense. Unities of sense . . . presuppose sense-bestowing consciousness which, on its own side, is absolute and does not exist through another bestowal of sense" — i.e., through having sense bestowed on it through some other source (*Ideen I*, §55, Biemel ed., p. 134).

Let us try to understand the above in terms of what it implies about the ultimate context and, hence, the guarantee of the subject-object correlation. In the *Logische Untersuchungen*, the context and guarantee are provided by the world in its ideal ontological structures. Such structures, understood as the laws of specific unity, apply to both subjects and objects. They thus establish the harmony of their correlation on an *a priori* basis (See above, p. 98). We can also say that the laws of specific unity, as all inclusive world-laws, give to the ontological sense of the world a definite epistemological function. It becomes, in its being, the ultimate ground of the subject's claims to knowledge having objective validity. Now, if we ask why the world in its sense of being must have this function, we come to the relation we initially specified between epistemology and ontology. The primacy of epistemology means that ontological considerations are shaped by epistemological goals. Thus, Husserl does not directly ask whether being in its structures permits objective knowledge.[11] He asks, rather, what the being of subjects and objects must be if objective knowledge is to be possible (See above, p. 2). This question is actually about the being of the world. For in the epistemological context, which denies the possibility of things that cannot become objects, the possibility of being is reduced to that of subjects and objects. Thus, the hypothesis of the possibility of objective knowledge becomes, in this context, a hypothesis about the world in its ontological structures or forms. The world becomes specified by the function it must perform if the epistemological standpoint is to be primary — i.e., if subjects are to have the possibility of valid knowledge of objects. It has simply the status of being the ultimate ontological condition of the valid subject-object correlation.

Granting this, the conclusion arises that a transfer of the function of providing a guarantee of the subject-object correlation implies a transfer of what counts as the being of the world. The transfer of the function is implied when we say that the correlation involving a subject's intentional experiences and its objective correlates is immanently grounded — i.e., grounded by the constitutive functions of consciousness. Insofar as consciousness in these functions can completely account for the correlation, it must, then, itself take on the ontological title of "the world." This shift may be expressed in terms of the shift in the predicative relation between consciousness and the world. In the *Logische Untersuchungen*, the *a priori form of the world*, by virtue of its function of correlating subjects and objects, is taken as the form of "sensibility and understanding as such" — in short, as *the form of consciousness*, this last being conceived of as a title for the *whole* of the intentional relation. It is, then, the world which requires, by virtue of the function of its formal structures, the title of consciousness. The doctrine of constitution put forward by the *Ideen* requires a reversal of this relationship. In this work, it is consciousness itself which requires, by virtue of its structures performing the exact same functions, the title of "the world."

This redefinition of what counts as the world is responsible for some of Husserl's most startling assertions. According to him, the most basic of ontological distinctions is no longer that between the world and what manifests itself within it. Instead, we have as "... the most radical of distinctions of being, *being as consciousness* and being as '*manifesting*' itself within consciousness...". In other words, we no longer have the world as something ontologically primary, something on which depend all special categories of being as categories or regions of the world. On the contrary, the phenomenological reduction gives us:

> ... the region of transcendental consciousness as a region of absolute being in a definite sense. It is the primary category of being in general (or in our way of speaking, the original region) in which all other regions of being have their roots, the region to which they are all essentially related and, thus, on which they all are essentially dependent (*Ideen I*, §76; Biemel ed., p. 174).

If we ask why consciousness must necessarily take up this position, we come to the account we have given of the failure of the worldly ontology of the *Logische Untersuchungen*. The doctrine that the ideal structures of the world serve as a determining *a priori* of real subjects and their objects cannot account for the subjective acts which are required to bring about their correlation. Indeed, as we mentioned at the end of our seventh chapter, the subject-object correlation appears, in terms of the conflicting ontological requirements for such acts, to be formally impossible. If we take from this situation the motivation of attempting to rehabilitate the correlation, then the tie between the correlation and what counts as the world gives a direction to this motivation. We have an incentive to transfer the title of "world" to what can ground the correlation. Here, we can say that consciousness achieves its unique position not just because of the failure of the old ontology of objective or worldly being. We have, in addition, the claim that consciousness considered as a world, i.e., as an ultimate ontological ground, can overcome the difficulty that leads to this failure. As we have said, the difficulty concerns the relation of the real and ideal. It concerns our understanding of the schema of species and instances that characterizes objective being. To ground an adequate correlation, we require their ontological identity. Thus must be an identity that does not sacrifice the position of the species as norms — i.e., their position as pure, as opposed to empirical, possibilities. How does the conception of consciousness as truly absolute — i.e., as the world — satisfy this?

To begin with, we note that the position of consciousness as the primary or original category of being naturally changes the focus of ontology, understood as the study of being. There is a necessary shift in its subject matter. This can be made more precise by defining onto-logy as the study of the *logos* or species of each of the *onta*. In the *Untersuchungen*, the *onta* are considered as worldly existents. The species themselves are understood as expressing the formal structures of objectives or worldly being. Now, the key element in Husserl's positioning of consciousness as the world is his statement that "... all ontologies, as we expressly demand, fall to the reduction" (*Ideen III*, §13; Biemel ed., p. 76). This reduction, as we earlier said, is a leading back of transcendent or objective being to the transcendental experiences that form its conditions. This means, then, that the schema of species and instances that delineates ontology's subject matter must be reinterpreted such that each particular ontology reappears in transcendental consciousness. In Husserl's words, the claim is that "... their basic concepts and axioms ... allow themselves to be reinterpreted as certain essential connections of pure experience" (*Ibid.*, §14; Biemel ed., p. 77). As he also expresses this a few lines later, "The transcendental interpretations of all ontologies would also belong here, the interpretation (to be accomplished through the phenomenological method) of each proposition of ontology as an index for quite definite connections of transcendental consciousness...". That this, in fact, gives consciousness its new position becomes apparent when we realize that the "basic concepts" of ontology are the species delineating, in a formal way, the various regions (or types) of being. The "propositions" or "axioms" of ontology are the laws of specific unity that ground the possibility and, hence, the being of the species. The reinterpretation, thus, signifies that the formal ontological structures of the world — the structures by which it is supposed to guarantee the subject-object correlation — are transferred to the constituting structures of consciousness.

This transference shows us how the first of our demands can be satisfied. We are referring to the ontological identity of species and instance required for genuine predication. The transcendental interpretation of ontology requires that we take the real instance as a unity of sense. The objective species is to be taken as the type of interconnection that grounds this unity in its specific character. As for the laws of specific unity, their transcendental interpretation follows from this. They are to be understood as laws for connecting experience so as to yield definite types — the types being the immanent representatives of what we objectively interpret as definite species. This immediately establishes the required identity. For, we are free to take the presence of a real instance as a presence grounded by the interconnections of experience. This means that the *types* of such interconnections are immanently correlated to the *types* of real instances these connections ground. It, thus, follows as a matter of course that they can be objectively interpreted as species delineating the types of such instances. This allows us — on a very different basis — to reaffirm the notion that Plato used to underpin the identity required for predication. We can correlate the possibility of apprehending an individual existent with that of predicating a species of it. The first, in fact, demands the second. This follows insofar as to think an individual existent is, on the transcendental level, to think a unity of sense — i.e., an immanently grounded point of unification. This, however, also implies the thought or the definite connections that establish this unity, the thought of their type being that of a species.

Ultimately, then, both species and instances have an ontological identity because *that by virtue of which both are* is one and the same. This is constituting consciousness with its types of connections and immanent unities established by these types. It is consciousness conceived as bearing the ontological sense of the world and, hence, its function of correlating subjects and objects. Does consciousness so conceived also allow us to ground the position of the species as norms? To ground them in their normative function is to establish them as pure possibilities. Here, we have to say that the pure thought of the species expresses only the possibility of instances falling under their concepts. In other words, the species specify — or norminatively define — their range of instances only in terms of the possibility of these receiving a definite concept as a predicate. This, as we observed, is the reverse of what happens in an empirical generalization where the concept is determined by actual apprehensions of actual objects. In this case, the species have an independence and self-subsistence that follows from their position as pure possibilities. Now if this independence, which is essential for a norm, can also be traceable back to the absolute character of consciousness — i.e., its position as bearing the sense of the world — then the ontological shift we have been describing will be successful. It will have established *both* the identity and difference of the species and instances.

To see how this is accomplished, we may begin by again observing that both the actual experience of an objectivity and the objectivity itself are correlated by being constituted in one and the same process. We also remark that the basis of this correlation is the dependence of both upon the connections of consciousness, connections which unite experiences in certain formal patterns so as to form points of unification. Now, in *Ideen I*, Husserl speaks of this situation as involving a *correlation of possibilities.* Possibilities involving types of objective worlds can be matched to those involving types of experiencing consciousness. In Husserl's words,

> ... the correlate of our factual experience, called the "actual world," shows itself as a special case of multiplicity of possible worlds which, on their side, are nothing other than correlates of essentially possible variations of the idea of "experiencing consciousness" (*Ideen I*, §47; Biemel ed., p. 111).

The implicit assertion in this is that the types of interconnections which give us a specific experiencing consciousness and also a specific objective world as its correlate *are themselves variable*. Because these connections in their specific forms *could have been otherwise*, the actual consciousness and its actual world are only special cases, i.e., "possible variations" grounded on the various forms of possible connections. We can also express this in terms of the claim that the multiplicities of experience which do, through their connections, give us an actual world, do not by themselves demand such connections. In other words, the necessity of such connections cannot be inferred from actual perceptual experience. As Husserl writes,

> The existence of a world is a correlate of certain multiplicities of experience marked out by certain essential formations. It is *not* clear, however, that actual experience could proceed *only* in such forms of connections. This cannot be inferred from the essence of perception in general or from the various types of empirical intuitions that play their role in this (*Ibid.*, §49; Biemel ed., p. 114).

It is easy to see that the species — now understood as *types of connections* — are once again conceived of as pure possibilities. Their thought does not demand the actuality of the world that would instantiate them; it involves only the possibility of this. The same point carries over to the laws of specific unity. Transcendental logic views such laws as laws for connecting experiences so as to give us definite types. If such types, as pure possibilities, do not demand their instantiation, we have to say with Husserl, "Transcendental logic — logic which as transcendental is led back to consciousness — contains the ground for a possible nature but not for an actual one" (*Erste Philosophie I*, "Beilage XX"; ed. R. Boehm, The Hague, 1956, p. 394).

The above, of course, establishes only the *fact* that Husserl once again considers the species as pure possibilities. It does not establish his *right* to consider them as such. Before we investigate the question of this right (a question which involves the tie of the species to the nature of consciousness), let us pause for a moment and reflect upon the significance of this fact. As we recall, the notion of the fitting or not fitting together of the individual experiences of consciousness receives its sense from the normative functioning of the types of experience. The statement that such types are, in themselves, to be regarded as species – i.e., as pure possibilities – allows us to justify this doctrine. A species has an ontological independence with regard to empirical reality. Its own being does not demand that such reality conform to it. In other words, its thought as a species is only that of the possibility of such reality – transcendentally expressed – the possibility of the actual connections that would establish this reality's presence. This means that it is determinative of reality only in a normative sense. We can take as an example the thought of the species of a spatial-temporal object. In its transcendental interpretation, this thought is of the type of interconnections that give us a perspectival ordering of perceptions. Given that this ordering simultaneously establishes both the intentional experience and its objective correlate, the thought, properly speaking is one of an *a priori* correlation between two possibilities: the possibility of an intentional experience based on this ordering, and the possibility of the presence of a certain type of object corresponding to this. Now, as expressing possibility, the thought does not demand that the perceptions we actually have fit into such an ordering. It does, however, by containing the notion of the correlation, normatively demand that all experiences of spatial-temporal objects be in terms of perspectival series. It, thus, serves as a norm for the correctness of our assertion that we are continuing to view a spatial-temporal object.

In considering the question of the right of the species to be taken as pure possibilities, we note first of all that this right does not conflict with the identity of species and instance as required by predication. This would be the case if both the identity and the difference between species and instance had not the same principle. The principle, however, is the same. It is the independence of consciousness insofar as it is conceived as an ultimate ground. The resolution of the conflict between the two arises, we can say, from what is signified by the notion of this ground. This becomes clear once we observe that the identity of species and instances refers to the constitution (or grounding) of a specifically given world. When the species are species of actual instances, both express the same principle of being — that of constituting consciousness. Thus, the *actuality* of the instance refers to the *actuality* of the type of connection that establishes its presence, and both refer to constituting consciousness in its function of actually grounding a given world. As for the distinction between species and instances, its reference is once again to constituting consciousness as its explanatory condition. This time, however, it is to its *independence as a ground* from that which it grounds. In other words, the position of the species as pure possibilities comes from the fact that consciousness, as an ultimate ground, can establish any number of possible worlds.

As the above indicates, the right of the species to be called pure possibilities is tied to the independence of absolute consciousness. Let us try to clarify this. Husserl writes: "*Immanent being is undoubtedly absolute being in the sense that in principle it needs no 'thing' in order to exist*" (*Ideen I*, §49; Biemel ed., p. 115). On the transcendental level, this becomes his assertion that "... *through the destruction of the world of things, the being of consciousness,* of the stream of experiences as such, *would be necessarily modified but not touched in its own existence*" (*Ibid.*). Now, the immediate reason for these assertions is the fact that the individual experiences which form the field of consciousness are *not themselves things.* They ground through their connections the world of things. That they themselves are untouched by the destruction of this world follows from the nature of this grounding. They establish through their connections the presence of "things" — i.e., transcendent realities that show themselves perspectively. As we said above, transcendent things are real unities — i.e., unities that Husserl takes as unities of sense. They are established by a point of unification, one whose inherent content includes the intentional anticipation of its indefinite persistence through the flow of experiences. Now, given that such a content can only be established on the basis of perspectively ordered experiences, the disruption of this ordering is the disruption of the presence of the thing which bears this content. This disruption, however, cannot touch the individual experiences that make up the elements of the thing's appearing. These last are distinguished from the objects they help constitute through the fact that they do not show themselves perspectivally. In other words, their own mode of presence (or being) is not such as can be affected by the disordering that disrupts the presence of a spatial-temporal thing.

We can also express the above in a less immediate form by putting it into the negative. If consciousness, in order to be, demanded the conditions that are required for the existence of thing-like realities, then it itself would be a thing-like reality. In other words, instead of being the ground of a world of things, it would require, along with this world, the same ground for its own existence. Here the conception of consciousness as a ground places its own conditions outside of those of the realities for which it serves as a condition. This can be put somewhat less abstractly by observing that if consciousness, in order to be, demanded a specific set of connections for its actual experience, then it would also demand, as a correlate of this, a specifically given actual world. At this point, the separation of consciousness from the world could not be brought about. Its own being would demand that of the world. If its connections set up a spatial-temporal world, it would be determined to interpret itself as a spatial-temporal part of this world. In any case, we would not be able to say that it needed no thing (or world of things) to exist, since, in fact, the conditions for its existence would be correlated to those of the latter.

The same point holds with regard to Husserl's assertions that the multiplicities of experience do not in themselves demand a specific form of connection and that transcendental logic gives us only the form of a possible world. Transcendentally regarded, the propositions of logic are indices pointing to the connections obtaining among the multiplicities of experience. They are normative rules for the types of such connections. Now, if we were to disregard their normative character and to consider them as actually determinative, two conclusions would follow. Logic would give us the form of a necessarily actual world and the multiplicities of experience would have to be seen as, in fact, requiring specific forms of connections. In other words, logic would be seen as necessarily determining both consciousness and the world. It would correlate them, after the manner of the *Logische Untersuchungen*, as dependent moments *of one concrete whole* which would itself receive *the title of the world*. In this regard, we can say that it is the later Husserl's attempt to break out of this context — a context that leaves unresolved the normative and the determining ontological functions of logic — which makes him turn to the notion of consciousness as an ultimate ground.

The above, in fact, may be summarized into three basic inferences, the last one leading to the right of the species to be called pure possibilities. We begin with the distinction between individual experiences and the objects these experiences constitute through their connections. This is at once a distinction between their modes of presence and also an ontological distinction. It permits us to consider the being of the individual experiences as independent of what they help constitute. In other words, it allows us to infer the independence of consciousness when consciousness is taken as a field of individual experiences. A second, though essentially related, inference is that the multiplicities of experience, regarded in terms of their individual elements, do not demand for their being specific forms of connections. From this, as we indicated, we can infer the right of the species (taken as types of connections) and transcendental logic (taken as rules for these types) to be described in terms of pure possibilities. In sum, the fact that the notion of constitution demands this distinction between individual experiences and what they help constitute means that this *right* (as based upon this *distinction*) is established by its ultimately flowing from the notion of constituting consciousness.

Two final reflections arise from the above. The first concerns the nature of the grounding (or establishing) which is accomplished by consciousness. Such grounding occurs through its types of connections. These types, as we indicated, have a *dual* ontological character. Thus, when consciousness is engaged in the process of constituting a given world, the types are really present in constituting consciousness. They, thus, show the aspect of actuality. The same process, however, demands that they also be considered as possibilities. This follows insofar as the process presupposes the distinction between experience and object and, thus, the independence of consciousness from what it constitutes. Now, taken together, these characteristics are reflected in the constituted world. As correlated to such types, it is *both* actual and possible. By this, we mean that it exists and yet it is possible for it not to exist. In other words, as constituted, it is *contingent*. This contingency, as we shall see, separates consciousness, considered as bearing the title of the world, from any given world. It leads to our second reflection. This concerns the notion of consciousness as the world in a more radical sense of "world" than we have hitherto considered.

As before, the starting point for our reflections is the notion of consciousness as the ground of the subject-object correlation. Now, for Husserl, the correlation involves the possibility of the dissolution of the world. In Husserl's words:

> It is conceivable that experience — and not just for us — teems with inherently unresolvable contradictions, that experience, all at once, thus shows itself as obstinately opposed to the demand that the things which it posits should ever harmoniously persist. It is conceivable that experience's connections forfeit the stable rules of ordering perspectives, apprehensions and appearances and that this actually remains *in infinitum* the case, in short, that there no longer exists a harmoniously positable and, thus, existing world (*Ideen I*, §49; Biemel ed., p. 115).

This possibility, as should be evident, is contained in the assertion that experiences *per se* do not demand specific sets of connections — i.e., "stable rules of ordering." Because of this, the actual world that they ground is contingent in the sense that it ". . . does not exclude in principle its non-being" (*Erste Philosophie II*, ed. R. Boehm, The Hague, 1959, p. 50).

Now, given that the subject, as an *individual experiencer* — i.e., as that which is *defined by the unity of an intentional experience* — is correlated to the *unity of what it experiences*, the dissolution of the latter involves the dissolution of the subject in this defined sense. In Husserl's words, "One can say that a complete dissolution of the world in a 'tumult' [of experiences] is the same as the dissolution of the ego . . ." (Ms. F. IV 3, p. 57a, ca. 1925). What this dissolution concerns is the ego taken as a unity of consciousness. It is, we can say, the ordering of experiences into such a unity which allows the ego to grasp its experiences as pertaining to itself. Experiences, when suitably ordered, give the ego what Husserl calls a "surrounding world" — one in which it is posited as its center. Its experiences become "its own" — i.e., point to it as a unique experiencer — insofar as they are arranged so as to situate it at what we may call the "zero point" marking the distances of its visual field. Thus, if we grant, with Husserl, that ". . . the pure ego is a numerical singular with regard to '*its*' stream of consciousness," then the dissolution of the conditions that would allow the formation of a personal stream becomes, at the same time, a dissolution of the ego as a numerical singular (*Ideen II*, §27, Biemel ed., p. 110).[12]

The conclusion to be drawn from this has been implicit in our whole treatment of the ontological shift. If consciousness, as a field of experiences, correlates both the subject and its world of objects, and if this correlation involves the possibility of the dissolution of both, then consciousness itself cannot be identified with either. In other words, the fact that it is not touched in its own being by the dissolution of the world implies, given the correlation, that it is also not touched by the dissolution of the numerically singular ego taken as an individual experiencer of this world. We have, then, the positioning of the field of consciousness as something beyond the individual experiencer and the objects this experiences.[13] It is situated as an independent ground of both. This allows us to say that the forms of the connections of consciousness — understood as species — function as norms not only for objects but also for experiencers of these objects. This means that, given an individual experiencer, certain of these norms can be viewed, after the manner of the *Logische Untersuchungen*, as forming a determining ontological *a priori*. We can never experience their violation — although this is always inherently possible; for if this were to occur, it would mean our own dissolution as individual experiencers.

As for consciousness itself, it achieves the title of the world in the sense in which Husserl defines this term in his last work. According to Husserl, ". . . the world does not exist like an existent entity or object. It rather exists in a singularity for which the plural is senseless" (*Krisis*, §37; ed. W. Biemel, 2nd ed., The Hague 1962, p. 146). Husserl's point here is that the world is properly characterized as that which has no beyond, that for which, as an absolute totality, there is no other. Individual objects, as singulars, imply the possibility of a plurality — i.e., the possibility of other objects which are the same or other than themselves. In distinction to this, the world, insofar as it does not have a beyond, has the character of a *unique* singular. With this, we can say that our investigation of the normative aspect of the species leads to the notion of consciousness as a world insofar as it gives us consciousness as a ground *of all possible existents* and worlds of existents. It is not just a world in the sense of being a ground of a definite subject-object correlation. It is one as grounding this in every possible variation. As including all possibilities, it *excludes* the possibility of something being beyond itself.

Understanding "subjectivity" as consciousness in this way, we have to say with Husserl that the "existing world" is to be regarded "... as a product of sense, as a product of a universal, ultimately functioning subjectivity." Expressing himself in the metaphors of "inner" and "outer", Husserl adds:

> It belongs essentially to its world constituting accomplishment that subjectivity objectifies itself as human subjectivity, as an element within the word. All objective consideration of the world is a consideration of the "outer" and grasps only what is outer, i.e., objectivities. The radical consideration of the world is the systematic and pure inner consideration of the subjectivity which externalizes ("expresses") itself in the outer (*Krisis*, §29; 2nd Biemel ed., pp. 115-16).

Thus, what is outer is all individual existents, including individual subjects. What is inner is a "universal, ultimately functioning subjectivity." This is something with which we can come into empirical contact when we directly regard our experiences and acknowledge all their inherent possibilities of combination. Insofar as the thought of the species leads to this, it contains something both empirical *and* ultimate.

NOTES

NOTES TO: 'INTRODUCTION'

1. *Logische Untersuchungen,* 5th ed., 3 vols. (Tübingen, 1968). The 5th edition is an unchanged version of the 2nd edition, the first two volumes of which appeared in 1913, the third appearing in 1921. Where there are substantial textual differences between this and the 1st edition, 2 vols. (Halle a. S., 1900-1901), we shall quote from the latter. Our translations from Husserl will in all cases be our own. The letter "F" refers to the pagination in the English translation, *Logical Investigations*, trans. J. Findlay (New York, 1970).
2. See *LU*, Tüb. ed., I, 224; F., p. 221; *Ibid.*, II/1, 21; F., p. 265. The assertions are repeated in *Die Idee der Phänomenologie*, ed. W. Biemel, 2nd edition, Husserliana II (The Hague, 1958), pp. 22-23, 32.
3. For a representative sampling, see H. Spiegelberg, *The Phenomenological Movement,* 2nd edition, Phaenomenologica, No. 5, 2 vols. (The Hague, 1971), I, 73; M. Farber, *The Foundations of Phenomenology,* 3rd edition (Albany, 1964), pp. 543-49; also Farber's *The Aims of Phenomenology* (New York, 1966), pp. 76-78; Theodor Celms, *Der phänomenologische Idealismus Husserls* (Riga, 1928), pp. 251-52; A. Osborn, *Edmund Husserl and his Logical Investigations,* 2nd edition (Cambridge, Mass., 1949), p. 109; P. Ricoeur, "Introduction du Traducteur," *Idées directrices pour une phénoménologie* (Paris, 1950), p. xxxi. The last two authors do not see any real opposition between the two works, while the rest stress, in varying degrees, their fundamental incompatibility. As will become evident, our own position is very closely allied to Theodor De Boer's "genetic method" for interpreting Husserl. According to De Boer, "This method makes it possible to understand the earlier work as an initial stage of the latter and the latter as an answer to the problematic of the earlier" ("Zusammenfassung," *De Ontwikkelingsgang in het Denken van Husserl,* Assen, 1966, p. 576). Unlike De Boer, our primary focus will be on the problematic of Husserl's ontology.

NOTES TO CHAPTER I: 'THE REFUTATION OF PSYCHOLOGISM'

1. In Husserl's words, "To being in itself correspond truths in themselves and to these correspond fixed and unambiguous expressions in themselves" (*LU*, Tüb. ed., II/1, 90; F., p. 322). Husserl also asserts in the same passage, "Everything that exists is knowable 'in itself' and its being is a being definite in content, one that documents itself in such and such 'truths in themselves' " (*Ibid.*, II/1, 90; F., 321). This sentiment, which is repeated throughout the *Logische Untersuchungen*, ill accords with De Boer's somewhat Kantian description of its epistemology: "The world in itself is for it unreachable" ("Zusammenfassung," *op. cit.*, p. 585). The position of the *Logische Untersuchungen*, on this point at least, is anti-Kantian. The dominant influence, here, stems from Brentano. As Iso Kern expresses the latter's position, "It also cannot be said that because the phenomena are codetermined by subjectivity these phenomena do not faithfully reproduce the things in themselves" (*Husserl und Kant*, Phaenomenologica, No. 16, The Hague, 1964, p. 7). As we shall see, Husserl's project of "epistemological clarification" involves understanding how subjectivity can both codetermine the phenomena and yet faithfully reproduce and, thus, know things in themselves.
2. Certain remarks of the late Wittgenstein seem to indicate that his position falls under this definition. The connection between the two is made through the identification of a logical law (or logical proposition), a form of facts (or, linguistically, a form of factual, empirical judgements) and a rule for testing these empirical judgements. Wittgenstein writes: "One could conceive that certain propositions, of the form of empirical propositions, were fixed and functioned as a channel for the non-fixed, fluid empirical propositions; and that this relation changed with time because fluid propositions became fixed and the fixed became fluid." ". . . at one time, the same sentence can be treated as one to be tested by experience, at another, as a rule for testing." "But, then, doesn't one have to say that there is no sharp boundary between logical propositions and empirical propositions? The unclarity is precisely that of the boundary between a *rule* and an empirical proposition" (*On Certainty*, §§96. 98, 319; eds. G.E.M. Anscombe and G.H. von Wright, trans. my own, New York, 1972). For Husserl, the "fluidity" of a logical law or rule makes it contingent.
3. See Husserl's citations from the works of Mill and Erdmann (*LU*, Tüb. ed., I, 81; F., p. 113; *Ibid.*, I, 137; F., p. 145).
4. See *LU*, Tüb. ed., I, 56-57; F., pp. 94-95 and *Ibid.*, 11/1, 347; F., pp. 536; also *LU*, Halle ed., II, 336; F., pp. 545-46.
5. See *LU*, Tüb. ed., I, 65; F., p. 101. Cf. Hume, *A Treatise of Human Understanding*, Bk. I, Part IV, sec. 1.
6. In terms of the analogy, the resemblance could at least be as slight as that between the statement of the electronic events inside the calculator and the statement of the arithmetical laws which the figures on its face

supposedly follow. The same disparity would occur in a calculator built on the principle of the gear and lever — i.e., a mechanical adding machine.
7. Gunther Stent extends the notion of this relativity to the very basic concepts of scientific laws — i.e., space, time and causality. See his "Limits to the Scientific Understanding of Man," *Science*, CLXXXVII (1974), 1054. Stent's position is not very different from those considered by Husserl in *LU*, "Prol.," §§52-56.
8. When we combine this with the Darwinian theory of the biological evolution of the subject, we achieve the type of scepticism described in *Die Idee der Phän.*; Biemel ed., p. 21. See also *LU*, "Prol.," §36, nos. 4-6.

NOTES TO CHAPTER II
'ESTABLISHING THE GUIDING MOTIVATION: THE REFUTATION OF SCEPTICISM AND RELATIVISM'

1. See Frederic B. Fitch, "Self-Reference in Philosophy," *Contemporary Readings in Logical Theory*, eds. I. Copi and J. Gould (New York, 1967), pp. 156-57.
2. This notion of Russell's has been generally accepted, though its consequence for his own theory of types is not generally noted. Fitch points out that to be meaningful as a theory of theories involving "maximum theoretical generality," it must involve some self-reference even though this violates its strictures against self-reference. Otherwise, it would not have the *sense* of a theory. See his "Self-Reference...," ed. cit., pp. 158-60.

NOTES TO CHAPTER III: 'THE CATEGORY OF THE IDEAL'

1. Cf. Heidegger's description of the "abyss" presented by Kant's transcendental imagination in the 1st edition of the *Critique of Pure Reason*. Heidegger describes "Kant's recoil" from this abyss in his *Kant und das Problem der Metaphysik*, §31.
2. It is also not the case, as E. Levinas asserts, that "Volume II of the *Logische Untersuchungen* builds a new ontology of consciousness to replace naturalistic ontology..." (*The Theory of Intuition in Husserl's Phenomenology*, trans. A. Orianne, Evanston, 1973, p. 13). This new ontology first appears some years after the publication of the 1st edition of the *Untersuchungen*.
3. See also Husserl's equation of real being with temporal being, *LU*, Tüb. ed., II/1, 123; F., p. 351. According to this, what is "in our thinking" — which is a temporal process — "... pertains to the sphere of real being, the sphere of temporality" (*LU*, Tüb. ed., II/1, 101; F., p. 330). The equation also leads Husserl to identify the mental content, understood temporally "in the subjective sense" with the content understood "in the

phenomenological sense, the descriptive psychological sense and in the empirically real sense" (*LU*, Halle ed., II, 52). See also *LU*, Halle ed., II, 332, 356 for the assertion that this temporal reality must involve causality. Some, but not all of the passages stressing the natural reality of consciousness were suppressed or altered when Husserl partially rewrote the 2nd ed. under the influence of *Ideen I*.

4. See also *LU*, Tüb. ed., I, 177; F., pp. 184-85; *Ibid.*, I, 68; F., p. 104.
5. See *LU*, Tüb. ed., I, 69; F., p. 104; *Ibid.*, I, 159; F., p. 171; *Ibid.*, I, 171-72; F., pp. 180-81.
6. Thus, Husserl writes of the objects of the arithmetical laws — e.g., the number Five: "In *no* case can it be comprehended without absurdity *as a part or side* of a mental experience and in this way as something real (*LU*, Tüb. ed., I, 171; F., p. 180). Similar assertions are made with respect to the propositional meanings which logic considers. See *Ibid.*, Tüb. ed., I, 175-76; F., pp. 183-84.
7. The question, here, is put by De Boer in terms of the acts of consciousness: "On the one hand, these are empirically necessary and determined; on the other, an idea is realized in them according to which they claim apodictic validity. How can both of these points of view be combined?" ("Zusammenfassung," *op. cit.,* p. 589).
8. This characterization, which is one of being one-in-many, is applied both to propositonal truths and to individual meanings considered as "ideal units." See *LU*, Tüb. ed., I, 99; F., p. 329; *Ibid.*, I, 128-30; F., pp. 149-50; *Ibid.*, II/1, 96-97; F., p. 327; *Ibid.*, II/1, 100-101; F., p. 330.
9. Husserl, in fact, doubts whether the empirical limits of language could ever allow of a completely definite description. See *LU*, Tüb. ed., II/1, 91; F., p. 322.
10. Without such a distinction and corresponding movement, a word is either a fixed expression or, *qua* occasional, it has no power to refer by acting as a mere indicator. The test for whether or not a word is fixed is made by observing whether we can form a definite presentation of its referent without regard to the circumstances of its use. Thus, to assert that a word like *lion* is essentially occasional is to assert that, independent of the particular circumstance of its use, it allows of no more definite presentation of its referent than a word like *you*. According to this test, not all words are essentially occasional. These last, rather, constitute an exceptional case. See *LU*, Tüb. ed., II/1, 83; F., p. 316.
11. We may note that if being is without an available objective sense, then all expressions have only an operative indicating function, but in a different sense than that described above. What they indicate is not specified by referring to the objective sense of the circumstances in which they are used. It is rather — to follow a current view — to be found in the conventions of the use of a particular language. In Strawsons's words, ". . . the meaning of an expression is not the set of things or single thing it may be correctly used to refer to: The meaning is the

set of rules, habits, conventions for its use in referring" ("On Referring," *Contemporary Readings in Logical Theory*, ed. cit., p. 113). If these rules for its use are described as contingent, if, for example, we say with Wittgenstein that it is an "empirical fact" that a certain word is used in a certain way (*On Certainty*, §305-§306), then in Husserl's view we slip into relativism. The relativism is of the basic form of making logic dependent on facts. Logic, which deals with propositional meanings, becomes contingent – i.e., empirically grounded – if these meanings are themselves contingent. So stated, the thesis, in Husserl's view, would lead to absurdity. Regarded as beyond the horizon of logic, the thesis would be unintelligible. Presented within the horizon of logic, the thesis would be inconsistent.

12. Wittgenstein writes, "It would be as if someone were looking for an object in a room. He opens a drawer and does not see it there. Then he closes it, waits and opens it again to see whether, perhaps, it may not now be there, and he continues in this manner" (*On Certainty*, §315, ed. cit., p. 40). The above point about reperformance seems implicit in this passage; through Wittgenstein's subsequent references to learning the linguistic game of seeking shows that he has a different way out of this impasse than either Kant's or Husserl's. Kant, it should be noted, differs from Husserl insofar as he does not assume that validity is established by an eidetic act. Denying the existence of such an act, he refers universal validity to subjective necessity – i.e., to "the universal and necessary connections of the given perceptions" by which we grasp what for us is the objective sense of an entity. As Kant makes clear, these subjective necessities can be considered quite apart from the inherent content of the entity; the last, in fact, "remains always unknown in itself" ("Prolegomena," §19, *Kants ges. Schr.*, IV, 298-99). This conclusion is probably responsible for Husserl's most sweeping criticism of Kant: "All the principal unclarities of the Kantian critique of reason are ultimately bound together by the fact that Kant never makes clear to himself the peculiar character of ideation..." (*LU*, Tüb. ed., II/2, 203; F., p. 833). According to Husserl, if we recognize ideation as a unique act that can grasp necessary universality, then an examination of subjective necessities of experience need not involve any abstraction from the question of the inherent sense of the object. In fact, as we shall see, the two must be correlated.

13. The claim that perception, by following its own inherent standard, can reach the object itself is made a number of times. See *LU*, Tüb. ed., II/2, 57; F., p. 713; *Ibid.*, II/2, 202, no. 3; F., p. 832. It is to be noted that adequate perception, which is defined as reaching the "full selfhood" of the object, is not equated with inner perception. Inner perception can lack evidence and outer perception can be evident. See *LU*, Halle ed., II, 704-705, 710-12, see also above, p. 80. One may compare this doctrine with the very different position of the *Ideen*, where there is ascribed an inherent "inadequcy" to the outer perception of things.

See *Ideen I*, §44; Biemel ed., p. 100; also *Ibid.*, Beilagen XII, XV; Biemel ed., pp. 398-99, 402-403.

NOTES TO CHAPTER IV: 'THE BEING OF THE IDEAL'

1. Thus, the thought of one in many is present in both the proper and the universal name. As Husserl writes: "What is usually designated as 'the universality of a word meaning' is a fact that in no way points to the universality attributed to concepts of kinds as opposed to concepts of individuals. On the contrary, it comprehends both in the same way" (*LU*, Tüb. ed., II/2, 30; F., p. 692). The distinction between the two is in what constitutes the many. For the proper name, as embodying the thought of an individual, the many refers to individual intuitions; for the generic name, it refers to individual objects. See *Ibid.*, II/2, 31-32; F., pp. 693-94. It is to be noted that the meaning signified by the proper name is, in a recognative synthesis, identifiable with the *fulfilling sense* of the perception of an individual object. As Husserl defines this last: "This is the *identical content* which, in perception, pertains to the totality of possible perceptual acts which intend the same object, i.e., intend it perceptually as actually the same" (*Ibid.*, II/1, 51; F., p. 291).
2. A much more extended accout of this point is made by R. Sokolowski in "Identity in Absence and Presence," *Husserlian Meditations* (Evanston, 1974), pp. 18-56.
3. Thomas Aquinas gives the classical formulation of this distinction in his *Quodlibetum*, II, 3c; ed. P. Mandonnet (Paris, 1926), p. 43. See also his *Le "De Ente et Essentia,"* Ch. 4; ed. M.D. Rolland-Gosselin (Kain, Belgium, 1926), p. 34.
4. Husserl is not above occasionally contradicting himself. At one point he writes: "The combination *a round square* really yields a unitary meaning. It is, however, apodictically evident that to this existing meaning no existing object can correspond" (*LU*, Halle ed., II, 312; see *LU*, Tüb. ed., II/1, 326; F., p. 517). As the context of this passage makes clear, Husserl sees the notion of a round square as inconsistent (widersinnig) but not as grammatically senseless (unsinnig). On a *grammatical* level of a substantive modified by an adjective, it does have a unity in its sense. Now, to speak of an inconsistent meaning as existing does not just contradict the passage quoted in our text, it also goes against Husserl's carefully worked out doctrine of the being of the ideal. As we shall see, Husserl will constantly assert that the ideal being of a species is the same as the ideal possibility of its instantiations existing. Thus, without the latter, we cannot speak of ideal being. Here, as always, the *Logische Untersuchungen*'s individual statements must be weighed in the context of its continuously expressed doctrine.

5. The distinction between the species as a concept and the species as an object is made in *LU*, Tüb. ed., II/1, 102-103; F., pp. 331-32. See also *Ibid.*, II/1, 222; F., p. 431.
6. In other words, objects are possible that are never actually grasped. See *LU*, Tüb. ed., II/1, 219; F., p. 428.
7. It is typical of Husserl's rather troubled relations with Frege that he makes only a general reference to this "Preface." See *LU*, Tüb. ed., I, 169, fn. 1; F., p. 179.
8. It is to be noted that this notion becomes fully defined only in the second edition of the *Logische Untersuchungen*. One may compare, e.g., Husserl's remarks on *LU*, Halle ed., II, 21 and his rewriting of these on *LU*, Tüb. ed., II/1, 21; F., p. 265.
9. The same assertion is made on the level of the predicability of a term. Universal predicability is a function of a term's specific unity. See *LU*, Tüb. ed., II/1, 148; F., p. 372.
10. The relation between possibility and unifiability is expressed by Husserl as follows: "In the limiting case of a single content, the validity of a single species may be defined as its unifiability 'with itself.' ... The difference between speaking of unifiability and possibility lies simply in the fact that while the latter designates the straightforward validity of a species, the former (prior to the widening of the concept to the limiting case) designates the relation of the component species in a species that counts as one" (*LU*, Tüb. ed., II/2, 106, 107; F., pp. 752, 753).
11. See also *LU*, Tüb. ed., II/1, 279; F., pp. 477-78; *Ibid.*, II/1, 283; F., pp. 480-81.

NOTES TO CHAPTER V: 'SUBJECTIVE ACCOMPLISHMENT: INTENTIONALITY AS ONTOLOGICAL TRANSCENDENCE'

1. This concept is extensively developed in the 1st edition, then largely omitted in the second. Accordingly, most of our references are to the 1st or Halle edition.
2. This position is the reverse of the 2nd edition's. The latter asserts that causal relations (as expressed in natural laws) do not pertain to the *a priori* of nature. In other words, they express only contingent truths, not truths grounded in the essence of an enduring entity. See *LU*, Tüb. ed., II/1, 290; F., p. 468.
3. Cf. *LU*, Tüb. ed., II/1, 16; F., pp. 259-60. The 2nd edition frequently substitutes *reelen* for the 1st edition's *actuellen*.
4. See also *LU*, Tüb. ed., II/1, 75; F., p. 310. It is to be noted that the sentence in the 2nd edition that follows the passage quoted in our text is not in the 1st edition. The abstraction from the question of the reality of the perceived object pertains to the later doctrine of the phenomenological epoché.

5. The 2nd edition substitutes *Sein* for *Dasein*. See *LU*, Tüb. ed., II/1, 382; F., p. 565. See also *LU*, Halle ed., II, 707.
6. What this means is that the subject-object relation is the relation of the subject to the sense of the object. The epistemological transcendence of the object is not by virtue of the object's real being, but by virtue of its ideal sense. This, we may observe, does not mean that the subject has a relation to one type of being through another, i.e., to a real being through the "ideal being" of its sense. As Husserl's whole doctrine of sense and reference is designed to show, sense *qua* sense is other than being; it is itself (or pretends to be) what being manifests when it is epistemologically present.
7. I am indebted to Professor Morrison in Toronto for the above formulation.
8. This inconsistency results in the 1st edition's rather curious treatment of the subject or ego. To consider it as an object is to consider it as a "founded" unity involving both formal and causal dependencies of content. Under this conception, the ego is a "bundle" of shifting acts and experiences. The fact that an ego has a relation to an object is explained by saying that ". . . intentional experiences also belong to the complex of experiences . . ." (*LU*, Halle ed., II, 342). As Husserl admits, this conception of the ego as a "bundle" does not tally with the evidence of "natural reflection." In the latter, what appears is ". . . not the individual act but the ego as a single point of relationship . . ." The ego appears to relate to its object by proceeding "through" its act experiences. One is thus led ". . . to posit the ego as the essential point of unity, one which in every act is everywhere identical" (*Ibid.*, II, 355). If one accepts this, then the ego, as we quoted Natorp, "cannot be a content," for it remains the same throughout the shifting contents of act experiences. Husserl's rather surprising response to this is to impugn the authority of natural reflection. When we perform an act of inner perception, ". . . the original act [which is the object of the new act] is no longer simply there, we no longer live in it, but rather attend it and judge it." What this means is that ". . . an essential descriptive change has occurred" (*Ibid.*, II, 357). Husserl's point on this and the preceding page seems to be that the notion of the ego as an unchanging center of relations does not correspond to a reality, but is rather an inevitable result of the objectifying interpretation that is inherent in perception. This doctrine, it is to be noted, ill accords with Husserl's statements that perception, even in the case of reflection on the ego, is a source of adequate evidence. See, e.g., *Ibid.*, II, 335. In summing this situation up, we can say that faced with the evidence that the ego is not an object, Husserl chooses to ignore this in favor of his ontological equation of being and object.

NOTES TO CHAPTER VI: 'THE SUBJECT-OBJECT CORRELATION

1. This position is repeated a number of times. See, e.g., *LU*, Tüb. ed., I, 171-2; F., pp. 180-81; *Ibid.*, II/1, 210; F., p. 141; *LU*, Halle ed., II, 144-45.
2. Husserl makes reference to his debt to James in *LU*, Tüb. ed., II/1, 208, fn. 1; F., p. 420.
3. It may be noted that these forms are sufficient to express formal implication. Thus, *p implies q* is truth functionally equivalent to the denial, *not both p and not q*. See Willard Quine, *Elementary Logic* (New York, 1965), p. 25.
4. That this, indeed, is the sense of the priority of epistemology (and of phenomenology, conceived of as a "method" of epistemological reflection) can be seen by comparing a number of Husserl's statements. See, e.g., *LU*, Tüb. ed., I, 160-61; F., p. 172; *Die Idee der Phänomenologie*; Biemel ed., pp. 22-23, 32; "Nachwort," *Ideen III*; Biemel ed., pp. 147-48.
5. Husserl follows this with the comment, "But enough of such arguments which are only different ways of expressing one and the same state of affairs (*Sachlage*), one which already guided us in the Prolegomena" (*LU*, Tüb. ed., II/2, 201; F., pp. 831-32). The *Sachlage*, we are maintaining, is that of the priority of the epistemological standpoint. It is a priority which, for Husserl, is established through the Prolegomena's refutation of scepticism and relativism.
6. As should be apparent, the sense is that of an *object*. See pp. 61-62, 69-70.
7. See also *LU*, Tüb. ed., II/1, 166; F., p. 386; *Ibid.*, II/1, 170-71; F., p. 390; *Ibid.*, II/1, 183; F., p. 400; *Ibid.*, II/2, 386; F., p. 568.

NOTES TO CHAPTER VII: 'CATEGORIAL REPRESENTATION'

1. Schérer's references are to Vol. II, Part 2, of the French translation, *Recherches logiques*, trans. H. Élie, L. Kelkel, R. Schérer (Paris, 1959-63). The corresponding references are *LU*, Tüb. ed., II/1, 399; F., p. 578; *Ibid.*, II/1, 413; F., p. 587. In the first of these, Husserl terms the intentional *matter* of an act, the act's intentional *content* when we do not include in this last the act's presentational quality. Thus, one may present to oneself an object as actual, probable, possible, doubtful, wished for, demanded, etc. In all these "qualitative modifications," the object as meant still has the same "matter" – i.e., the same objectively describable features (See also *LU*, Tüb. ed., II/1, 415-16; F., pp. 588-89). This matter cannot be confused with the real content of the act. As Husserl says, we must make "the important distinction ... between an act's *real or phenomenological* (descriptive psychological) *content* and its *intentional content*." The examination of real content "... is the task

of purely descriptive psychological analysis" (*LU*, Halle ed., II, 374; cf. *LU*, Tüb. ed., II/1, 397; F., p. 576). As for the intentional content (or matter), its examination belongs to logic. This position is abandoned in the second of Schérer's references where Husserl writes, "All differences in the manner of objective reference are descriptive differences in the relevant intentional experiences." Since the manner of objective reference has been said to be a function of the act's intentional matter, such matter is now referred to the experience as opposed to the objectivity. In other words, it is considered not as something transcendent to the act, but as something immanently describable within it. This becomes even more explicit when Husserl finally declares that presentational quality as well as "matter" exist "... as a real (*reales*) moment in the descriptive content of an act of presentation" (*LU*, Halle ed., II, 470; cf. *LU*, Tüb. ed., II/1, 506; F., p. 657). Note that the 2nd edition substitutes *reel* for *real*. This is its common practice.

2. When eidetic perception is directed, not to a species of individual objects, but to that of a feature of them – e.g., to a species of color – the immediate basis for the identifying act is provided by "sensuous abstraction." This is a "setting in relief" of the features whose species is to be eidetically perceived. See the reference cited in our text.

3. As Rene Schérer expresses this, "One can relate a collection to other collections and so continue *ad infinitum*. In such purely formal complications, which are constitutive of new objects, one is no longer required to return to the sensible at each state of the formalizing abstraction." Instead of speaking, as we have done, of presentation and nominalization, Schérer justifies this conclusion in terms of an "abstractive consciousness." By virtue of this, we can say that in ascending the ladder of foundations, "... the agreement with sensible objects undergoes a displacement. The 'materials' no longer directly refer to the intuition of an individual ..." (*op. cit.*, p. 326). For our position, see pp. 111-113.

4. Contents of reflection are formally defined "as those contents which are either themselves act characters or are founded in act characters" (*LU*, Tüb. ed., II/2, 180; F., p. 814). Strictly speaking, if we distinguish, in the "realm of inner sensibility," between object and sense contents through which the object is presented, we have to say that these contents are contents *of* the act characters.

5. See p. 79, n. 2 of our text; see also *LU*, II/1, 383; F., p. 566 where Husserl writes, "I can see nothing more evident than the distinction that comes forward here between content and act ...".

NOTES TO CHAPTER VIII:
'ONTOLOGICAL DIFFICULTIES AND MOTIVATING CONNECTIONS'

1. See *Phaedo* 78d. We here follow Etienne Gilson's interpretation of this passage. See his *Being and Some Philosophers,* 2nd ed. (Toronto, 1952), p. 12.

2. Husserl puts this in the following way: "Just as every law that arises from experience and the induction from individual facts is a law for facts, so conversely every law for facts is a law from experience and induction; consequently, as has been shown above, assertions with existential content are inseparable from it." This is the premise for Husserl's conclusion that non-inductively derived laws cannot be overthrown by facts. As Husserl says of the ideal, logical laws: "Their 'origin' — or, more precisely put, the basis which justifies them — is not taken from induction. Thus, they do not carry with them that existential content which is attached to all probabilities as such, even the highest and most valuable. What they assert has complete and entire validity" (*LU*, Tüb. ed., 73-74; F., p. 107).

3. De Boer comes to the same conclusion, though he does not tie it directly to Husserl's ontology. He writes: "Husserl overcomes the 'naturalization of the ideas,' but not yet the 'naturalization of consciousness.' This consciousness, which is placed under the command of the validity of ideal norms, is at the same time a part of 'nature' and, as such, is subordinated to the necessity of natural laws. Symptomatic for the *Logische Untersuchungen* is the simultaneous presence of two methods: a phenomenological, descriptive analysis of essences and a natural scientific explanation of consciousness. This methodological dualism reaches a crisis in the description of the logical acts. On the one hand, these acts are empirically necessary and determined; on the other hand, an idea realizes itself in them through which they claim apodictic validity. How can both these views be combined?" ("Zusammenfassung," *op. cit.*, p. 589).

4. In a manuscript dating from 1907, Husserl writes: "The 'Logische Untersuchungen' lets phenomenology stand as descriptive psychology (even though its decisive interest was epistemological). This descriptive psychology, understood as empirical phenomenology, must, however, be distinguished from transcendental phenomenology . . . What was designated in my 'Logische Untersuchungen' as descriptive, psychological phenomenology concerns the simple sphere of experiences according to their inherent (*reelen*) content. The experiences are experiences of an experiencing ego insofar as they are empirically referred to natural objectivities. For a phenomenology that desires to be epistemological, for an essential doctrine of (*a priori*) knowledge, however, the empirical relation remains suspended" (*Die Idee der Phän.*, "Einleitung des Herausgebers"; Biemel ed., p. ix). The empirical relation referred to here is one between an empirical (real) subject and its objects.

5. This is why the eidetic reduction, when performed by itself, is considered by Husserl as insufficient for reaching the new ontological level to be investigated by the *Ideen*. In Husserl's words, "If the phenomenological region would so immediately and self-understandably offer itself as does the region of the standpoint of the experience of nature, or if it could be made to yield itself via a simple move from this to the eidetic standpoint

(as perhaps the geometrical region does when we start from the empirically spatial), then there would be no need for any involved reductions with the difficult considerations that belong to them" (*Ideen I*, §61; Biemel ed., p. 145).
6. The 2nd edition of the *Logische Untersuchungen* seems to embrace this position in Investigations VI, §10. The section, however, is not present in the 1st edition.
7. Paul Ricoeur writes of the constitution of *both* sense and presence, "This ultimate episode in the *Ideen* is of capital importance. ... To constitute reality is to refuse to leave its 'presence' *outside* of the 'sense' of the world" ("Introduction du traducteur," *Idées directrices pour une phénoménologie,* Paris, 1950, pp. xxiv-xxv).
8. This doctrine first appears in the lectures on internal time consciousness. Husserl writes: 'In the same impressional consciousness in which perception is constituted, the perceived is also constituted through this [process] ... The thing constitutes itself in the flowing off of its appearances, which are themselves constituted as immanent unities in the flowing of the original impressions. Necessarily the one constitutes itself with the other. The appearing thing constitutes itself because in the original flowing both unities of sensations and unitary interpretations constitute themselves; there is, thus, continually consciousness of something, exhibiting, or rather, presenting of something and, in the continual sequence, the exhibition of the same thing" (*Zur Phänomenologie des inneren Zeitbewusstseins,* §43; ed. Rudolph Boehm, The Hague, 1966, pp. 91, 92-93).
9. See *Zur Phän. d. inn. Zeitbewusstseins,* §10-§11, §43.
10. See pp. 57-58, 84, 100; see also *LU*, Tüb. ed., II/2, 126; F., p. 768.
11. Indirectly, of course, this question is faced in the refutations of psychologism and relativism.
12. Since such a dissolution is always inherently possible, the individual ego cannot *per se* be considered to be the constitutive ground of the world. Its own being as a numerical singular – i.e., as an "actual ego" – depends upon the possibility of the constitution of the "surrounding world" that permits it to be posited. In other words, as a singular ego, it does not ground, but is rather grounded by the possibility of constituting the world that surrounds it. This leads Kern to speak of the constitutive acts of the ego in the following way: "We can say in interpreting Husserl that it does not lie within, but is rather 'grace' for it that it can productively constitute a cosmos and precisely *this* cosmos. It is always in 'danger' of having this grace withdrawn, i.e., of having the cosmos extinguish itself in a chaos of sensations, of collapsing as an ego that has a world and, thus, as an actual ego" (*Husserl u. Kant*, ed. cit., p. 298). Here we may note that we do not conclude from this, as Kern apparently does, that consciousness itself, i.e., consciousness regarded as pre-individual and pre-objective, is in danger of dissolution. See Kern, *op. cit.,* 297-98.
13. This position first makes its appearance in the 1905 lectures on internal

time consciousness. Husserl writes: "The phenomena that constitute time are, thus, evidently and in principle different objectivities from those that are constituted in time. They are not individual objects nor individual processes and the predicates of these latter cannot with sense be applied to them" (*Zur Phän. d. inn. Zeitbewusstseins*, S36; Boehm ed., pp. 74-75; see also *Ibid.*, "Beilage VI," No. 3, p. 112).

BIBLIOGRAPHY

LIST OF WORKS CITED

Aquinas, Thomas. *De Ente et Essentia,* in *Le "De Ente et Essentia."* Ed. M.D. Roland Gosselin. Kain, Belgium, 1926.
—. *Quodlibetum.* Ed. Pierre Mandonnet. Paris, 1926.
Celms, Theodor. *Der phänomenologische Idealismus Husserls.* Riga, 1928.
De Boer, Theodor. "Zusammenfassung," in *De Ontwikkelingsgang in Het Denken van Husserl.* Assen, 1966. 575-601.
Farber, Marvin. *The Aims of Phenomenology.* New York, 1966.
—. *The Foundations of Phenomenology,* 3rd ed. Albany, 1964.
Fitch, Frederick B. "Self Reference in Philosophy," in *Contemporary Readings in Logical Theory.* Eds. Irving Copi and James Gould. New York, 1967. 154-161.
Frege, Gottlob. *Translations from the Philosophical Writings of Gottlob Frege.* Eds. and trans. Peter Geach and Max Black. Oxford, 1970.
Freud, Sigmund. *The Future of an Illusion.* Ed. James Strachey. Trans. W.D. Robson-Scott. Garden City, 1964.
Gilson, Etienne. *Being and Some Philosophers,* 2nd ed. Toronto, 1952.
Heidegger, Martin. *Kant und das Problem der Metaphysik,* 2nd ed. Frankfurt/M., 1951.
Hume, David. *A Treatise of Human Nature.* Ed. L.A. Selbey-Bigge. Oxford, 1973.
Husserl, Edmund. *Die Idee der Phänomenologie.* Ed. Walter Biemel. 2nd ed. Husserliana II. The Hague, 1973.
—. *Die Krisis der europäischen Wissenschaften und die transzendentale Phänomenologie.* Ed. Walter Biemel. 2nd ed. Husserliana VI. The Hague, 1962.
—. *Erste Philosophie (1923/24), Erster Teil, Kritische Ideengeschichte.* Ed. Rudolf Boehm. Husserliana VII. The Hague, 1956.
—. *Erste Philosophie (1923/24), Zweiter Teil, Theorie der phänomenologischen Reduktion.* Ed. Rudolf Boehm. Husserliana VIII. The Hague, 1959.
—. *Formal and Transcendental Logic.* Trans. Dorion Cairns. The Hague, 1969.
—. *Ideen zu einer reinen Phänomenologie und phänomenologischen Philosophie, Erstes Buch.* Ed. Walter Biemel. Husserliana III. The Hague, 1950.
—. *Ideen zu einer reinen Phänomenologie und phänomenologischen Philosophie, Zweites Buch.* Ed. Marly Biemel. Husserliana IV. The Hague, 1952.

—. *Ideen zu einer reinen Phänomenologie und phänomenologischen Philosophie, Drittes Buch.* Ed. Walter Biemel. Husserliana V. The Hague, 1971.
—. *Logical Investigations.* Trans. J.N. Fidlay. New York, 1970.
—. *Logische Untersuchungen,* 1st ed. 2 vols. Halle/S., 1900-1901.
—. *Logische Untersuchungen,* 5th ed. 3 vols. Tübingen, 1968.
—. "Nachwort," in *Ideen zu einer reinen Phänomenologie und phänomenologischen Philosophie, Drittes Buch.* Ed. Walter Biemel. Husserliana V. The Hague, 1971. 138-162.
—. *Zur Phänomenologie des inneren Zeitbewusstseins (1893-1917).* Ed. Rudolf Boehm. Husserliana X. The Hague, 1966.
James, William. *Psychology, Briefer Course.* New York, 1948.
Kant, Immanuel. *Kants gesammelte Schriften.* Ed. Königliche Preußische Akademie der Wissenschaften. 23 vols. Berlin, 1910-1955.
Kern, Iso. *Husserl und Kant.* Phaenomenologica, No. 16. The Hague, 1964.
Levinas, Emmanuel. *The Theory of Intuition in Husserl's Phenomenology.* Trans. André Orianne. Evanston, 1973.
Osborn, Andrew D. *Edmund Husserl and his Logical Investigations,* 2nd ed. Cambridge, Mass., 1949.
Plato. *Platonis Opera.* Ed. John Burnet. 5 vols. Oxford, 1900-1907, reprinted, 1957.
Quine, Willard. *Elementary Logic.* New York, 1965.
Ricoeur, Paul. *Husserl: An Analysis of his Phenomenology.* Trans. Edward G. Ballard and Lester E. Embree. Evanston, 1967.
—. "Introduction du Traducteur," in *Idées directrices pour une phenomenologie.* Paris, 1950.
Schérer, René. *La Phénoménologie des Recherches Logique de Husserl.* Paris, 1967.
Sokolowski, Robert. *Husserlian Meditations: How Words Present Things.* Evanston, 1974.
Spiegelberg, Herbert. *The Phenomenological Movement,* 2nd ed. Phaenomenologica, No. 5. 2 vols. The Hague, 1971.
Stent, Gunther. "Limits to Scientific Understanding of Man," in *Science,* CLXXXVII (1974), 1052-1057.
Strawson, Peter Frederick. "On Referring," in *Contemporary Readings in Logical Theory.* Eds. Irving Copi and James Gould. New York, 1967. 105-127.
Tugendhat, Ernst. *Der Wahrheitsbegriff bei Husserl und Heidegger.* Berlin, 1967.
Wittgenstein, Ludwig. *Über Gewissheit – On Certainty.* Eds. G.E.M. Anscombe and G.H. von Wright. Trans. Denis Paul and G. E. M. Anscombe. New York, 1972.

NAME INDEX

Aquinas, T., 198
Aristotle, 81, 86

Brentano, F., 194

Celms, Th., 159

De Boer, Th., 158, 172, 179, 193, 194, 196, 203
Descartes, R., 7, 52

Erdmann, B., 17, 194

Farber, M., 193
Fichte, J.G., 162
Fitch, F., 27, 195
Frege, G., 53, 54, 63, 64, 112, 113, 154, 199
Freud, S., 22

Gilson, E., 202

Heidegger, M., 195
Hume, D., 49, 194

James, W., 101, 102, 201

Kant, I., 10, 49, 86, 87, 88, 89, 102, 197
Kern, I., 194, 204

Levinas, E., 195
Lipps, Th., 13, 14, 17

Mills, J.S., 14, 17, 194
Morrison, J., 200

Natorp, P., 92, 200

Osborn, A., 193

Plato, 102, 152, 153, 183

Quine, W., 201

Ricoeur, P., 193, 204
Russell, B., 195

Schérer, R., 135, 138, 144, 175, 201, 202
Sokolowski, R., 140, 198
Spiegelberg, H., 193
Stent, G., 195
Strawson, P., 196, 197

Tugendhat, E., 140

Wittgenstein, L., 194, 197

SUBJECT INDEX

apriori, 89f, 98, 121ff, 151, 191
authentic thought, 101, 103
being
    1) and essence, 57f
    2) as determined by the sense of predication, 150ff
    3) as object, 61f, 69f, 92, 161, 164
    4) as presence, 116, 164f
    5) ideal being – as a pure possibility, 62ff, 154ff, 184ff – as a species, 43 – as distinct from the real, 95f, 129, 146, 154ff – as expressing the ontological sense of the world, 97, 180 – as functioning in epistemological transcendence, 83, 129, 167f – as immanent in the real, 97, 128, 146ff, 152f – as limiting the real, 98, 125ff, 152 – as not predicable of the real, 154 – as posited, 60f, 150 – as predicable of the real, 150ff – of the intentional content, 78, 83 – role in the intentional relationship, 95ff
    6) in itself, 10f, 44
    7) in the sense of truth, 58
    8) irreal being, 8, 93, 163f, 170, 176
    9) objective being, 9ff, 44
    10) real being – as causal, 73 – as temporal, 45, of the subject, 74, 162f
    11) unity of being, 130, 149

categorial
    1) acts, 103
    2) intuitions, 101ff, 107ff, 117ff, 134ff
    3) objects, 117, 119f
causality
    1) and psychologism, 20ff
    2) and temporality, 73f
    3) and the objectifying act, 85, 158
    4) and the real ego, 74, 160f
    5) as not applicable to the irreal, 163, 170
    6) Kantian notion of, 86f
constitution, 78ff, 90, 124f, 166ff, 171, 178f

epistemological motivation, 28f
epistemological standpoint as primary, 33, 115f, 162f
epistemology and metaphysics, 2
epoché, 7, 91

founded acts, 110, 136ff
fulfilling sense, 75, 198

genetic explanation, 4f
grammatical laws of categorial activity, 106ff

intention and fulfillment, 58, 84f, 105, 133ff, 170ff, 177ff
intentional matter (interpretive sense), 135, 138ff, 147, 175ff, 201f
intentional object, 75, 77f, 82
intentional relationship
    1) as an ideal world form, 98ff, 125ff

SUBJECT INDEX

2) as opposed to a real relation, 75ff, 83
judgement
   1) of experience, 49
   2) of perception, 49
   3) vs. presentation, 112

knowledge
   1) objectively valid, 9ff
   2) objectivity of, 1f

ladder of foundations, 110ff, 140
law of non-contradiction, 10f, 18, 96
logic of content, 66f, 100f
logical laws of categorial activity, 108ff
logically adequate language, 113f

metabasis, 9, 14ff
motivated path, 2ff, 159ff

names as bearing senses, 54ff, 198
natural attitude, 36, 86, 162
norms, 157f, 184, 191

objectifying, interpretative act, 79ff
occasional judgements, 44f
ontology, 182f
original givenness, 51f
outer vs. inner perception, 80

perception as interpretation, 80, 134f
positing on the basis of truth, 60f, 68ff, 116, 118f
possibility, 62ff, 101, 184ff
psychologism, 12ff

reduction
   1) eidetic, 7, 91
   2) phenomenological, 7f, 91, 159f
relativism, 11f, 16, 21, 23, 31ff
reperformance of cognative acts, 49f

scepticism, 27f
sciences of the real vs. the ideal, 40f, 65, 95f
sense and reference, 53ff
specific and real unity, 157f

teleology, 3f
thing in itself, 62, 87ff
transcendence, 83, 129, 167ff, 171, 173
truth in itself, 10, 44

verification, 48ff, 70f, 110

"weight of being" in the intentional relation, 85ff, 124
world, 180ff, 190